MILL GIRLS
AND STRANGERS

MILL GIRLS AND STRANGERS

Single Women's Independent Migration
in England, Scotland, and the United States

1850–1881

Wendy M. Gordon

State University of New York Press

Published by
State University of New York Press, Albany

For information, address State University of New York Press,
90 State Street, Suite 700, Albany, NY, 12207

Production by Diane Ganeles
Marketing by Jennifer Giovani

Library of Congress Cataloging-in-Publication Data

Gordon, Wendy M., 1967–
    Mill Girls and strangers: single women's independent migration in
England, Scotland, and the United States, 1850–1881 / Wendy M. Gordon.
    p. cm.
    Includes bibliographical references and index.
    ISBN 0-7914-5525-4 (alk. paper) – ISBN 0-7914-5526-2 (pbk. : alk. paper)
    1. Women textile workers—England—Preston (Lancashire)—
History—19th century. 2. Women textile workers—Scotland—Paisley—
History—19th century. 3. Women textile workers—Massachusetts—
Lowell—History—19th century. 4. Women migrant labor—
England—Preston (Lancashire)—History—19th century. 5. Women
migrant labor—Employment—Scotland—Paisley—History—19th century.
6. Women migrant labor—Massachusetts—Lowell—History—
19th century. I. Title.

HD6073.T42 G692 2002
305.43'677—dc21
                                                                    2002021816

10 9 8 7 6 5 4 3 2 1

Contents

Figures

Acknowledgments

Completing this project would not have been possible without the support and advice of colleagues, friends, and helpful strangers on both sides of the Atlantic, for whom mention here is far too little recognition. The committee that oversaw *Mill Girls*'s first incarnation as a Doctoral Dissertation, Dr. Carol Green-Devens, Professor T. M. Devine, Dr. James Schmiechen, Dean Susan Conner, and Dr. Leslie Page Moch brought their wildly different specialties to bear in suggestions and critiques that vastly improved the final product. Leslie Page Moch did additional service in reading and commenting on the book manuscript, and deserves particular thanks for suggesting many alternatives to the word *migrant*. My classmates in the Central Michigan University/University of Strathclyde joint Ph.D. program, Carrie Hoefferle, Susan Pyecroft, and Ruth Mills provided invaluable support, sympathy, advice, and judicious amounts of beer at crucial moments. My colleagues at Plattsburgh State University have since rendered many of the same services. Annette Davis, Jo Milne, and Margaret Hastie all helped to smooth the wheels of bureaucracy. Michael Anderson, Thomas Dublin, and Geoffrey Timmins responded graciously to my requests for help. Emma Currie, Lynn Hepburn, and Michael Stephenson all had roles in creating the many maps; Peter Friesen helped with the lovely graphs.

Everywhere I went I encountered helpful archivists and library staffs. In the United States, the volunteers at the Mount Pleasant Michigan LDS Family History Center welcomed me into their ranks, and the staff at the Baker Library, Lowell National Historic Park and Martha Mayo at the Center for Lowell History made it possible for me to get the maximum amount of information in the shortest possible time. Nancy Reinhardt at Colby College was terribly understanding of my illogical need to see and handle original documents. In England, the staffs at the Lancashire Record Office and the Harris Library patiently burrowed through stacks that "just might" contain useful sources. In Scotland, David Roberts at the Paisley Museum and the staff at the Paisley Library gave tremendous help, as did the staff at the Scottish Record Office, especially Dax and Morna at West Register House and Robert Fotheringham who patiently answered multiple e-mails. Murdo MacDonald, archivist for the Argyll and Bute Region, very kindly gave me access to his holdings and an excuse to visit beautiful Lochgilphead. Great thanks to all these archivists and librarians, who devote their lives to helping other peoples' research.

Formal acknowledgment and thanks go to the Baker Library of the Harvard Business School; the Special Collections Department of the Miller Library at Colby College, Waterville, Maine; and the Keeper of the Records of Scotland for permission to access and cite from documents in their care.

And thanks of course to my family—Tom and Pat Gordon and Charlie Guenther for their unfaltering support and encouragement, and Chet Guenther for providing a most agreeable distraction during the revision process. Finally, I always thought it was trite when book writers saved their greatest thanks for their spouse, "without whom none of this would be possible." I don't think so any more. My greatest thanks goes to Ed, without whom none of this would be possible.

CHAPTER 1

Transitions in the City:
Independent Female Migration,
1850–1881

Grace Campbell was fourteen years old when she moved from Campbelltown, Argyllshire to Paisley, Renfrewshire, Scotland, in the late 1830s. She went to work at the Lounsdale bleachworks just outside Paisley and lived there with dozens of other young female migrants in accommodations provided by the bleachworks. Thirty years later and across the Atlantic another young woman, Mattie Weymouth, was the first of her friends to move from Readfield, Maine, to Lowell, Massachusetts. Mattie went to work for one of Lowell's textile manufacturers, living in a private boardinghouse close to the mill with many other mill workers. Both of these women left rural homes in favor of industrial employment, knowing exactly what type of jobs they would find. In Paisley and in Lowell they joined communities of fellow female migrants, some from their home towns, some from even farther afield. In Preston, England, Esther Jackson was attracted by a different sort of opportunity. Probably born in rural Lancashire, Esther came to Preston around 1845 and found work as a domestic servant. Preston-born women preferred employment in the city's textile mills, which left a demand for servants in the homes of the middle class. Esther had traded her own country family for the chores of an urban one, but in Preston her wages were her own. Between 1845 and 1851 she was able to put away £47 8s.3d. in her savings account.[1]

None of these young women came from wealthy homes; all of them were probably economic contributors to their parents' families before migration. In moving, however, they were leaving the protection of their families. They also potentially incurred suspicion from the middle classes, many of whom believed that young women of all classes needed adult supervision to protect them from moral corruption.[2] Grace, Mattie, and Esther took advantage of systems of residential labor that by providing such supervision permitted

1

them to migrate while still having some protection from the dangers of urban industrialization.

These three women and thousands like them were part of an often overlooked group in the story of British and American industrialization: independent female migrants. Migration was a central feature in the creation of the great textile centers of the nineteenth century. Workers flooded from the countryside into textile factories, bleachfields, and bourgeois kitchens. Understanding the migrants who constituted that flood is crucial to grasping the dynamic of the textile cities themselves.

The largest portion of the migrants in Britain, the United States, and much of Europe in the nineteenth century were young, unmarried people, including women.[3] Examining these single female migrants reveals a crucial segment of women's life course, the transition from their parents' families and to adult roles of their own. Independent migration was one of the most important ways women might accomplish this transition. It is important to note that these migrants also offer the opportunity to study women *without* reference to their familial roles—in the historical record single female migrants take on individual identities as workers or friends rather than relational identities as wife, mother, or daughter. Yet women living outside family relationships, especially in cities, were viewed with suspicion. Single women were perceived to need protection and control, whether from their families or other institutions. This social constraint distinguished female migrants' experiences from their male counterparts and necessitates a gendered historical analysis. Studying female migrants in their host communities thus also gives insight to how nineteenth-century urban populations coped with women who were on their own.

Finally, very little is known about migrant women's own experiences, though historians have frequently addressed their role in helping to support rural families. How did potential migrants assert their personal agency within the family to get permission to move? How did migration change a daughter's role in her family? What made one type of job more appealing to female migrants than others? What did the migrants do with their wages and what were their personal goals in migration? What dangers did the single female migrant face in the city, and how could she avoid those dangers? At a basic level, analyzing the experience of single female migrants in textile cities expands our knowledge of the process of migration and contributes to a more complex understanding of the textile cities that transformed the nineteenth-century landscape.

Mill Girls and Strangers is a comparative examination of single women's internal migration to three cities, each a model of the textile industry in its own country: Preston (Lancashire, England); Paisley (Renfrewshire, Scotland); and Lowell (Massachusetts, United States of America).[4] Each city has different sources extant and thus brings a distinct perspective to single women's migration, highlighting in turn employers' influence, the migrants' own desires, and the unpredictable dangers of city life. This variety of perspectives reveals young women's migration to textile cities to be a far more complex problem than previously acknowledged. Comparing the three cities shows both a surprising degree of overall uniformity and tremendous complexity in the details of the migration experience. Young women in each country were affected by the same general factors, but those influences fluctuated in importance to produce a wide variety of individual experiences.

Historians have most often described single women's migration into textile cities in the context of the family economy, usually focusing on the young women's occupational choices to the exclusion of other elements. The most common historical model of single women's migration into textile cities in the second half of the nineteenth century was summarized by Leslie Page Moch in her excellent survey of European migration, *Moving Europeans*. Drawing on research in Roubaix, France, and Verviers, Belgium, the model described the wide variety of female migrants into those cities in the nineteenth century. Those who moved in family groups were more likely to remain in the cities, and more likely to work in the cities' textile mills. Young single women without their parents, on the other hand, were highly mobile, likely to stay in the city for only a few years, and worked almost exclusively as domestic servants. Many of these women migrated after the death of their parents; they chose domestic service because it provided them with food, shelter, and a surrogate family setting.[5]

While this model is generally accurate, it has notable shortcomings. First, it implies uniformity in single migrant women's employment from city to city and country to country. In fact, young migrant women entered a wide range of situations, which varied from one location to another. It analyzes female migrants almost wholly in economic terms, concentrating on choice of occupation as their primary difference from nonmigrant young women. In doing so, it fails to address the purpose migration served in the development of young women's lives and their progress from girlhood dependence to adult responsibilities. Finally, because it does not address questions of why migrants might be desirable employees, this model does not consider the social functions single migrant women filled in the textile cities.

There was a need in textile cities for a specifically female, specifically migrant workforce, and not only in domestic service. Preston's middle classes compensated for the high factory employment of local women by recruiting "country girls" to work in their homes. In Paisley and Lowell, industrial textile employers needed migrants to supplement the native-born labor force. Both of these cities actively recruited young women from rural areas up to several days' travel away. They persuaded parents and ministers of the suitability of industrial labor for their daughters, and enticed the young women with promises of good wages and a chance to see the city. Thus urban employers' needs drew single women to the cities while their beliefs about respectability demanded they control the migrants' behavior.

Migration also served the needs of the young women. Between their late teens and mid twenties, young women were in transition between their parents' families and their own adult families. For working-class women these years were marked by active, unpaid participation in a family endeavor (most commonly farming) or wage earning and, for some women, migration. Those women who left their parents' homes went most often to protected accommodations provided by the employers who needed migrant workers: middle-class homes or corporate-sponsored boarding houses. All too often, historians have addressed nineteenth-century single women only within the context of the nuclear family.[6] The study of industrial family structures generally integrates daughters into a family economy, where every member contributed to a common goal, even in the cases when those daughters lived away from the family.[7] A family-based analysis, though crucial, denies individuals their own desires and frustrations within the family milieu. Evidence from Preston, Lowell, and Paisley suggests that migrant women were in fact economically as well as physically separate from their families.

Family studies also tend to acknowledge only young women's economic roles, giving an artificially flat portrait of lives that included friends, dreams, and disappointments as well as work. In addition to wages, young women sought intangibles like friendship and adventure in the cities. After a period as a migrant, a young woman was more likely to marry and form her own family than to return permanently to her parents' home. Thus, migration could serve more to facilitate the creation of the migrants' adult families than to sustain their parents'. Migrants used employment opportunities in the cities for their own ends, enabling their transition to independent adulthood.

In a society in which the family was the primary supportive framework, young women away from their families were vulnerable in spite of the supervised positions to which they migrated. So long as there was work and they were healthy, independent female migrants stood a good chance of successfully making the transition between their parents' families and their adult families. Adversity in the shape of unemployment, disease, or an unwanted child could shatter a migrant's independence, sending her back to her parents' home, to a poorhouse, to prison, or worse. The process and success of an individual's migration was dramatically influenced by factors beyond either a migrant's or her employer's control such as social mores, homesickness, and communicable disease.

Clearly, single women's migration was not a simple equation of economic need and available employment. As Moch concluded, "The role played by migrants in the textile cities of the industrial age . . . was more complex, and perhaps more interesting, than we have imagined."[8] Given the intricacy of the process, comparative history is particularly useful in studying independent female migration. Young women in general left comparatively few sources, and their migration, looked at in any single nation, appears to be nearly nonexistent, unremarkable, or (in the case of Lowell), absolutely extraordinary. Comparison across national borders gives a broader perspective, revealing complexity and commonalities where single cases produce a deceptively simple or overly rigid model. Comparison also facilitates using a combination of sources and methodologies. A quantitative methodology provides the statistical groundwork for this project, after which qualitative sources illuminate individual women's experiences from different perspectives, including insight into their goals and feelings regarding migration. In tandem, the qualitative and quantitative sources reveal a picture of single female migrants with multiple dimensions, revealing their hopes and failures as well as their economic roles.

Beyond the censuses that give a uniform base to the study, vastly different sources survive for the three groups of migrant women. Primary documents referring to single female migrants in Preston were decidedly scarce, while those in Paisley were plentiful but generated wholly by middle-class observers and authorities, not the migrants themselves. The City of Lowell, in contrast, preserved a plethora of personal letters and corporate records that cast light on the daily lives and thoughts of the migrant workforce. Based on the qualitative sources available I have devoted one chapter to each city, each building on the one before and each contributing a different perspective on single women's migration. In Preston the sources that have survived point to the importance of employers' needs in the choices migrants made. Therefore, the focus of chapter 2 is the influence of employers in determining women's migration patterns. The highly detailed sources from Lowell, on the other hand, provided intimate details of the lives and motivations of individual migrants. Chapter 3 thereby adds to information on employers' influence with an exploration of how the migrants' personal situations, desires, and contacts contributed to their decisions to migrate and their experiences as migrants. In Paisley official records and reports illustrate the ways in which migrants interacted with their host community and the dangers they faced as women outside families. After examining the migration to Paisley from the perspectives of employers' needs and migrants' personal situations and desires, chapter 4 investigates how migration was influenced by factors beyond the control of either the migrants or their employers. Finally, the conclusion directly compares the three cities, analyzing the variations but finding an overall similarity. Comparative analysis presents a three-dimensional description of single women's independent migration to textile cities with a previously unavailable degree of nuance and complexity.

Although I have avoided jargon as much as possible, it is necessary for me to provide definitions of some terms. Technically, any person who makes a change of residence is a migrant, making *migration* a potentially troublesome term that requires a strict definition to be useful.[9] I defined *migration* in this study based on boundaries crossed, rather than on actual distance traveled. The migrants I am concerned with were internal migrants who crossed county or state, but not national, boundaries. The term *migrant* will always refer to such internal migrants. Immigrants who came to a city from outside the country will be specifically identified as such. The United States' census recorded only the state in which an individual was born, and state of birth has been used to identify migrants in Lowell. To obtain a degree of detail similar to the United States, county of birth was used to define migrants to Paisley and Preston. Due to the geographic location of the cities in relation to state and county borders "migrants" from adjacent regions might actually have moved shorter distances than "nonmigrants" from elsewhere in the same region (see maps in chapters 2, 3, and 4). Nevertheless it is the moving that defines a migrant, not the distance that is moved. Using this method to identify migrants will tend to *under*identify, not *mis*identify them. Thus the numbers presented here should be taken as a minimum.

Identifying migrants by place of birth alone is effective, but it does not distinguish between recent migrants, who came to the city in the few years preceding a census, and those who had been in residence for many years. Although anyone might migrate at any time, especially in periods of economic distress, throughout the nineteenth century unmarried young adults were the most mobile segment of the population in Britain and the United States.[10] In order to describe the experiences and volume of relatively recent arrivals to the city, I used migrants between fifteen and thirty years old as the cohort of "recent" or "current" migrants, those most likely to have migrated independently in the ten years between censuses. An "independent migrant" was defined as one who moved without her parents, and "migration experience" included all her experiences during the time she was most likely to migrate, that is, from the time of her first migration, through her search for work and accommodation, integration into a host community and possible remigration, until she married or aged outside the current migrant cohort.[11] To be practical, I identified independent migrants in the census by their residence in a household that had no one else with the same surname who was of an age to be the migrant's parent.

Migration itself takes place between two points: the point of origin and the destination.[12] In many cases a discernible migration stream develops between points as new migrants follow paths they know by acquaintance with old migrants rather than striking out to wholly unknown territory. There are often fruitful avenues for the historian in both origin and destination points, and full understanding of where and why migration streams exist and how they change is best achieved by examining the whole migration pattern in a region, mapping migrants in both their homes and the host environment. This work, however, is primarily a destination-point study which, except for a very few cases, does not trace the careers of individual migrants. It was possible to place women at the time of each census, but the short-term nature of most single women's migration, the scanty survival of records from origin points and the frequency with which certain surnames appeared (particularly in Scotland) made it impractical to either link individual migrants to their families or follow them through consecutive censuses.

Thus, this study is limited to questions that could be answered with sources generated after migration. These included the migrants' place of birth and in some cases previous migration history, their choices of occupation and housing, the communities they formed after the move and the problems they could face, the use of their wages and—so far as possible—their general reasons for migration. Some of these questions, notably those about migrants' communities and reasons for migration, are necessarily answered through inferences made from evidence of the young women's behavior at the destination, for example, living close to other migrants or placing the bulk of her wages in a savings account. These inferences are educated, but they are ultimately guesses at the migrants' motives. There are also important questions to which destination-point sources cannot even infer answers. There is no definitive information on the birth families of female migrants, such as economic status, religious affiliation, composition, or size. Exact age at first migration, immediate catalysts to migration, and parental reaction can only be guessed at unless explicitly mentioned in letters or official records. Nevertheless the sheer bulk of data available from the censuses and destination-point sources gave a more accurate picture of single migrant women's experience in the cities than would chance-surviving individual histories that could more precisely integrate origin and destination.

Comparison of these data is a vital component of this research. Simultaneously examining the three cities of Preston, Lowell, and Paisley gives a breadth to the study of single women's migration that could not be achieved in any one city. Addressing all three cities with the same set of questions reveals general similarities about influences on women's migration to textile cities in the third quarter of the nineteenth century and their experiences there, but it also shows clear differences in circumstances and hence the patterns of women's migration to each city. My use of comparative analysis as an integral part of this study is informed by others' theoretical and practical work in comparative history, which has long intrigued historians and other social scientists.

There has been considerable discussion about how comparison is explicitly used by historians, but in truth all history is implicitly comparative, in that it relates the past to the present or indicates what distinguishes one country or region from all others.[13] Histories in which the comparison is implicit often suffer from setting the case against a poorly defined standard or a set of assumptions that are not grounded in reality. Explicitly comparative history, on the other hand, develops two or more distinct, well-defined cases which when compared to one another give a much clearer presentation of both generalities and divergences within the phenomenon under study. Comparison allows analysis to become more than the sum of its parts, providing large-scale context, possibly revealing general patterns of causation or truly unique developments. As William Sewell, Jr., concluded in 1967, "The adoption of a comparative framework enables [the historian] to detect errors or inadequacies in hypothetical explanations which would seem unimpeachable if viewed in one single historical or geographical setting."[14]

Historians of the United States have been particularly prone to exceptionalist histories, even when placing the United States in comparative perspective. In recent years, however, comparative history has emphasized that most comparable nations are neither identical nor truly exceptional. Thus "cross-national comparative history can undermine two contrary but equally damaging presuppositions—the illusion of total regularity and that of absolute uniqueness."[15] Part of comparison's role in this study is to test the exceptionalism of the case of the Lowell Mill Girls. Comparing Lowell with Preston and Paisley locates it historically as one of many cities that attracted single female migration, not a peculiarly American phenomenon.

Recent theorists of comparative history have largely ignored Marc Bloch's proposal of "the possibility of filling in certain gaps in documentation by means of hypotheses based upon analogy."[16] In my statistical data I have a large, eminently comparable body of evidence from each of my subject cities—identical questions were asked of samples drawn in an identical manner from nearly identical sources. Qualitative information, however, varies widely in content and quality from city to city. In constructing my analysis, where the statistical evidence in each of the three cities is similar but qualitative data from one or more is missing, I use the qualitative material that I do have to fill in patterns where documentation does not survive. Similar behaviors do not mandate similar motivations, but in the absence of complete qualitative data from every case, suppositions based on data from a quantitatively comparable case has more basis in fact than suppositions based on no data at all. While such a "transitive property" cannot work as neatly in history as it does in algebra, it is a sound method to hypothesize answers where none are available in the historical record. In this way comparison produces a more complete description of single women's migration experiences than is attainable through individual case studies.

I chose the United States, Scotland, and England for this comparison because they were nations with their own economic and social peculiarities yet with close historic, cultural, and economic ties. In the nineteenth century England, Scotland, and New England were all in the throes of industrialization, all Protestant communities with a strong work ethic (at least among the employing class). By midcentury all three also had a substantial and growing Roman Catholic Irish population, which formed strong subcultures in the communities. Although similar, the countries were far from identical. New England society developed from English Puritans transplanted to American soil in the seventeenth century, but it changed over the centuries through repeated waves of immigration and the introduction of republican democracy. Scotland and England since 1707 were joined in a political union, but Scotland industrialized later than England and was generally less urban and less affluent. Once begun, industrialization and urban growth occurred much more rapidly in Scotland, which amplified the inherent stresses to population and infrastructure.[17]

Preston, Paisley, and Lowell are comparable as representative textile cities of their respective nations, although they varied considerably in size.[18] All three cities were built around variations of the cotton industry. Preston and Paisley developed textile industries in the late eighteenth century, Preston producing plain goods while Paisley specialized in thread and patterned shawls. Lowell, built with the explicit intention of bringing rural values to a factory setting (in contrast to the "English" system in which industrialization begot immoral urban squalor), was not established until 1826, but thanks to industrial espionage all three cities were at an approximately equal level of industrialization by 1850.[19] Each had several major textile corporations that participated in the worldwide cotton market and used roughly similar technology.[20] The industrial communities fostered by the textile mills were similar in all three cities. The mills were the cities' largest employers, especially of young people. There was a smaller sector of shops and craftspeople, and a still smaller group of middle-class employers. Preston, as a port city, was notably larger than the other two and also supported a substantial mercantile class, which affected migrant women's employment opportunities.

Independent female migrants made up from 8.6 to 12.5 percent of the entire migrant population in Preston and Paisley from 1851 to 1881, and throughout those years comprised approximately one quarter of those who migrated in the past ten years in those cities (Figures 1.1 and 1.2). In Lowell young single women were an even more important component of the migrant population. Unmarried

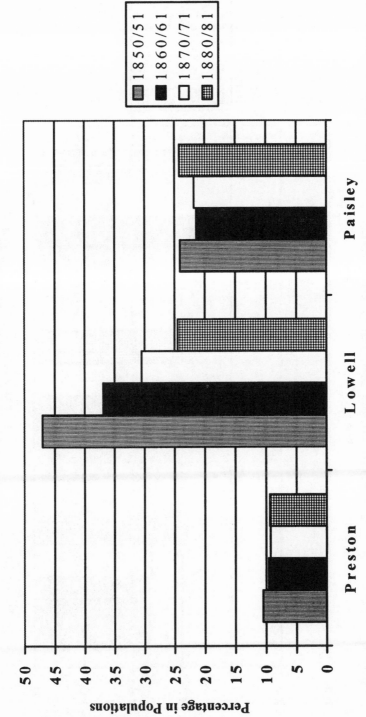

Figure 1.1

Percentage of migrants in total populations.

Preston, Lowell, and Paisley, 1850–1881.

Legend:
- 1850/51
- 1860/61
- 1870/71
- 1880/81

(Y-axis) Percentage in Populations: 0, 5, 10, 15, 20, 25, 30, 35, 40, 45, 50

(X-axis categories) Preston, Lowell, Paisley

Source: Data derived from *Census of Great Britain, 1851, Census of England and Wales, 1861–1881*, Preston Borough; *Census of Scotland, 1861–1881*, Paisley Burgh, both microfilm; Genealogical Society of the Church of Jesus Christ of Latter Day Saints, Salt Lake City, Utah; and *Seventh, Eighth, Ninth, and Tenth Census of the United States*, Lowell, Mass., microfilm, National Archives.

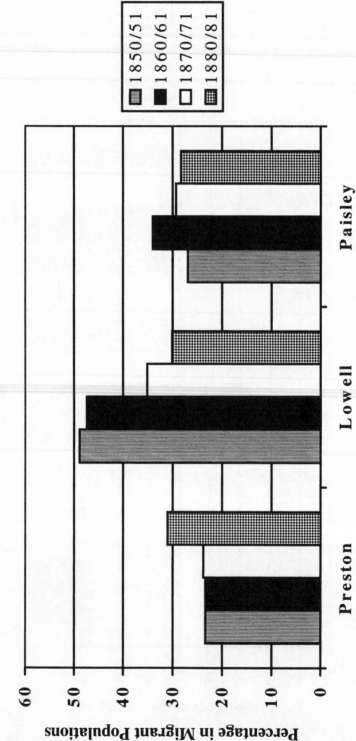

Figure 1.2
Percentage of independent female migrants in recent migrant populations.
Preston, Lowell, and Paisley, 1850–1881.

Legend:
- 1850/51
- 1860/61
- 1870/71
- 1880/81

X-axis categories: Preston, Lowell, Paisley

Y-axis: Percentage in Migrant Populations (0, 10, 20, 30, 40, 50, 60)

Source: Data derived from *Census of Great Britain, 1851*, *Census of England and Wales, 1861–1881*, Preston Borough; *Census of Scotland, 1861–1881*, Paisley Burgh, both microfilm; Genealogical Society of the Church of Jesus Christ of Latter Day Saints, Salt Lake City, Utah; and *Seventh, Eighth, Ninth*, and *Tenth Census of the United States*, Lowell, Mass., microfilm, National Archives.

women were 32 percent of Lowell's whole migrant population in 1850, and nearly half of the recent migrants. Their proportion in the population fell in the ensuing decades, but in 1880 they still made up more than 12 percent of the whole migrant population, and 30 percent of the recent American-born migrants.

Migration to all three cities between 1850 and 1881 was affected by two major historical events, the Potato Famine in Britain and the American Civil War. Beginning in 1845 and continuing for nearly a decade, Ireland and parts of the Scottish Highlands were struck by a blight that partially or wholly ruined potato crops, subjecting millions of people to the danger of starvation. In Scotland the menace was less severe than in Ireland, and was less subject to bungling by the government and charitable organizations. In both countries the famine exacerbated existing problems and prompted large-scale migration.[21] In Ireland, where in some regions the peasant class was already on the bare edge of survival, for many the only recourse was emigration. Refugees flooded first into industrial cities in Scotland and England, particularly Glasgow and the cities of western Lancashire. As they were able to save funds for the Atlantic passage hundreds of thousands migrated again, this time to the United States, especially to New England's industrial cities. Desperate for support, the Irish immigrants in Scotland and England competed for industrial work, and also drew on Poor Relief systems where they could.[22] In New England the Irish went into the factories, and the single women among them found a niche as domestic servants, a position that was shunned by native-born American migrants.[23] In 1850 Preston, Paisley, and Lowell all had substantial Irish populations, which grew through the next decade and a half, and the immigrants changed the face of the industrial workforce. In doing so they changed internal migration patterns, directly or indirectly filling the labor vacuum that had drawn many rural young women into the cities.

Less than a decade after the end of the Potato Famine, the American Civil War threatened the very existence of the United States. By drawing young men into arms the conflict discouraged young women's migration in New England, since they were required at home to help tend family farms. The Union blockade of Confederate ports also meant that the world's major supplier of raw cotton was unable to export its product, causing a Cotton Famine. Not only American but English and Scottish cotton mills were forced to shut down, depressing the economies of the cities that depended on them.[24] The 1860s saw a decline in internal migration to all three cities as potential employers faltered. Cotton exports resumed in 1865, but economic security did not return until the 1870s.

Comparing textile cities of three industrial nations lends strength to answering questions about migration to textile cities in general. For example, under what circumstances did employers' needs exercise more influence on single women's migration, and when were the women's own needs and desires a stronger factor? What experiences were common to all textile cities, and which were specific to the city or region in which they occurred?

Comparison also benefits the historiography of the individual cities in ways single case studies could not. Perhaps most important, placing Lowell in the study tests its rarity as a case of large-scale independent female migration. The thorough (and well-deserved) research on Lowell has to this point resulted in a perception of the mill girls' experiences as unique in the history of industrialization. Comparison with other textile cities puts Lowell's unusual features into a more realistic context. Preston, unlike Lowell, has little surviving information about single female migrants, although the census reveals without doubt that they existed. The comparative method allows meaningful conjecture to be made about those migrants' experiences, by drawing on surviving sources from cities with similar data. The least-studied city in this work is Paisley, and an individual case study of that city alone would indeed be a meaningful contribution to the historiography. However, by carrying out the study in a comparative context there is added breadth and significance to the information, since it is clear how the Scottish migrants' experiences fit into a more general pattern of single women's industrial migration.

Single Female Migrants in Historical Perspectives

This is primarily a work of migration history and has its strongest roots in that historiography. E. G. Ravenstein's analysis of the 1881 census established him as the father of migration history, and in it he set a pattern that to some extent still defines the discipline.[25] More than the experience of migration—how individual migrants chose when and where to migrate, how they found jobs, how they interacted with their host community—Ravenstein and those who followed him were interested in the gross motion of people, how population was moving in Britain and what rules governed that movement. Such analysis of migration patterns on a very large scale is essential in describing how migration is related to other factors and it emphasizes the importance of migration in international relations and development. The drawback to such a macroanalysis is the loss of detail. Aggregate statistics reveal important patterns, but they also obscure variation at regional and personal levels. In macroanalyses of migration, individuals often disappear entirely.

Even in a community with strong economic or social pressures toward migration a decision to move was made at the level of the individual, who had her own reasons for choosing to go or not to go based on such things as family circumstances, communication with previous migrants, and personal preferences for adventure or security. Analysis of individual experience is as crucial as economic analysis in understanding why and how migration occurs. A "micro" study concentrates on the experience of individuals or specific communities without necessarily tying them into the larger picture of national or world history. Microanalyses cast light on the personal inner workings of migration and so illuminate larger patterns. In Oscar Handlin's words, "The origins of a social process of any importance must be sought 'in the internal constitution of the social milieû.' . . . Only by considering immigrant adjustment on the local scale can the influence of the *milieu* be given full weight."[26]

In *Mill Girls and Strangers*, comparison provides an alternative to the macro-micro dilemma in migration history.[27] By incorporating research on three different cases into one analytical framework I am better able to support a generally applicable description of single women's migration than I could with a single case study. The comparative method gives the individual migrants' experiences context, showing that single women's migration into all three cities was similar in form and function, though different in detail. Thus I utilize a level of analysis that is not so broad as large-scale economic cycles and political shifts, yet has wider significance than a single community study. Comparison cannot replace the need to connect personal experience with large social and economic patterns, but it does allow analysis of differences in personal experience and gives individuals context on their own scale.

The comparative method also gives broader significance to the study of internal migration, which has received less attention in recent decades than international movement. In great part the focus on internal migration was dictated by my subjects; young white women in the nineteenth century were simply far more likely to move internally than to emigrate. Yet I chose these subjects because they were able to address questions regarding the effect of migration that are obscured in studying the personal experiences of international migration. For example, internal migrants did not (with the possible exception of Scottish Highlanders) face as large a linguistic or cultural change as did international migrants; questions of assimilation or acculturation have less meaning in discussions of internal migration. With the possibility of ethnic (though not class or gender) bias against the migrants largely removed, patterns of behavior can be more firmly connected to an individual's status as a migrant, rather than to cultural preferences. Comparing the internal migration experience in different countries allows generalizations about what behavioral choices were a product of migration, and which were more likely cultural preferences. With a more complete understanding of internal migration, it may be possible for other scholars to determine which features of immigrant experience are due to cultural differences, and which may be the product of migration itself.

Single women's migration is not only a problem of demographics, but of economics, class, gender, and the family. During the eighteenth and nineteenth centuries in both Britain and the United States patterns of labor and family relationships changed as the primary economic activity for many families shifted from agricultural subsistence to waged industrial labor. During this process young women's economic roles in the family changed as well, generally from assistants in a family enterprise to wage earners in their own right.[28]

The single female migrants were a distinct labor group in nineteenth-century textile cities, fulfilling particular roles. Although most were working class, employed in factories or as domestic servants, there were social differences among them.[29] For example, in Preston some migrants were able to work as boarding-school teachers or in dressmaking shops, both of which required more educational and economic resources than working as a domestic servant. Migrant teachers and skilled workers most likely came from a different social level than did migrants who were servants. In Lowell, most migrants were the daughters of small landowners and were literate, both factors that place them at a different class level than most English and Scottish migrants.[30] All female migrants, furthermore, were expected to conform to middle-class moral principles. Domestic servants could be immediately dismissed for violating their employers' standards, and strict standards of behavior were imposed on corporate boardinghouse residents.

In spite of the influence of class on migrant women's lives in the occupations they chose there is little evidence of class conflict among female migrants in the period of this study, at least as expressed through labor activism. The early generations of Lowell workers organized labor protests, but female-headed unions had faded by midcentury, when this study opens.[31] In Paisley, migrant women showed more regional identification (especially those from the Highlands) than class affiliation, and there is no record of women attending organizational meetings, even when arguments were made on their behalf.[32] In both British cities, the majority of migrant women worked in isolation as domestic servants, a profession that was not organized in any sense until the last years of the nineteenth century. Economics, on the other hand, most certainly affected young migrant women's lives, in their need to work at all and in the positions they chose. Some sense of their position in the community was almost certainly present, displaying itself in their occupations, in the clothes they wore and their leisure-time activities. There is no doubt that they knew to what level of society they belonged, but there is no evidence of conflict over that position.

Bound up with the issue of class is the issue of gender.[33] Both were social systems that controlled behavior, the one based on economic status, the other on biological sex. Just as there was little class-based conflict evident in the migrants' lives, I have found no evidence of women's-rights agitation among the migrants.[34] There is no surviving evidence that they questioned the validity of the gender structure in which they lived, though they may have seen migration as a means to escape some aspects of rural women's lives. Migrants were in the process of transition between two realms of womanhood, from dependent "girl" to adult, married "woman" who though still dependent on a husband's authority was expected to manage her own household and exercise some control over her children and servants. In the meantime they occupied a third, median position, identified by paid labor, partial independence from all family groups, and hence vulnerability to misfortune. The migrants identified themselves primarily as female, and as such they felt they were bound to certain standards of behavior and appearance to maintain their respectability. Respectability was equated with "proper" behavior, but definitions of respectability varied depending on class status.[35] Governed by middle-class employers, migrant women were expected to maintain middle-class standards of working-class respectability in terms of dress, cleanliness, decorum, and choice of companions. When migrants transgressed these boundaries—through flamboyant dress, unseemly fraternization with men or nonattendance at religious services—they were subject to ridicule, scorn, even censure by their employers. While a domestic servant might expect to have sex with a suitor before they were married, consistent with her rural, working-class background, her middle-class employers would be appalled at such behavior, and the misunderstanding could easily cost the servant her position.[36] If the migrants aspired to personal and economic independence, they nearly always did so within the limits set by their gender and class expectations.

Evidence in this study, particularly from Lowell and Paisley, suggests that the limitations of gender encouraged single female migrants to form networks of friends in their destination cities whenever possible. Chain migration, the practice of one migrant sending money, encouragement, or both for others to join her, contributed to the development of such support systems. These networks both made migration more enjoyable, by providing social contacts, and helped young women to negotiate such difficulties as finding jobs or managing through a period of illness or pregnancy. The chance of unmarried motherhood was just one danger faced by independent female migrants, and one reason they were a source of anxiety to the urban middle class. Women alone were suspected of turning to prostitution to supplement meager wages or, conversely, they were seen as vulnerable to corruption from bad company.[37]

Migrant women *were* vulnerable, but they were not helpless. Within options limited by their social position (mostly working class, female, young) they exercised their own agency, choosing situations that served their individual needs in the transition from past and to future family groups. It is today widely recognized that migration was historically common in young women's lives, but what that meant for the women is little understood in any but the most general terms. My description is one based in the opportunities, desires, and problems of the migrants themselves, showing that a woman did not need to be incorporated in a nuclear family to function successfully in a nineteenth-century textile city. Throughout the third quarter of the nineteenth century, single female migrants did more than respond passively to economic and social forces. They used the opportunities they found to extend the boundaries of their lives, asserting independence from parents and moving toward their own adulthood.

CHAPTER 2

Preston: The Unseen Migrants

In July of 1858 the grocer R. Hignet advertised in the *Preston Guardian* for a "female servant of all work, in a situation where there is no family. One from the county of Westmorland or Yorkshire would be preferred."[1] There is no record of the young woman who filled Hignet's requirements, but he almost certainly found one. Preston and its neighbors attracted single female migrants from Westmorland and Yorkshire, as well as from rural Lancashire, precisely because employers like Hignet preferred "country girls" as household servants. Domestic service was equated with migration, whether from the parental home to another household in the same town or across parish and county boundaries to an industrial city like Preston.[2] This migration did not excite comment from contemporary middle-class observers and rarely sparked fears that women separated from their families would turn to lives of sinfulness and crime.[3] Nor were migrant women as domestic servants problematic for historians like Louise Tilly and Joan Scott, who described domestic service as the typical employment for migrant daughters in the family economy model of young women's work. Similarly, historians who examined individuals' life courses, like George Alter, were comfortable finding female migrants working as domestic servants.[4] Since these important works, very little has been published that examines American or European migrant women's roles in family economies. Single women's migration to cities like Preston was "normal" to both contemporaries and modern historians. Comparison to statistics compiled by other historians show that Preston was a generally typical British city. Yet under closer examination the single female migration pattern in Preston was not as simple as contemporaries and historians believed it to be.

Preston nevertheless, with its well-integrated, unremarkable migrant community, serves as a baseline against which to compare migration into Lowell and Paisley, where migration did prompt comment. At the same time it challenges the common perception of female migrants to textile towns. Independent female migrants to Preston showed different occupational patterns than nonmigrants and family-based migrants, but domestic service was far from the only occupation they chose, and many of them retained a portion of their wages for their own use rather than contributing to a family economy. A complete description of single women's migration thus must begin with a fresh examination of the migrants' actions, discarding the preconception that all migrants followed a single behavioral pattern that did not change over time. The sources in Preston particularly illuminate the importance of employers' needs in drawing migrants to a city, showing that young women were recruited to Preston from both rural and urban areas for specific but varied employment opportunities, and that the migrants changed their behavior according to what options were available.

Preston, on the Ribble river in central Lancashire (see maps, Figures 2.1a and 2.1b) was one of the birth places of the cotton industry. Mechanized cotton spinning was well established in the city by the end of the eighteenth century, and legions of handloom weavers in the surrounding countryside made the area a center of textile production. By 1850 cotton factories dominated the city physically and economically. Rapid population growth had outpaced construction; working-class housing was overcrowded and appallingly unhealthy. Cotton manufacturers were the primary employers in Preston at midcentury, directly employing at least 25 percent of the city's adult population in 1851, and more in construction, maintenance, and management.[5] In spite of cotton's dominance it was not the only employer in Preston, nor the only strong economic sector. Preston had been a port city before it was a textile city, and trade remained important. Trading in various goods employed about 8 percent of the city's adult men, and more than 14 percent were craftworkers producing goods from shoes to umbrellas. The railway was also important to Preston, employing men as laborers, clerks, and engine drivers. The strength of trade in Preston gave the city a strong middle class, which in turn supported a substantial service sector.[6]

Women in Preston did not work in as many different occupations as men. Forty-three percent of Preston's adult women reported no waged employment at all, though most were occupied in caring for their homes and children and may have engaged in sporadic income-producing labor that they or the census enumerators did not consider an "occupation."[7] Just over 9 percent of Preston's

Figure 2.1a
Map of England and Wales showing county boundaries

Figure 2.1b
Map of England and Wales with places mentioned in the text

women worked in the female-dominated service fields, as residential domestic servants, charwomen or laundresses. Five percent of women in Preston plied a needle for their living as dressmakers, milliners, or plain seamstresses. Of the paid occupations women followed, work in the city's textile factories was by far the most important, employing 36 percent of Preston's adult women. In the whole of Great Britain, the numbers of women working in textiles was second to those in domestic service, but it was not unusual in industrial cities for there to be many more operatives than servants.[8]

Preston's textile industries, like others in Lancashire, relied on a burgeoning working-class population to supply workers for their factories. When the first of the large cotton spinning mills opened it was staffed by orphan and apprentice labor, but that was a limited labor supply.[9] As the mills grew and new technology was developed, employers turned toward family-based labor, the supply of which was sustained by rural-urban migration.[10] Men worked as mule spinners (a skilled job that initially required a grown man's strength) and overseers, their sons as doffers and piecers, and their wives and daughters as power loom weavers, throstle spinners, winders, warpers, slubbers and rovers, among other specialized tasks.[11] Well after the mid-nineteenth-century employment in the cotton mills continued to attract migrants from the countryside around Preston, a fact which was used by contemporaries to explain Preston's relatively low wages.[12] Single women made up nearly a quarter of all the recent transcounty migrants (those under age thirty) in Preston from 1851 through 1871, and in 1881 that proportion rose to over 30 percent. Although migrants were a small portion of the total population, independent young women were always a substantial segment of that portion.

Michael Anderson's close study of Preston's 1851 census determined that most of the English-born migrants in Preston came to the city from thirty miles or fewer away. About 25 percent of these migrants were from neighboring cities such as Blackburn, but a majority had moved into the city from rural areas of Lancashire.[13] Lancashire's large rural sector and industrial centers contributed to urban growth without forcing transcounty migration. Seventy-nine percent of Preston's adult population in 1851 had been born in Lancashire, and another 9 percent was Irish-born, many of whom were refugees from the Potato Famine. A mere 1.5 percent of Preston's inhabitants were from elsewhere outside England (including Scotland). That left 10.3 percent of Preston's population in the sample who were migrants from within England and Wales.[14]

In this internal migrant community 8.6 percent were independent young women who had come within the last ten years, a proportion that remained relatively stable until 1881. Most of the migrants came from England's northern counties (Cumberland, Northumberland, Westmorland, and Durham) and Yorkshire to the east. The remaining smattering of migrants, about 3 percent of the total population, came from all across England, with higher concentrations from counties closer to Lancashire and London.

Methods of cotton production in Lancashire may have worked to somewhat limit migration within the region. Although cotton spinning was entirely mechanized by the early nineteenth century, mechanized weaving continued to present a problem. The increase in yarn production initially resulted in a proliferation of hand-loom weavers, instead of an immediate shift to powered weaving. Early power looms produced only coarse, plain cloth, and were unsuitable for textiles other than cotton. Until well into the mid-Victorian years, there was a niche for hand-loom weavers in producing high-quality fabrics.[15] Hand-loom weaving was primarily an outwork industry, carried out in a loom shop attached to the weaver's home. Though there were communities of urban hand-loom weavers, there were also country weavers who combined weaving with agricultural or pastoral occupations. Duncan Bythell maintained that their ability to gain a textile-based income while avoiding migration was one reason for hand-loom weavers' preference for that occupation.[16] Arthur Redford described migration as the last resort of families that were no longer able to support themselves in declining trades such as hand-loom weaving. They avoided this as long as possible and when it was finally necessary they moved as short a distance as possible.[17] Until it was impossible to maintain a living through hand-loom weaving, a family's shift to textile production did not mandate migration.

Young single people from rural areas of England, however, were quite likely to leave their parents' homes in favor of the cities. Michael Anderson discovered that in rural areas of Lancashire, only slightly more than half of the children remained in their parents' homes until marriage. Almost all children whose parents lived in cities, on the other hand, lived with their parents until they married.[18] This implies that a lack of profitable employment in England's rural areas prompted many young men and women to either find a position in another rural household or move to one of the growing cities in search of work. Anderson's findings suggested that most young migrants were moving either to the closest city or, if they made a longer move, to where friends or family would help them find work.[19]

The small proportion of transcounty migrants in Preston's population reflected a tendency for short-as-possible-distance migration in a region with many potential destinations. Although many young people made rural-to-urban migrations, most moved into cities within their own counties. As illustrated in Figure 2.2, recent independent migrants comprised just 2 to 5 percent of the whole single adult population in the years 1851–1881.[20] Figure 2.3, however, shows the gross numbers (derived from the samples) of independent, recent migrants in Preston. Although migrants were sometimes found in higher concentrations among single men in Preston, true to Ravenstein's law female migrants always exceeded the male in volume.[21]

In his study of internal migration and emigration throughout England and Wales between 1861 and 1900, Dudley Baines found that both urban- and rural-born women were more likely than men to be internally mobile. Rural-born men, on the other hand, were more likely to emigrate out of the country entirely.[22] The consistent presence of more female migrants than male in Preston agrees with Baines's findings, and emphasizes the differences between male and female migration. The same social beliefs that demanded young women live and work under the supervision of adults restricted their ability to move overseas in search of opportunity. A large number of British young women may have migrated internally because regardless of personal desires virtually none of them were able to emigrate independently, while young men who were inclined to emigrate were more readily able to do so.[23] Internal migration could be a secondary choice for independent single men, while it was the only migration choice available to many young women.

Single male migrants in Preston peaked, both proportionately and numerically, in the 1861 census, when recent migrants were nearly 5 percent of the single male population. Single women's migration to Preston also rose numerically from 1851 to 1861, but the increase was not so dramatic. Indeed, Figure 2.2 shows the proportion of independent migrants among Preston's single women remained stable in the 1850s, and fell slightly in the 1860s. A substantial rise in the number and proportion of female migrants only began in the 1870s. In the first half of the 1860s the great Cotton Panic that accompanied the American Civil War severely curtailed opportunities for migrants to Preston and across Lancashire. The crisis was exacerbated by a glutted cotton export market at the beginning of the decade. Thus demand (and hence employment and

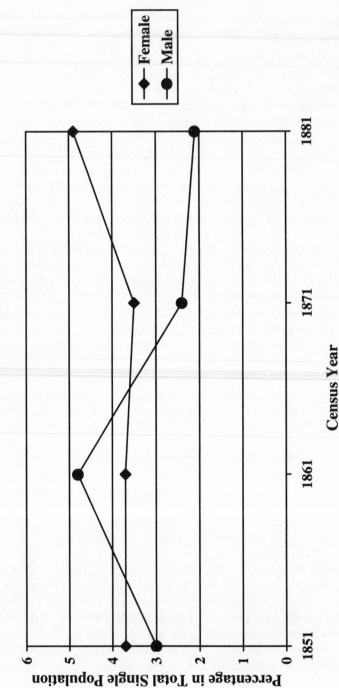

Figure 2.2
Recent independent migrants in the single population. Preston, 1851–1881.

Female
Male

Census Year

Percentage in Total Single Population

6
5
4
3
2
1
0

1851   1861   1871   1881

Source: Data derived from *Census of Great Britain, 1851* and *Census of England and Wales, 1861–1881*, Preston Borough, microfilm, and Genealogical Society of the Church of Jesus Christ of Latter Day Saints, Salt Lake City, Utah.

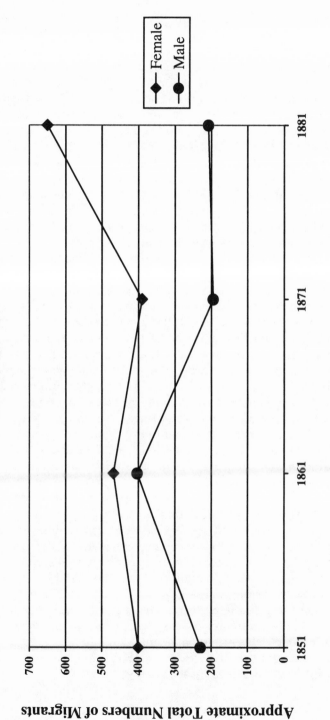

Figure 2.3
Volume of recent independent migrants.
Preston, 1851–1881.

Legend: ◆ Female ● Male

Y-axis: Approximate Total Numbers of Migrants (0, 100, 200, 300, 400, 500, 600, 700)

X-axis: Census Year (1851, 1861, 1871, 1881)

Source: Data derived from *Census of Great Britain, 1851* and *Census of England and Wales, 1861–1881*, Preston Borough, microfilm, and Genealogical Society of the Church of Jesus Christ of Latter Day Saints, Salt Lake City, Utah.

production) had already begun to fall when the American war raised the specter of raw material shortages.[24] The uncertainty of the following years, when raw cotton was more valuable than finished and investors were haunted by fears that an early end to the war would produce a new glut of raw materials and loss of investment, brought the Preston cotton industry to a virtual standstill.[25] Contemporaries reported that cotton operatives had "removed to other parts of the country, and large numbers emigrated to Queensland, America, Australia, &c."[26] Even after the supply of raw cotton was restored to Lancashire, a financial crisis brought on by overproduction kept the region's economy in the doldrums.[27] Preston's population grew by fewer than three thousand over the course of the 1860s. Compared with a growth of more than thirteen thousand between 1851 and 1861, the decade of the Cotton Famine was clearly a period of reduced migration to Preston.[28]

Widespread unemployment in the city undoubtedly discouraged migrants from traveling to Preston, and may have prompted young migrants to return to their parents' homes. In addition, more Lancashire-born single women resided with their parents in Preston in 1871 than in 1861 (62.9 percent compared to 56.9 percent). This reflects the reduction of independent female migrants from rural Lancashire and thus the economic difficulties of the decade, as single women were less able to support themselves. After 1871, however, the economy improved; the number and proportion of female migrants in Preston rose correspondingly.

In the 1881 census of Preston, nearly 5 percent of the single women in the city, more than six hundred individuals, had recently migrated from outside the county boundary.[29] Baines reported that internal migration from most rural counties to urban ones rose in the 1870s, which he attributed to the "attraction of the urban areas."[30] The 1870s were indeed kind to Preston, especially in comparison to the widespread distress of the Cotton Famine years.[31] Perhaps more important, however, were continuing changes in England's economy and infrastructure. Agricultural depression and change meant that fewer and fewer young women stayed with their families in rural areas.[32] In addition, investment in the English and Welsh railway system increased after 1870.[33] The railways made travel easier in general, and Preston's central location on the west coast line made it an easy destination. Independent women's proportion among the recent migrant population reflected these changes, rising to 29.2 percent in 1881 after hovering around 23 percent in the previous three censuses.

In spite of fluctuations in response to economic change, internal migration to Preston was remarkably stable throughout the period from 1851 to 1881, with migrants (single and in families) making up between 9 and 10.5 percent of the entire population in each census year. Within this percentage single women's migration was more variable but still remarkably steady, neither rising to a flood nor trickling away altogether in response to the city's or the nation's economic shifts. The rise after 1871 corresponded with an increasingly frantic demand among England's middle class for reliable, inexpensive servants—precisely the sort of young woman R. Hignet had in mind when he placed his advertisement in 1858.[34] Young women after 1871 became a larger proportion of the migrants in Preston. Many of the women who migrated to Preston likely came in response to the demand for domestic servants, realizing that they were desirable employees. Indeed, the two counties Hignet specified, Westmorland and Yorkshire, were consistently the largest sources of migrants to Preston. The female migrants' birthplaces inclined them to particular occupations, with rural-born migrants far more likely than those from urban counties to enter domestic service.

For the first two-thirds of the period, most independent female migrants to Preston came from counties that either immediately bordered Lancashire or, in the case of London-born migrants, were connected by a direct rail line.[35] Only after 1871, when many new rail connections were completed, did larger numbers of women begin to migrate from more distant counties. (See maps, Figures 2.4–2.7.) Furthermore, the migrants came primarily from counties designated by Dudley Baines as either rural or "urban with significant rural parts."[36]

Westmorland was the largest overall contributor of single female migrants to Preston. This rural county sent more than a quarter of all the recent migrants to Preston prior to the Cotton Famine, and accounted for 17.5 percent of all the recent female migrants in the period. Westmorland bordered Lancashire to the north and had little industrialization of its own that could work to keep potential migrants within the county boundaries. The numbers of migrants to Preston from Westmorland dwindled sharply after the 1860s, however, while more migrants were coming from farther afield. Yorkshire, which neighbored Lancashire to the east, had some substantial industrialization but also had considerable rural area. Yorkshire sent a steady flow of migrants into Preston, the numbers surpassing Westmorland in 1871 and 1881. Overall the volume

Figure 2.4
Origin of single female migrants to Preston 1851.

Figure 2.5
Origin of single female migrants to Preston 1861.

Figure 2.6
Origin of single female migrants to Preston 1871.

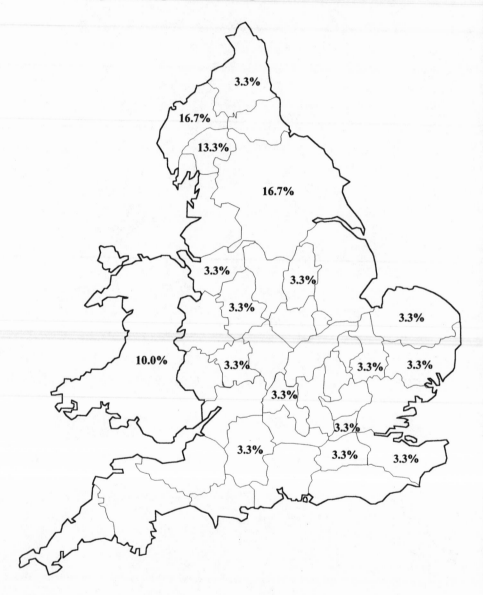

Figure 2.7
Origin of single female migrants to Preston 1881.

from Yorkshire nearly equaled that from Westmorland, accounting for almost 17 percent of Preston's female migrants over the entire period.

After these two major contributors, Cumberland, the other primarily rural county in northern England, sent the most consistent stream of migrants into Preston. Although migrants from Cumberland had to pass through Westmorland to reach Lancashire, the lack of industry in that county helped to keep them from stopping. Cumberland natives made up nearly 11 percent of Preston's recent independent female migrants from 1851 to 1881. Welsh natives, many from Flintshire, Wales's northernmost county, accounted for 8.4 percent of these recent migrants, and women from London just over 7 percent. The Welsh presence in the city increased throughout the period, while migration from London was relatively stable except during the Cotton Famine years.

Because of the overall low proportion of independent female migrants in Preston's total population it is risky to point out strong migration streams into Preston in the later censuses, when as few as two or three migrants in the sample from one county represented a significant percentage of migration from that county. It is apparent, however, that the migrant population in 1881 traveled longer distances to Preston than the migrants had in 1851. The primary birthplaces of migrants in 1851 were concentrated in the ring of counties immediately surrounding Lancashire, with secondary groups from Cumberland to the north and London.[37] By 1881, however, the origins of migrants were more diffuse, coming from the second ring of counties outside Lancashire and beyond as expanding railway networks facilitated longer-distance moves. These data suggest that proximity to a migrant's place of birth and ease of travel were considerations in moving to Preston, but without additional data on how many young women from the northern counties made the trek to London or other cities it is impossible to declare just how significant they were. Continuing distress in agriculture limited opportunities in rural areas and, as I discuss below, there was an increasing demand for female labor in Preston. Both of these factors could override an easy journey in the selection of a destination.

Dudley Baines found that in all of England and Wales rural-born women were more likely to migrate internally than urban-born women, if only because the employment opportunities for women were expanding primarily in urban areas.[38] The data from Preston bears out that conclusion, showing that 59 percent of all independent female migrants in the city between 1851 and 1881 came from rural counties.

Statistically, migration into Preston conforms very neatly with migration patterns throughout England and Wales, but actual movement is only part of the story. While accepting Preston as typical it is also necessary to redefine what is meant by "typical" through a far more detailed examination of the single female migrant population. As Baines suggested, young women from rural areas may have had a greater propensity to migrate simply because the relative lack of opportunity to earn wages in rural England made migration necessary for survival. Yet the migration streams into Preston correlated to the needs of employers, not distress in the countryside; if there were few opportunities, as in the Cotton Famine years, fewer people chose Preston as a destination.

Although employment opportunities in the city were crucial for migrants, not all migrants were willing to take any available position. The type of region in which a migrant was born presaged the occupation she was likely to fill in Preston. As Hignet's advertisement suggested, women from Westmorland and Yorkshire, as well as other rural areas, were likely to find positions in domestic service. Migrants from urban areas, however, pursued different avenues. Figure 2.8 illustrates that migrants from urban counties were less likely than other migrant groups to enter either domestic service or the textile mills. The "other" occupations they preferred were frequently in the arts, as performers or music teachers (17.6 percent of urban migrants) or trained craft workers such as dressmakers (also 17.6 percent). A considerable proportion of urban migrants had no income at all (11.8 percent), which suggests that they were dependent on friends or relations for support.[39] In contrast, migrants from rural areas far preferred residential domestic service.[40] The migrants from counties with both urban and rural areas, as might be expected, showed traits of both urban and rural migrants, with a large number in domestic service but also represented in textile mills and other occupations. The high proportion of urban/rural migrants in Preston's cotton mills may signal the migration of experienced mill workers from Yorkshire (an urban/rural county) textile cities. Such migrants would be more likely to find work in the industry with which they were already familiar rather than in domestic service.

Migrants overall were deeply underrepresented in textile work. The "Lancashire" set of columns in Figure 2.8 shows that averaged across the period, two-thirds of Lancashire-born single women

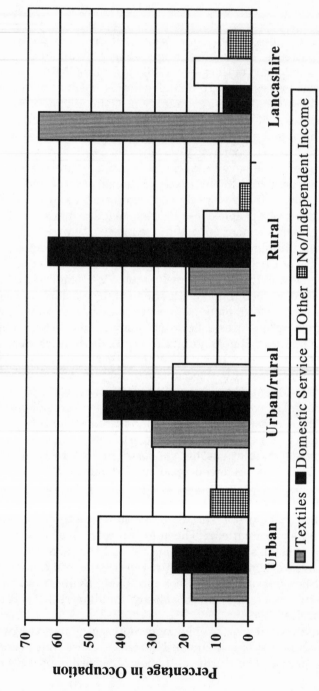

Figure 2.8
Single women's occupations by place of birth.
Preston, 1851–1881.

Textiles ▨ Domestic Service □ Other ▨ No/Independent Income

Urban counties include: London and Middlesex, Warwickshire and Staffordshire. Urban/rural include: Yorkshire, Durham, Northumberland, Cheshire, Nottinghamshire, Gloucestershire, Essex, Kent, Surrey, Hampshire, Sussex, and Monmouthshire (Wales). All other counties of England and Wales are included in Rural. "Lancashire" includes all unmarried Lancashire-born women under thirty years old.

Source: Data derived from *Census of Great Britain*, 1851 and *Census of England and Wales*, 1861–1881, Preston Borough, microfilm, Genealogical Society of the Church of Jesus Christ of Latter Day Saints, Salt Lake City, Utah.

under thirty years old were employed in cotton (mostly), silk, or linen (a few) mills, with only about a quarter choosing domestic service or another occupation. Only 22 percent of migrants, on the other hand, worked in any kind of textile industry, and independent migrants accounted for less than 3 percent of the Preston mills' total female workforce. The importance of family and acquaintance in obtaining positions in the mills certainly had some influence on the type of occupation migrants found in Preston; young women born in or near the city were more likely to have connections that would help them find work.[41] About 20 percent of the few recent migrants to Preston who worked in the textile mills lived in a household headed by a relative, compared to just 7 percent of those who did not work in the mills.[42] Urban-born women may have scorned domestic service because of the subservience the job required. Rural-born women, on the other hand, might also resent the lack of freedom in domestic service but they valued more highly the relative simplicity of finding food, lodging, and a wage under the same roof in an unfamiliar environment.[43]

Textile work also bore a question of respectability for migrant women. From the early nineteenth century the archetypal "factory girl" occupied her own class/gender category typified by the middle classes as an irresponsible, spendthrift character who spent too much money on clothes inappropriate to her station and did not display a deference appropriate to her position in society.[44] An officer of Preston's Penny Savings Bank was thinking of factory girls in 1859 when he declared, as related by a newspaper reporter, to an enthusiastic crowd,

> Mr. Moore asked if it were not a fact that . . . the large majority of the females of the working classes in this town dressed as well, or rather as showily, as ladies of the first rank. (Here, here) Their money was spent for the most part in dress—in mere tawdry finery—(here, here)—in order to make up an appearance; . . . Now, people who did that were not looked on as respectable.[45]

Note the distinction Moore made between the working-class "females" and the respectable "ladies of the first rank." Though they may wear the same clothes, without the proper status those clothes became "mere tawdry finery." The irresponsibility working-class women showed in squandering their wages on clothes was extended, in middle class perception, to disregard for such things as moral standards.

Factory workers were also seen as susceptible to moral corruption because of their low wages and their frequent contact with male supervisors. Linda Mahood found that Glaswegian moral reformers looked with particular suspicion at factory girls in their effort to control prostitution, and the same suspicion must have existed in Preston.[46] The stereotype of textile work as unrespectable, even immoral, may have worked to prevent rural migrants, concerned with their good names and unfamiliar with urban society in any case, from even seeking employment in the mills.

Fluctuations in migrants' employment patterns, addressed in more detail below, suggest that migrants' choices were based at least as much on the opportunities presented to them as on a preference for certain types of occupation. The aggregate statistics used to compile Figure 2.8 are useful in discerning overall trends, but it is important also to note that migrants' behavior varied from census to census, depending on conditions in the city. In 1871, for example, one-third of the young women from rural counties worked in textile mills and all of the (very few) urban-born migrants in the sample worked as domestic servants.[47] In the next census the migrants' employment statistics returned to a more familiar pattern, with only 7 percent of rural migrants in textile mills and more urban migrants working as actresses or musicians than in either textiles or domestic service.

The young women who migrated to Preston from outside Lancashire not only showed different employment patterns than Lancashire-born women, they also found different forms of accommodation. Figure 2.9 illustrates independent single women's relationships to the heads of the households in which they lived, divided by the type of county in which they were born. The differences in employment patterns between urban and rural migrants were repeated in housing choices. Rural and urban/rural migrants were more likely to live with an employer than in any other arrangement. Urban migrants, on the other hand, were slightly more likely to choose private lodgings over living with their employer. Yet all three groups of migrants were more likely to live with an employer than were independent Lancashire-born women, who preferred to board with unrelated families.[48] Figure 2.9 shows again that although single female migrants did behave differently than nonmigrants, they also did not follow a single, predictable pattern. Being able to live with an employer was important to a majority of the migrants, but not to all of them.

About 10 percent of the recent female migrants from urban or rural counties lived with relatives, as did nearly a quarter of the

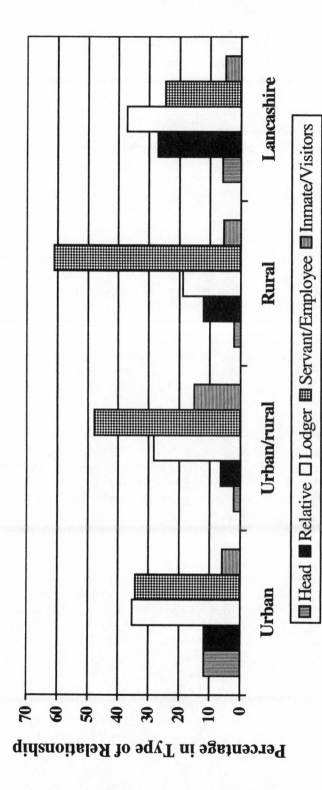

Figure 2.9
Single women's relationship to head of household.
Preston, 1851–1881.

Legend: ▦ Head ■ Relative ☐ Lodger ▦ Servant/Employee ▥ Inmate/Visitors

"Lancashire": includes single women less than thirty years old and not living with their parents.
Head: includes head of household and persons living alone.
Relative: includes any specified relationship other than child.
Lodger: includes boarders and lodgers unrelated to head.
Servant/Employee: includes domestic servants, apprentices, assistants, and other employees.
Inmate/Visitors: includes visitors, boarding-school students, prisoners and patients in prisons, hospitals, and poorhouses.

Source: Data derived from *Census of Great Britain*, 1851 and *Census of England and Wales*, 1861–1881, Preston Borough, microfilm, Genealogical Society of the Church of Jesus Christ of Latter Day Saints, Salt Lake City, Utah.

Lancashire-born independent single women. Michael Anderson, examining migration at the parish level, determined that 'parentless' young kin in 1851 Preston were primarily migrants from rural areas who depended on relatives in the city to find employment. That is a likely explanation for the Lancashire-born women and rural migrants living with relatives throughout the period.[49] Ninety percent of the rural migrants who lived with relatives reported an occupation, most of them (60 percent) in cotton mills. The urban migrants living with relatives, however, generally had no regular income, which suggests that they were members of Preston's middle or upper classes.[50] The suggestion that urban migrants who lived with relatives were more likely to be middle class is strengthened by the fact that in 1871, when Preston's economy had still not recovered from the effects of the Cotton Famine, no urban-born migrants were shown to have either lived with relatives or had independent incomes. Many more single urban-born women than migrants from other regions, it seems, were middle-class women dependent on and moving with family members.

The differences between rural and urban/rural migrants' relationships to the families with which they lived are best explained by the same factors that explain the differences in employment patterns. Migrants from other textile cities can reasonably be expected to behave more like Lancashire-born independent single women than rural-born migrants. The unavoidable combination of rural and urban migrants in the urban/rural category naturally resulted in patterns that combined characteristics of both.[51]

Overall, Preston showed a gradually changing pattern of women's independent migration from 1851 to 1881 that conforms neatly with prevailing models of English migration and single women's migration in the nineteenth century. Migrants were predominantly but not exclusively from rural areas, tending to come from further afield as the period progressed. Many single female migrants chose to work as domestic servants, apparently shunning textile factory labor. Yet Preston's very conformity to the old models makes the variations there more important. Not all the migrants to Preston were country girls; a substantial proportion had apparently come from other textile cities. Since the type of county in which a migrant was born influenced her choices in the city, all single female migrants cannot be lumped into one homogeneous group. Rural migrants did show a propensity for domestic service, but that tendency was tempered by rural and urban/rural migrants who chose textile work or urban migrants who found still other occupations. A substantial number of the migrants who worked in industry or other occupations lived as lodgers, choosing not to reside with relatives or employers as might be expected. Preston was a typical case in England; the variety of experience evident there must be at least posited for all English and perhaps all nineteenth-century textile cities.

Migrants and Domestic Service in Preston

Although far from all migrants were domestic servants, service was the most common experience for migrants to Preston in the years from 1851–1881, and young women who chose domestic service provide the largest block of information about single female migrants to Preston. A closer study of domestic service and migrants' role in the domestic labor pool gives depth to the story of single women's migration by highlighting the interplay of employer demand and migrant response. As Hignet's expressed preference implied, middle-class ideas about gender and urbanization made young rural women more desirable employees than urban-born girls. Domestic service was the easiest occupation for migrants to find in industrial cities, and the demand for servants rose steadily through most of the nineteenth century due to the rising affluence of the middle class.[52] There was a labor vacuum in the middle-class home that worked to draw migrants into the city, in addition to an expectation that servants would be migrants. Examining the question of why rural women chose domestic service but those from urban areas were more likely to choose other occupations, finally, further emphasizes the diversity of migrants' experiences, even in the face of limited opportunities.

Young rural women were desirable employees to the middle classes not only because they would work for low wages in a subordinate position but because of the ideology that surrounded them. Nineteenth-century ideals for single women specified that they would be virginal, submissive to authority and diligent at their tasks. These qualities were amplified by a rural background, while they were tarnished by urban life, giving rise to the despised "factory girl." Middle-class women sought domestic servants untainted by the independence and materialism associated with urban workers. Country girls were assumed to be used to parental control, unused to handling their own wages, and quite likely healthier overall than children who had grown up in the disease and pollution of the city.

In spite of some employers' preference for servants born outside Lancashire and the large percentage of migrants who chose domestic service, young women from outside Lancashire did not come close to filling all of the available positions for servants in Preston. Sixty-eight percent of all the unmarried, female domestic servants in Preston's 1851 census were born in Lancashire.[53] Many of the Lancashire-born servants, however, were migrants from rural areas outside Preston, and had much in common with the transcounty migrants.[54] The next largest group, from the rural northern counties of Westmorland and Cumberland, distantly trailed the Lancashire born at 12.6 percent. They were followed in turn by migrants from elsewhere in England (10.1 percent), particularly Yorkshire. The remaining 9 percent of servants were immigrants, primarily from Ireland.

Most of Preston's domestic servants were the only hired help in the household, listed in the census as housemaids or simply "general servant." These women had responsibility for every aspect of housekeeping, under the supervision of their mistresses.[55] A minority of the servants worked in larger households and had more specialized duties such as housekeeper, nursemaid, cook, or kitchenmaid. Most servants, 89 percent in 1851, worked for individual families, but about 6 percent worked in boarding houses, hotels or taverns, and a few were employed at schools or other institutions. The servants were generally young: in 1851, 79.5 percent were under thirty years old, including 33 percent who were between fifteen and nineteen.[56]

Through the next thirty years, transcounty migrants increased their proportion in Preston's servant population while the total number of domestic servants in the city fell. In 1851 approximately 1,500 single, female domestic servants were enumerated in the census, of whom about 350 (23 percent) were transcounty migrants (many more had probably migrated from rural Lancashire). By 1881 the census recorded only about 1,100 unmarried female servants, but nearly 420 of them, 36 percent, were migrants from outside Lancashire. Domestic servants were becoming increasingly difficult to find in England's cities as the century progressed; migrants were not only able to find employment as domestic servants in Preston but the labor vacuum in middle-class houses actually pulled migrants to the city as potential employers actively recruited country girls.[57]

Domestic service was the easiest sort of job for migrants to find. Kinship was crucial to gaining employment in England's cotton mills, a factor which automatically put a large group of migrants at a disadvantage for industrial employment.[58] Nor was there a wide variety of other occupations open to young women at midcentury. Domestic service and textile work together accounted for three-quarters of all employed women in Preston. Most of the remainder were in another sort of factory work or were business proprietors— options that were either limited by the same kin-preference systems as textiles or required an investment most migrants could not supply. Domestic servants, on the other hand, were expected to be migrants. Their very lack of contacts in the city was a factor in their desirability, since employers believed they would have fewer reasons to lark off rather than attending to their duties.

The system by which servants found work in Preston could not have been better designed to aid migrants. Young women often found work in their own village or on neighboring farms through word of mouth, and throughout the period women continued to get employment via personal connections.[59] By mid century there was also a formal structure through which potential servants and hopeful employers could find each other. Registry offices specializing in matching servants with employers were well established in Preston by 1850, and they proliferated in the next thirty years as the competition for good servants became more heated. The *Oakey's Commercial Directory of Preston* in 1851 listed three Registry offices, including Mrs. Mary Bannister's establishment at 107 Church Street, which continued under a series of owners until at least 1881.[60] While the Registry at 107 Church was thriving, it could not keep up with demand. The number of registries in Preston rose to a peak of seven listed in Gillette's directory of 1869, and there were still five in Mannex's 1880 directory.[61] Registry offices were sometimes objects of distrust for both employers and potential employees, since they could charge fees from both parties and did not necessarily guarantee placement. Nevertheless, the existence and proliferation of such offices indicates a keen demand for their services.[62]

The presence of servants' registries in Preston through 1880 suggests that employers were having a difficult time finding servants through less formal contacts. The total number of domestic servants in Preston fell between the 1851 and 1881 censuses, but that decline was not necessarily due to a fall in demand. In England as a whole the demand for domestic servants in middle-class England did not begin to fall until the 1890s, when smaller families, modern conveniences, and an increased sense of the sanctity of the private family home made resident domestic servants both less necessary and less desirable.[63] The advertising pages of Preston's newspapers, meanwhile, showed an increasingly competitive search for servants between 1850 and 1880 as well as expanding employment opportunities for young women in general.

The use of newspaper advertisements to find jobs and employees in the nineteenth century also indicates that the traditional method of finding workers through family or acquaintance was not sufficient to fill employers' demands. Hence people without connections in Preston, like recent migrants, were more readily able to pursue the positions. The rise in advertisements for women's jobs other than domestic service shows that there were more opportunities for young women in Preston as the century progressed. As more Lancashire-born women chose occupations other than domestic service, migrants were more likely to fill the service openings.

Newspaper advertisements also disclose the employers' preferences regarding their servants. Most employers were satisfied to specify only that a servant be "of good character," but some were extremely specific in their requirements. An advertiser in January 1857 knew exactly what he was looking for:

> Wanted, to fill the situation of Housekeeper, to a single gentleman, a respectable, middle-aged woman. She must be a person of steady, careful, sober, industrious, cleanly, and orderly habits, and a member of the Established Church. A person from the country will be preferred.[64]

Like R. Hignet, some advertisers specified that servants from the counties of Westmorland or Yorkshire were preferred, or only that applicants must be English.[65] A survey of the change in the volume and text of advertisements from the 1850s to 1880, along with the fluctuating census data, potently illustrates the changes that were transpiring in the supply of and demand for domestic servants.

Advertising for servants was relatively rare in the *Preston Guardian* in the early to mid-1850s. There was an occasional advertisement for a registry office, like Mrs. Bannister's, which by labeling itself a "*Ladies* Register Office for Servants" seemed to cater to the employing class rather than actively recruiting servants.[66] In July of 1855, only one position for a domestic servant was advertised in the *Guardian*, and that one was a specialized case: a Catholic family looking for a cook "of like faith" who was also "knowledgeable in the dairy."[67] In spite of the lack of advertised openings and few formal registries, there were more domestic servants in the 1851 census than in any later one. This indicates that there were sufficient young women to fill the available positions, that they were willing to do so, and that it was relatively easy for an employer to find a servant when he or she was in need of one. There were also no other positions for young women advertised in the newspaper. Migrants and Lancashire-born women alike were restricted to a very few types of occupation.[68]

The number of positions advertised for servants multiplied in the following decades, with advertisements by registry offices becoming more common as the 1860s progressed. The tone of the advertisements also changed through the decade. In 1860 an advertiser dictated terms: "Wanted, as under Nurse, a girl, about 16 years of age; satisfactory references required." Five years later, however, a Mr. Lord was careful to reassure applicants of the desirability of a position in his household, and that a servant would not be additionally burdened by child care: "Wanted, a thoroughly good general servant, in a Weslyan family. There are two children, and a nurse girl is kept. Wages no object to a thoroughly satisfactory person. References required."[69] A good character was still crucial, but domestic service was no longer entirely a buyer's market. The ads placed by registries were also catering to attract servants rather than potential employers. Advertisements now billed the offices as "*Servants'* Register Offices," and listed the type and number of open positions available rather than the servants in search of employ.[70] Mrs. Mercer, who ran a registry in Blackburn, actively encouraged young women in Preston to make the short migration to Blackburn: "Cooks, housemaids, general servants of good character wanting situations can be engaged immediately at Mrs. Mercers."[71]

By 1870 there were not only more servants' registries and more advertisements for servants, there were more openings for young women in other fields. One July weekend in 1870 saw, in addition to six advertisements for various female servants and one for an assistant to a laundry, three ads for milliners or dressmakers, two for teachers, one for both experienced and apprentice gold flatters, and one recruiting female emigrants to Queensland, "a large number required in the colony."[72] By the census evidence, migrants were primarily attracted to the service and possibly millinery positions, but the wider range of options made the entire female labor market tighter.

In the 1871 census, only 46.7 percent of all the recent female migrants in Preston were employed as domestic servants. Thirty percent worked in textile mills, a higher proportion than in any other census, and 10 percent were dressmakers, milliners, or seamstresses. Migrant women accounted for more than a quarter of all the city's domestic servants, but only one-eighth all of Preston's servants had probably come to the city within the last ten years. There were overall fewer recent female migrants in Preston in 1871 than in any other census year, totaling not quite four hundred. Economic troubles for Preston's middle classes, which depended on the health of the cotton trade for their prosperity, affected the demand for domestic servants and hence the impetus for migrants to choose Preston over other destinations.

Through the 1870s the supply of servants began to catch up with demand. The number of registries in Preston decreased, and the number of unemployed servants advertising for positions increased. Other types of employment were also on the rise. In 1875 Lancashire mills were actually advertising for throstle spinners, reelers and cop winders, predominantly female positions, which is a sign that the traditional modes of recruiting were no longer meeting their needs. In July of that year employers were also looking for dressmakers, apprentice confectioners, and "a young girl to assist in a wholesale warehouse."[73] By 1880 there were approximately equal numbers of employers and potential servants advertising their positions. The equality of Preston's supply of and demand for domestic service in the 1880s coincided with the beginning of the tidal shift away from keeping domestic servants in England. The country's servant population did not begin to fall until the twentieth century, but after 1871 it was no longer rising at a double-digit pace.[74]

Registry offices were by the late 1870s actively promoting both sides of their business, some recruiting "select servants in all capacities," others promoting servants registered with them, such as Mrs. Pateson's "tall, superior housemaid."[75] They were also more actively recruiting migrants than in previous years. In the 1860s advertisements were rarely from further away than Blackburn or at a stretch Blackpool, five and twenty miles from Preston, respectively. By 1876, however, Miss Atkinson's Servants' Registry in Kendal, Westmorland, was advertising in Preston that she had "on her list disengaged good cooks, housemaids, and general servants."[76] Atkinson apparently had found it was effective to recruit potential servants where they were plentiful, and send them as needed to other areas. A few years later, Mrs. Hurst's Registry and Servants' Home in Manchester saw a potential trolling ground in the smaller city of Preston: "Established 1864. Good country servants of all capacities wanted. . . . Ladies waiting daily at the office. Luggage-room free. No charge till suited. Lodgings for clean servants."[77] Mrs. Hurst's advertisement, with its luggage room and lodgings, implies she expected servants to pack their things and arrive in Manchester by their own means, trusting her to find them a position.

Young migrant women were readily able to find work as domestic servants, and in 1881 transcounty migrants accounted for one-third of Preston's single female servant population. For the first time since 1851, more than half of the recent migrants were employed as domestic servants. Meanwhile, opportunities for women were expanding rapidly. In 1880 the *Guardian* ran advertisements searching for, among the now commonplace dressmakers and confectioners, "an expert Lady Swimmer . . . to teach swimming at the baths," and "a young lady of ability to collect accounts" for the Wheeler and Wilson Sewing Machine Manufacturing Co.[78] New employment opportunities for women meant there were more openings in service that migrants could fill. The renewed influx of young women to Preston in the 1870s shows the migration flow responding to conditions in the city as it recovered from the Cotton Famine.

Tracing fluctuations of migration in relation to domestic service helps to describe the interrelationship of migrants and the labor needs of the city. The fluctuating volume of migrants in Preston, correlated with the city's economic health, shows that migrants were at least generally aware of conditions in their destination city before they set out. They did not simply move to the closest available city in times of distress, as Michael Anderson's work implied, or the volume of migrants would not correspond to economic fluctuations in the city.[79] Rather, they chose their destinations in response to opportunity.

After this extended discussion of domestic service, however, it is important to reiterate that in the latter half of the nineteenth century only about half of all the young women who moved to Preston went into domestic service, and those were mostly from rural areas. The next most common employment was industrial textile work, at which the migrants probably differed little from their Lancashire-born counterparts. There were also clusters of migrants in dressmaking and drapers' establishments, when those establishments met the migrants' need for supervised accommodations.

Most drapers' and dressmakers' shops in Preston (and their number was considerable: 4.2 percent of all employed adults in Preston were drapers, tailors, dressmakers, or milliners) were small establishments, including only the proprietor and perhaps an assistant, usually a son, daughter, or other relative.[80] A few shops, however, were much larger, employing five, ten, or even two dozen assistants who boarded on the premises. In these shops which provided housing for the assistants, male and female migrants dominated. Studying dressmakers in New England, Wendy Gamber found that the practice of keeping "indoor" apprentices and assistants declined throughout the nineteenth century: if the same was true in England, these few establishments with migrant apprentices could be the remnants of an older tradition.[81]

The largest of these establishments in Preston was a draper's shop owned by Frederick Bayliss, a native of Northhampton, in 1861, and after 1871 by Frederic Thorp, from Herefordshire. The shop occupied 19, 20, and 21 Fishergate, in the heart of Preston's business district, at least into the 1880s. In each of the census years, the draper employed eleven or more female staff and an equal number of men in addition to four or five domestic servants. Ninety percent of those female employees (not including the servants) were migrants from outside Lancashire. In other establishments, such as Hannah and Jane Wearnings' dressmaking shop and Ann and Edward Wade, dressmaker and upholsterer, the percentage of migrants among their employees varied from 58 to 100 percent. Beyond the census there is no record of these businesses, and currently no way to determine if these employers were actively recruiting migrants, if they also employed nonmigrants who lived elsewhere, or if the migrants had been actively searching for a position that offered them both employment and accommodation. Their concentration in these business is significant, though, showing that there were alternatives to domestic service or common lodgings for migrants who did not have relatives in Preston.

Not all of the alternatives to domestic service were available or appealing to all migrants. The positions for educators and the "lady swimmer" implied a need for education and a certain class standing, which migrants from rural families would be less likely to have. An apprentice to a dressmaker or confectioner, for example, often worked for the first several months without wages, and may even have had to pay her employer.[82] This situation would have been untenable for a young woman whose family had no surplus income or who needed her to contribute to a family economy. Women from urban areas, such as those who came to Preston from London, were likely to avoid domestic service. With the exception of the 1871 census, London-born migrants to Preston were recorded working as performers, dressmakers, or teachers more often than as domestic servants, suggesting that these women were of a class with education, resources, or a sense of position that precluded them from such work.

The Migrants' Economy

Most independent single women, migrants or Lancashire-born, whatever occupation they chose, were employed. Only 3.2 percent of all recent migrants were not employed in the census year following their arrival. The need to earn their own living was certainly a strong motivation to migration for rural-born women, and there was less demand for their labor in their home communities as the century progressed.[83] Domestic service required long hours, hard work, and submissive obedience, but it offered significant benefits that could be enough to make it appealing to many young migrants.

Recruitment was a two-way street, of course. Not only did young women need to please potential employers; the demand for servants was such that a migrant could potentially choose among several possibilities. The advertisements for servants hint at what features, in addition to room, board, and a cash wage, attracted women to particular positions (or at least what the advertisers thought should attract them). The most common additional feature mentioned in the advertisements was family composition, including the number of children. To this was most often added other servants kept, particularly if a Cook or Housekeeper could expect to have a girl or two under her or if a nurse would relieve a general servant of any child care. Advertisers might also mention the family's status ("Wanted, in a Gentleman's Family"), religion ("in a Wesleyan family"), or a desirable location ("for a gentleman's family [small] in the country").[84] Some of these advertisers may have been practicing full disclosure in an attempt to limit servant turnover, as in the family which was looking for a "strong, active Nurse; four young children; good Needlewoman; Protestant; wages £16," an advertisement that (unusually) ran for several weeks.[85] Most, however, specified the ease or prestige of the position—that the family was small, there were other servants to share the workload, or that the employing family was of particularly good character. These characteristics were seen, at least by the employers, to be as important in choosing a position as the wage paid.

Nevertheless, the realities of working-class life meant that the primary consideration for the migrant women had to be income. The wages paid to servants ranged widely over the period, depending on the position, age and experience of the servant. Like the grocer Hignet, most advertisers did not state a wage, preferring more ambiguous phrases such as "good wages will be offered to a trustworthy person," "Liberal wages will be given," or simply offering "a comfortable home."[86] Enough advertisers did specify wages, however, to get a general idea of how Preston's domestic servants' income changed over the years. Using wages offered or requested in *Guardian* advertisements, Figure 2.10 illustrates the general upward trend of domestic servants' wages from 1857 (the earliest wage rate available) to 1880.[87] The British economy was booming in this period, with little to no inflation, so the increase shown represents a genuine increase in servants' income.[88]

Over the twenty-four years covered by Figure 2.10 a good general cook saw her annual wages increase from about thirteen pounds to sixteen pounds.[89] General servants who were paid ten pounds in 1850 would be likely to find a position paying thirteen pounds or fourteen pounds in the mid-1870s, and possibly as much as twenty pounds if she cooked as well. Rising wages for servants were the rule in England in the nineteenth century, indicative of growing middle-class wealth and high demand for good servants.[90] Servants' wages in Preston may have been depressed in the Cotton Famine years, but by 1880 a "disengaged, first-class Cook" could demand a wage of thirty five pounds per year.[91]

The cash wages earned by domestic servants were on average lower than women's potential earnings in the cotton mills. One estimate in 1850, drawn from an employer's letter to the *Morning Chronicle*, placed female power-loom weavers' wages in neighboring Yorkshire at 12 s. per week. Assuming full employment, that gave a young woman more than thirty pounds annual income.[92] Since that report came from an employer it was probably generous, but there are few contemporary estimates against which to measure it. In the mid-1830s female cotton workers in Lancashire from ages sixteen to thirty six were reported to earn from 7 s. 3½d. to 8 s. 9½d. per week, for a yearly wage of £18 18 s. to £22 16 s. Ten years later, female power-loom weavers in Manchester took home up to 16 s. 8 d. each week (£43 6 s. per annum), after paying their helpers.[93] Other letters to the *Morning Chronicle* at midcentury recorded wages for female textile workers that ranged from £14 6 s. to £26 per year. There was considerable fluctuation in factory

Figure 2.10
Domestic servants' wages as reported in *Preston Guardian*, 1857–1880.

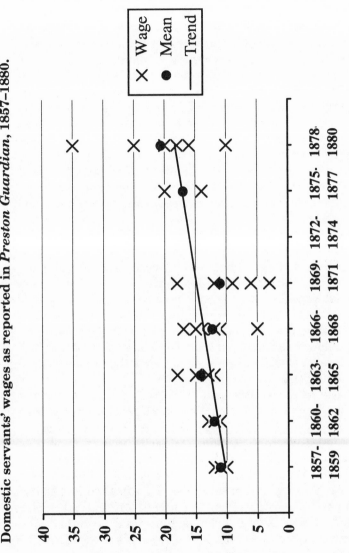

Source: *Preston Guardian* 3 January, 30 May, 27 June, 4 July 1857; 1, 29 December 1860; 5 January, 2 February, 9 March 1861; 9, 23 September, 21 October, 1 November 1865; 3, 10, 24 March, 9 May 1866; 14 May, 4 June, 2, 16, 30 July 1870; 8, 12 January, 1876; 29 September, 2, 9, 13 October 1880.

wages, depending on the type and amount of work and how low a wage an employer could offer and still retain an adequate workforce, which was in turn affected by the size of the city in which the mill was located. Even the lowest-paid textile worker at midcentury was paid more than the average wage for a domestic servant in the 1850s, but it must be remembered that domestic service always included room and board, a benefit that was estimated to be worth as much as twenty pounds per year.[94] If that estimate of living expenses was at all accurate, a mill worker making fourteen to fifteen pounds per year probably could not easily survive on her own. Rather, the census shows that single female textile workers usually lived with their families or relatives, likely contributing all or most of their wages to family economies.[95] When food and housing are included, domestic servants' wages compare favorably to what a factory worker could make.

Domestic servants have usually been analyzed as part of a family economy, with emphasis placed on money returned to their families, but saving money for their own use was important to many servants in Preston. Since their employers paid for their immediate needs, servants' wages could be spent on luxuries, saved, or sent to their families. Such contributions could have been a boon to rural families trying to make ends meet.[96] The records left by Preston's Savings Bank, however, show that many servants accumulated substantial sums over periods of years, money that these women were saving, not passing on to their parents.

One of those servants, Catherine Billington, accumulated a balance of £25 11 d. between 1850 and 1852, which she gradually drew out over the next year and a half. Esther Jackson came from Forton, about twenty miles north of Preston. She made regular deposits of five or six pounds—possibly as much as half her annual wage—every February from 1845 until 1850, when she withdrew a lump sum of £47 8 s. 3 d. Marie Craven, from Ribby (between Preston and Blackpool) accumulated the impressive sum of £109 13 s. 1 d. between 1845 and 1856. Mercy Clayton, who gave no residence other than Preston, kept her account open for nearly ten years without making a single withdrawal, but she only managed to accumulate £1 3 s. 6 d. with interest.[97] The bulk of her wages may have gone to her family, or she may have spent them in preference to saving. There is no record of what these women did after they withdrew their savings. They may have married and used their savings to furnish their new homes, or simply moved on to employment in another part of the country. With funds as ample as Craven's, however, they could have purchased an apprenticeship or opened a small shop of their own. Indeed, one scholar found to her surprise that most of the single female shopkeepers in Preston were migrants.[98] The Preston Bank records show that these shopkeepers may very well have acquired their initial stake by saving their wages from domestic service.

A great many servants kept savings accounts in Preston. The bank reported in 1845 that eight hundred fifty-six female domestic servants had savings accounts, making up the largest class of female depositors. The Preston census sample for 1851 produced a total estimate of seventeen hundred female domestic servants in the city; extrapolating from the 1845 bank figures almost half saved part of their wages for later use. Although some, like Mercy Clayton, either made few deposits or withdrew as regularly as they deposited, the average balance of the domestic servants' accounts in 1845 was twenty three pounds. Only 184 female cotton workers, by contrast, had bank deposits in that year, although there were more than 8,000 of them recorded in the 1851 census.[99] Some migrants, indeed, may have chosen domestic service over mill work expressly because they were better able to accumulate savings from a servants' wage.[100]

Nor did the servants who saved their wages face scorn for failing to send the money home. Indeed, the governing classes of Preston believed it was suitable, possibly even preferable for young women to save money on their own account rather than turning it all over to their families. At a public meeting promoting the newly established Penny Bank in 1859, Mr. Moore, one of the bank officers, bemoaned the tendency for working women to spend their wages immediately, especially on clothes. He much preferred to see them putting their wages "to good purpose," which was conspicuously not turning it over to their parents:

> if a girl had £30 or £40 in the bank she could look any young man in the face when he proposed, and say "yes" or "no" as suited her inclinations. But how many girls said "yes" when they felt they would like a home of their own, though they did not like the person who "popped the question?" Let her have £30 or £40 in the bank and she could say "no" because she would feel independent.[101]

Although the bank's founders did not address migrant women explicitly, their emphasis on young people, especially young women, is significant. They saw Preston's single women as economically independent, with control over the wages they received.

Moore recognized that personal funds gave a woman a degree of power in her relationships with men and contributed to her independence from her parents. Similarly, a letter to the editor of the *Preston Guardian* regarding the "Dangers of Crinoline" noted,

> Emancipated from household control, the female workers in mills and factories are more especially privileged to err in matters of dress. If they foolishly spend money, they have acquired the power of doing so by first earning it, and injure only themselves.[102]

If domestic servants were truly separated from their parents' economies, then they, too, would be "privileged to err" in how they spent their money.

The amount of money women kept for themselves and how they spent it (or saved it) is a strong indication of how economically separate the women were from their parents' families and has significance for understanding the migrants' roles in their families and the communities to which they migrated. Unfortunately, aside from scattered comments like Moore's, no evidence survives in Preston of exactly how migrants divided their wages between family, self, and savings. Sources from Lowell and Paisley suggest in more detail how Preston's migrants may have used their income.

Moore, like R. Hignet and the thousands of others who employed domestic servants, expected young women to migrate and participate in Preston's economy. Over the period of this study, the volume of single women's migration to Preston fluctuated, but the patterns of their behavior stayed essentially the same. Young migrant women did not generally work in Preston's mills, and they did not excite comment from the city fathers on the dangers of unsupervised women in the city. A thorough search of Preston's archives revealed no mention, disapproving or otherwise, of English-born women migrating into the city. This lack of comment is not proof that women's migration did not exist; rather, it is evidence that young women's independent migration was a normal and accepted part of Preston's culture. Just as Preston-born women were accepted as wage earners in the textile mills, independent migrant women were accepted in the surrogate families of their employers, relations, and even, in small numbers, as boarders. Migration was normal female behavior in Lancashire, and hence nearly unnoticed.

Preston shows that the volume of single women's migration fluctuated in conjunction with the needs of employers in the city. Although migrants tended to be pushed by rural pressures and to make the easiest possible journey to the closest city or to the one on a convenient rail line, their decision when and where to migrate was also related to the availability of employment. Most migrants would be able to find a position as a domestic servant with little difficulty, but when other opportunities were present they took them. Migrants found employment in textile mills, as dressmakers, or in more esoteric occupations, boarding with their employers or with private families. Some succumbed to the dangers of the city, entering the record as inmates of prisons and poorhouses. These migrants who did not follow the "normal" path of domestic service and coresidence with employers or relatives must be incorporated into the historical description of single women's migration to a typical nineteenth-century textile city.

Unfortunately, in Preston there are few sources from which to describe these or any migrants' lives in greater detail. Details from Lowell and Paisley, compared with data from Preston, illuminates the experiences of all single female migrants, including what drove their choices of occupation and accommodation and what dangers threatened their ability to support themselves. Lowell in particular offers a wealth of personal accounts that evoke the subjective experience of migration. Driven by their own preferences and dreams, girls from New England's rural areas flocked to the city to work almost exclusively in the textile industry, quite unlike the English migrants. Women's migration in New England *did* excite comment: the Lowell mill girls were anything but invisible.

CHAPTER 3

_____

Lowell: The Mill Girls

While young women were migrating to Preston in response to employers' demands for domestic servants, women in New England were enticing one another to move to industrial employment. In May 1866 Emma Page, working in her uncle's woolen mill in Readfield, Maine, received a letter from a friend who had gone to work in Lowell, Massachusetts. Her friend, Mattie Weymouth, wrote, "I wish you was up here Em tell Hat Malissa sais thare is plenty of chances whare she works she and Hanah had 80 cts per day the first month." By the end of the summer Emma had joined Mattie in Lowell, becoming part of a migration that had begun almost forty years earlier and would continue into the 1880s.[1]

Yankee women's migration to Lowell was begun by employer demand in the late 1820s.[2] As in Preston, the volume of migration to Lowell increased and decreased in response to employers' needs, but the migrants themselves were also a crucial component in maintaining the migration. In the decades after the Civil War, when Lowell's cotton manufacturers were relying more and more heavily on family-based, immigrant workers, single female migrants from New England continued to encourage their friends to come to the city, maintaining a migration stream that the employers had ceased to recruit. The sources that survive in Lowell bring to the fore an influence on single women's migration that was obscured in Preston's record: the migrants' own needs and desires.

_____

The Lowell workers were referred to as "mill girls" both by contemporaries and themselves, but the term is a somewhat uncomfortable one for historians, with its implications of youth and dependence. In fact, quite mature, independent women worked in the Lowell mills. I have retained the term in this chapter both for ease of use and because, as I argue, "mill girl" represented a specific transitional category of womanhood separate from both "girl" and "woman."

57

Figure 3.1a
Map of New England and New York showing state borders.

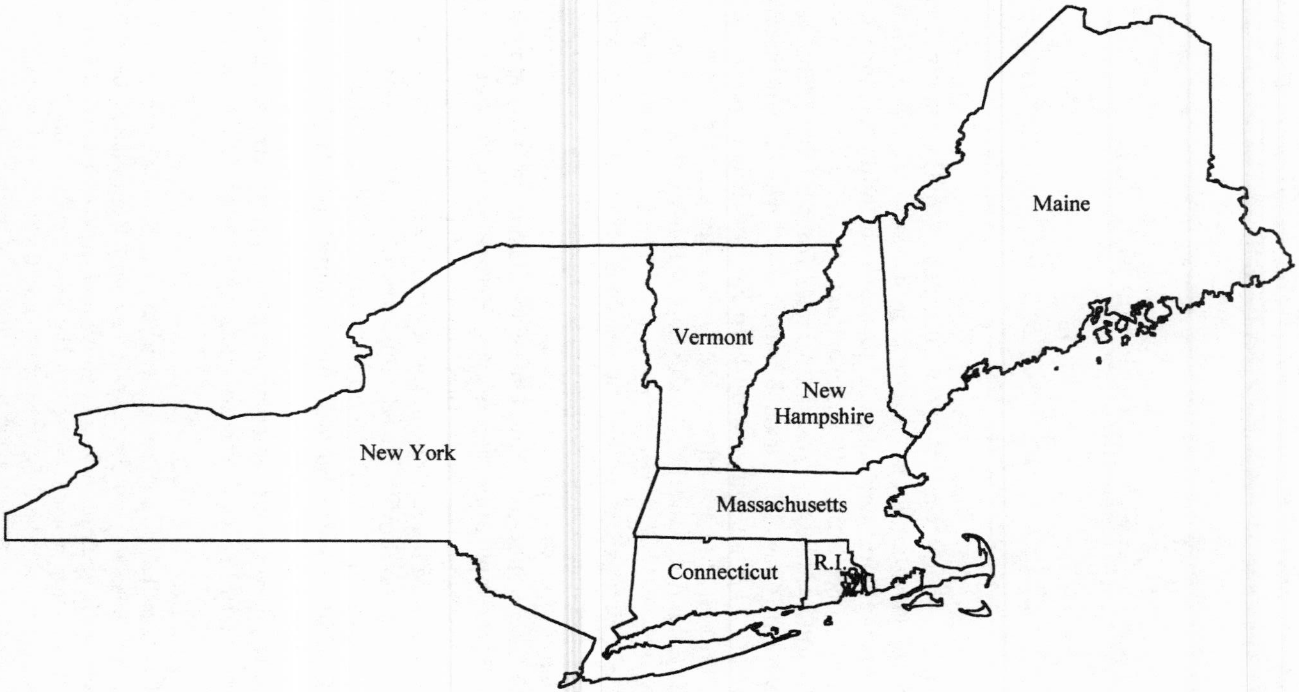

Figure 3.1b
Map of New England and New York with places mentioned in the text.

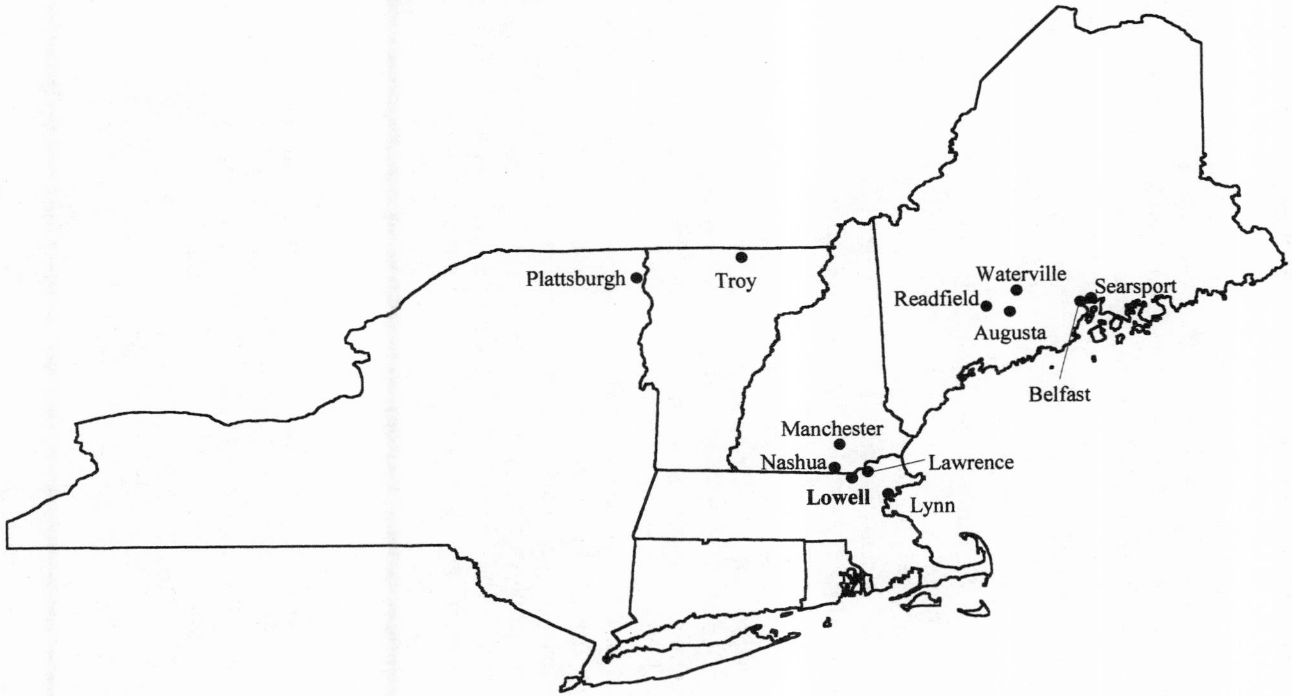

Lowell's history has been very well documented, not least because single female migrants were a highly visible portion of the city's population, so an extensive retelling of that history is not necessary here. Suffice it to say that the tiny farming community of East Chelmsford, located at the junction of the Merrimack and Concord rivers in northern Massachusetts (see maps, Figures 3.1a and 3.1b), was targeted by the Waltham company in 1821 to be transformed into Lowell, the flagship industrial textile city of the United States in the 1820s and 1830s. In contrast to the English factory system, which had been copied in earlier New England mills, the Waltham-Lowell system did not rely on workers who migrated in family groups. Instead, with a high level of capitalization, a dearth of available labor, and a suspicion of the crowded squalor of British cities, the company constructed boardinghouses and recruited the respectable adolescent daughters of Yankee farmers to work in the new mills.[3]

Unlike the migrants to Preston, these female migrants attracted notice. Far from the imagined degradation of British working-class factory girls, these were the respectable daughters of landowning farmers, supposed to be the protectors of republican ideals for future generations. Not only did their move from rural homes to the factory town tap into social fears about industrialization, the market economy, and the growth of cities in general, but the Lowell mill workers turned out not to be the docile workforce their employers expected.[4] Mill girls led industrial actions in Lowell in the 1830s and 1840s, protesting against declining wages and deteriorating conditions.[5] The migrants were also literate, which further increased their visibility. In addition to writing copious letters to friends and family, mill workers edited and published a monthly magazine, *The Lowell Offering*, in the early 1840s. The *Offering* publicized Lowell as a model industrial city, in great part due to the high moral character of its migrant operatives.[6] Although the mill girls' various activities prior to 1850 gave somewhat conflicting views of Lowell, they made the migrants a visible and important part of the history of America's industrialization.

After 1850, when this study begins, New England migrants were a declining segment of Lowell's mill-working population, but the Yankees did not stop coming to Lowell entirely.[7] After midcentury the mills gradually turned to a predominantly immigrant workforce, first employing refugees from the Irish Potato Famine, later French Canadians, and still later immigrants from central and eastern Europe. The *Lowell Offering* ceased publication in

1845, apparently due to lengthening work days and the departure of sympathetic readers and writers from Lowell.[8] Women's participation in labor protest in Lowell declined in the 1850s, which Thomas Dublin tied to the replacement of Yankee workers by immigrants with different concerns.[9] By the time of the Civil War there was a clear change in the direction of Lowell's development, from a model factory town to a modern textile city dependent on immigrant families rather than independent migrants. However, young women from New England continued to move to Lowell for decades after they no longer dominated the mills' workforce. Concentrating on the history of the migration rather than on the history of the city of Lowell, this chapter shows the process of change in the migration pattern and examines reasons for its endurance as well as its decline.

The unparalleled survival of primary sources in Lowell makes it possible to address questions about female migrants that cannot be so readily explored anywhere else, including common reasons for moving and the effects of migration on the mill girls. The unique insight into the migration experience possible from Lowell's qualitative sources will, in turn, help to interpret the less complete records left in Preston and Paisley. In addition to corporate records and observers' reports, the Lowell migrants' high literacy rate resulted in vast numbers of letters written by and to mill workers, letters that give more insight into the personal experience of migration than any other source.[10]

The definitive study of migrants in Lowell before 1860 is Thomas Dublin's *Women at Work: The Transformation of Life and Work in Lowell, Massachusetts*. It details the experience of single women working in the Lowell mills, with particular emphasis on the migrants from rural New England. Between completing school and marrying, young women from towns in Vermont, Maine, New Hampshire, and elsewhere in Massachusetts migrated to the company boardinghouses of Lowell. The mill girls were from relatively prosperous families, neither the wealthiest nor the poorest in their communities. These families did not need a daughter's income or labor to survive, but they were not so wealthy that a dowry was assured or that a daughter working for wages was beyond the realm of respectability.[11]

Respectability, roughly defined by class- and gender-appropriateness, was undoubtedly important to nineteenth-century female migrants and especially to those in Lowell, for whom migration was less likely to be an economic necessity. The workers in

Lowell were, like the migrants to Preston, in transition between their parents' families and their own adult families. Contemporaries saw the young women as vulnerable to corruption, and feared for their moral safety when they were separated from their parents. A respectable destination was crucial to the women's ability to migrate at all. In rural New England, where mill work was associated with the poverty and perceived squalor of cities such as Preston, there were lingering doubts of its respectability for young women. Lydia Bixby, a mill worker in Nashua, New Hampshire (just across the border from Lowell), wrote to her mother at midcentury, "my overseer wantet I should get him more Groton girls to work for him I told him they was all Ladys up there and would not work in the factory."[12] Lydia's imputation was that due to either their class or gender standing the "Groton girls" believed mill work (and hence possibly Lydia herself) was beneath them. In order to recruit their preferred workforce, the manufacturers in Lowell had to make the work and the city acceptable to the workers' moral standards.

The city of Lowell was designed to appeal to the Yankee farming community, including the daughters but also the parents whose permission was necessary for at least the first trip to the city. The boardinghouses, especially in Lowell's early years, were self-consciously respectable, designed to keep the American workers at a moral level a step or two above their British counterparts.[13] In contrast to the squalid slums that housed Preston's factory workers, the Lowell boardinghouses were "finished off in a style much above the common farmhouses of the country, and more nearly resemble the abodes of respectable mechanics in rural villages [this despite the fact they were three-story tenements]. These are constantly kept clean, the buildings well painted . . . at the corporation's expense."[14] At least until midcentury, the corporate managers were well aware that keeping factory work respectable was vital to maintaining their female workforce. John Aiken, observing the mill systems in England and the United States in 1849, drew an explicit connection between migration, Lowell's boardinghouses and the city's respectable reputation:

> As a matter of course [factory labor in England] is less reputable for females than domestic service; and those only go into factories to work who cannot find more reputable employments, or where tastes are satisfied by such as are disreputable. . . . English girls . . . refused to place themselves under the supervision and guardianship of a matron, or the regulations of a boarding house.[15]

In fact, between 70 and 80 percent of all single female mill migrants and nonmigrants alike, in Preston from 1864 to 1881 lived with their parents or another relative, doubtless well supervised. So far as independent female migrants went, he was generally correct about their choice of occupation, if not their motivations. His implication, however, was clearly that the American girls were more virtuous than the English, concerned with respectability and so willing to submit to regulations. Not coincidentally, such respectable passivity would ideally create a more controllable workforce than was found in the rapidly unionizing English cotton industry. However, the boardinghouse community seems to have actually aided the labor actions of the 1830s and 1840s in Lowell, rather than hindering them.[16] Nevertheless Aiken continued,

> In small communities, where all the operatives could board at home [the English factory system] might answer. But in a manufacturing town like Lowell, where the great mass of female operatives are separated from home and parental oversight, I regard the boarding-house system as *indispensable*. By the aid of these houses, unworthy persons can be discovered and excluded, and the well-disposed and virtuous can, in a very good degree, be protected from evil companionships, and other degrading influences. . . . Let [the Lowell system] be abandoned, or in any considerable degree relaxed, and it requires no prophet's ken to foresee that most deplorable consequences must ensue.[17]

Regulations designed to protect the workers' respectability were posted at the boardinghouses, rules including a ten o'clock curfew and the stipulation, "The Keepers of the Boarding Houses must give an account of . . . their boarders . . . ; and report the names of such as are guilty of any improper conduct, or are not in the regular habit of attending public worship."[18] To distract the young women from degrading influences there were cultural opportunities including evening schools, circulating libraries, lectures, concerts, and the creative outlet of the *Lowell Offering*. The mill workers were also famous as voracious readers.[19] Thus Lowell was far removed, physically and culturally, from chaotic industrial Preston. The city's founders successfully made factory labor an occupation for which young American women—in less coercive economic situations than their English counterparts—were willing to move.

Throughout the 1830s and 1840s Yankee migrants were the primary source of labor for the Lowell mills. At Lowell's Hamilton Corporation in 1836, 96.6 percent of the female workforce had been born in the United States and most of those workers had migrated from other states (especially New Hampshire) or elsewhere in Massachusetts.[20] Before the mid-1840s Irish immigrants were not widely employed in the mills, although there had been a small Irish population in Lowell since they helped to build the city in the 1820s. The potato blight that struck Ireland in 1845, however, drove hundreds of thousands to starvation, and hundreds of thousands more to emigrate. By 1850 there was a strong Irish presence, starting to dominate (according to one historian) "the look, feel, and smell of Lowell."[21] Nevertheless, when Mattie Weymouth persuaded Emma Page to come to Lowell in 1866 she gave no hint that Yankee mill workers were in competition with Irish women for their jobs or cultural control of the city. The Irish workers did not so much push the native-born women out of the mills as fill in the positions the Yankees were already leaving. On the other hand, the growing number of immigrants did make it possible for the textile corporations to maintain wages and conditions that were intolerable to the American-born migrants.[22] The general pattern of Lowell's population change from 1850 to 1880 was one of rising numbers of immigrants and Lowell natives, and falling numbers of internal migrants. Within that generalization, however, individual young women continued to move to Lowell with all the eagerness and optimism that had inspired earlier migrants.

The 1850 census recorded approximately 22,700 individuals over age fifteen in Lowell. The cotton mills were the most important business in town, employing approximately 32 percent of all the men in the city. Eighteen percent of the men gave their occupation as "laborer," many of them probably working with the 11 percent of the city's men employed in the building trades.[23] Thirty years later the situation was little changed. The textile mills continued to employ 30 percent of all the city's adults, male and female. The city's service sector had expanded in response to its growing population, and 9 percent of all men were still employed in construction, but fabric production remained Lowell's economic heart.

In 1850, 47 percent of Lowell's adult population had been born in the United States outside Massachusetts, most migrants coming from Maine, New Hampshire, and Vermont. Almost one-third of those internal migrants were independent women under thirty years old.[24] Another 18.9 percent of the total population had been born within Massachusetts's boundaries, and that group also contained many migrants from outside Lowell. Irish immigrants accounted for more than 25 percent of the city's adult population, and the remaining 9 percent came from elsewhere outside the United States, including Great Britain, Canada, and parts of Europe.[25]

As Lowell's population grew internal migrants became a much smaller proportion of the town's labor force. By the time of the 1880 census, immigrants made up nearly half of the city's population and Massachusetts-born residents, many of whose parents were immigrants, composed almost 29 percent. The proportion of internal migrants in Lowell's adult population had fallen to just under a quarter and only a small fraction of that quarter were recent independent female migrants.[26] Among the recent migrant population, single women had dropped from almost half to just 30 percent.

The stream of internal migrants into Lowell was composed of men and women of all ages, married and widowed as well as single, but most of the American-born migrants to Lowell were single women in their late teens and twenties. In 1850, 45.5 percent of all the single women in Lowell under thirty years old were internal migrants, compared to 35 percent of the city's single men (Figure 3.2). By 1880, migrant women still made up 15.4 percent of Lowell's single women, while men were 11.4 percent. There were obvious similarities in the general trends of male and female migration into Lowell. The proportions of both groups in the population tumbled after 1850, then remained comparatively stable in the period following the Civil War. A closer look at the volume, however, shows that there were real differences between men's and women's migration patterns to Lowell. Figure 3.3 shows the gross estimated numbers of unmarried recent migrants in Lowell for each census by sex.

There was a consistently stronger pull to Lowell for single women than for single men.[27] Though that difference was most obvious before the Civil War, when single migrant women were the major component of the Lowell mills' workforce, women's migration also rebounded more strongly after the war, while single men's migration levels remained stagnant. Male migrants reported a wide variety of occupations, unlike the female migrants who were predominantly employed in Lowell's textile mills (and for whom there were many fewer options). Some of the single male migrants may have moved to Lowell specifically in search of textile work, but many more had a trade or profession that they could have pursued in any city or, in many cases, on the western frontier. Migration to the West served much the same function in nineteenth-century New England as emigration did in Preston: it was an appealing alternative to short-distance industrial migration.[28] The lack of any particular employment opportunity in Lowell for men largely

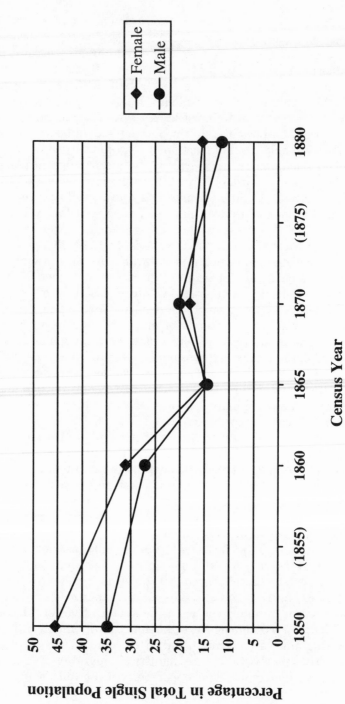

Figure 3.2
Recent independent migrants in the single population.
Lowell, 1850–1880.

Source: Derived from *Seventh, Eighth, Ninth,* and *Tenth Census of the United States,* Lowell, Mass., microfilm, National Archives; and *Massachusetts State Census, 1865,* Lowell, microfilm, Massachusetts State Archives.

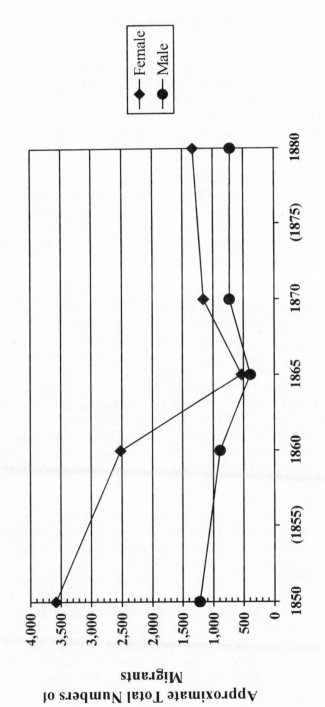

Figure 3.3
Volume of recent independent migrants.
Lowell, 1850–1880.

Source: Derived from *Seventh, Eighth, Ninth, and Tenth Census of the United States*, Lowell, Mass., microfilm, National Archives; and *Massachusetts State Census*, 1865, Lowell, microfilm, Massachusetts State Archives.

accounts for the disparity of numbers between male and female migrants.

Young women, on the other hand, were attracted by the unique opportunities Lowell offered. Female migrants to Lowell showed an even stronger occupational preference than the migrants in Preston, but in this case with obvious partiality for textile work. Figure 3.4 illustrates the average proportions of migrant women in the major female occupations from 1860 to 1880, comparing them to women in the immigrant and nonmigrant communities. Figure 3.4 also emphasizes the tremendous importance of textile work for all of Lowell's single women.[29]

From 1860 to 1880, the lowest percentage in any single census of female migrants who reported textile work was 58 percent (in 1880). In that census more women in Lowell than ever before worked as clerks, salespeople, dressmakers, milliners, seamstresses, or domestic servants. Nevertheless, there were still relatively few alternatives to textile work for single women in Lowell. Women born on American farms or in villages, unlike rural English migrants in Preston, generally shunned domestic service because of the long hours and subservience it required.[30] In 1860, fewer than 2 percent of the Yankee migrants found positions as domestic servants and those women represented only 12.5 percent of all the servants in Lowell. Surprisingly, the proportion of American women in service rose over the following decades until they were 29 percent of the servant population in 1880, with 14 percent of all Yankee migrants working as domestics. Meanwhile the relative demand for household servants grew only slightly; in 1860 there was one domestic servant in Lowell for every fifty nine adults in the population, and by 1880 there was one for every fifty six adults. The growing tendency for American-born women to take positions that earlier migrants had shunned reflects both changes that made the textile industry less clearly superior to service and a possibly greater economic need among migrants in the decades after the Civil War. On balance, however, textile work remained the most important occupation for Yankee migrants to Lowell, and most probably the occupation that drew them to the city.

Independent female migrants' housing patterns in Lowell corresponded with their occupations even more strongly than in Preston. In 1860, 85.5 percent of the recent migrants to the city lived in boardinghouses associated with the cotton mills. Among the migrants who worked in the mills, more than 90 percent took advantage of the corporate or private boardinghouses. In contrast, in the same year only 48.3 percent of all the immigrants and

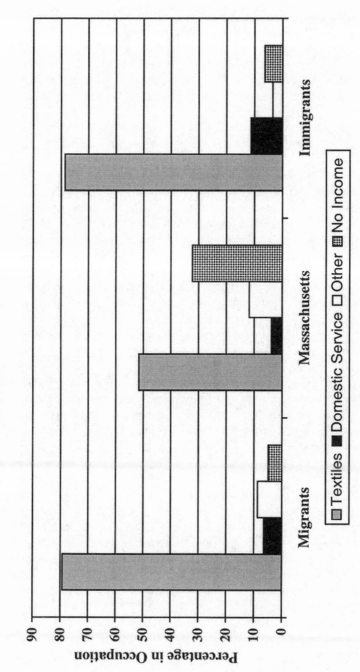

Figure 3.4

Single women's occupations by place of birth.
Lowell, 1860–1880.

Percentage in Occupation

□ Textiles ■ Domestic Service □ Other ▦ No Income

Migrants   Massachusetts   Immigrants

"Massachusetts": includes all unmarried Massachusetts-born women under thirty years old.

Source: Derived from *Seventh, Eighth, Ninth,* and *Tenth Census of the United States*, Lowell, Mass., microfilm, National Archives; and *Massachusetts State Census*, 1865, Lowell, microfilm, Massachusetts State Archives.

nonmigrants under thirty years old who worked in the mills lived in boardinghouses. The migrants' preferences for boardinghouses associated with the mills (even after those houses had been sold to private parties) continued through 1880. Figure 3.5 compares the migrants' housing pattern to the immigrant and nonmigrant independent single women in Lowell, distinguishing between those who lived with families and those who resided in boardinghouses with at least four tenants.[31]

After about 1860 mill workers who did not have parents in Lowell were no longer required to live in company-run accommodations. Indeed, the corporations began selling off the housing they owned to private individuals, relinquishing direct control of the boarders.[32] The native-born migrants nevertheless continued to prefer the community of a boardinghouse to living with an unrelated family. Independent women born in Massachusetts and immigrants were more likely to live with relatives than the Yankee migrants were, which helps to account for the larger number of those women living in family groups.[33] Lowell's domestic servant population also came primarily from women born in Massachusetts or outside the United States. The migrants preferred employment in the textile mills, and unlike single migrant women in Preston, they preferred to live in boardinghouses.[34]

The pattern of female Yankee migration was remarkably stable in terms of origins over the period from 1850 to 1880. Thomas Dublin found that most of the migrants who worked at the Hamilton Corporation in the first six months of 1836 came from New Hampshire, but after midcentury women from Maine were the largest contingent of migrants.[35] New Hampshire girls represented 30 percent or less of Lowell's migrants and young women from Maine were 40 percent or more in every census except the 1865 state count. Emma Page and Mattie Weymouth came to Lowell from Readfield, near Augusta in Kennebec County, Maine, and many of their friends in the mills were from that area. A recruiter for the Hamilton Corporation in 1865 brought migrants on the steamer from Searsport, Maine, and they must have included young women from the same south-central region of the state.[36] Figures 3.6–3.10 show the shifting proportions of single female migrants' origins in more detail.

Migrants from Maine's southern regions could have been encouraged by both their geographic proximity to Lowell and a lack of alternatives closer by. Emma Page's uncle owned a woolen mill in Readfield, which apparently attracted women from surrounding

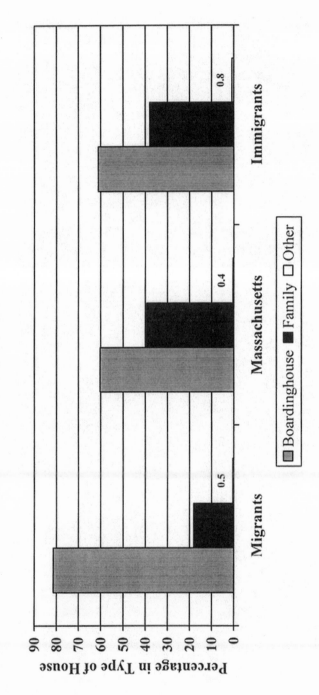

Figure 3.5
Type of housing chosen by independent single women.
Lowell, 1850–1880.

"Massachusetts": includes single women less than thirty years old not living with their parents.
Boardinghouse: includes houses with four or more nonrelated boarders.
Family: includes houses with zero to three nonrelated boarders.
Other: includes hotels and institutions.

Source: Derived from *Seventh, Eighth, Ninth,* and *Tenth Census of the United States,* Lowell, Mass., microfilm, National Archives, and *Massachusetts State Census,* 1865, Lowell, microfilm, Massachusetts State Archives.

Figure 3.6
Origin of single female migrants to Lowell, 1850.

42.2%

31.3%

24.3%

1.4%

0.3%

Other US – 1.9%

Figure 3.7
Origin of single female migrants to Lowell, 1860.

43.3%

26.3%

20.6%

0.5%

2.6%

6.2%

Other US - 0.5%

Figure 3.8
Origin of single female migrants to Lowell, 1865.

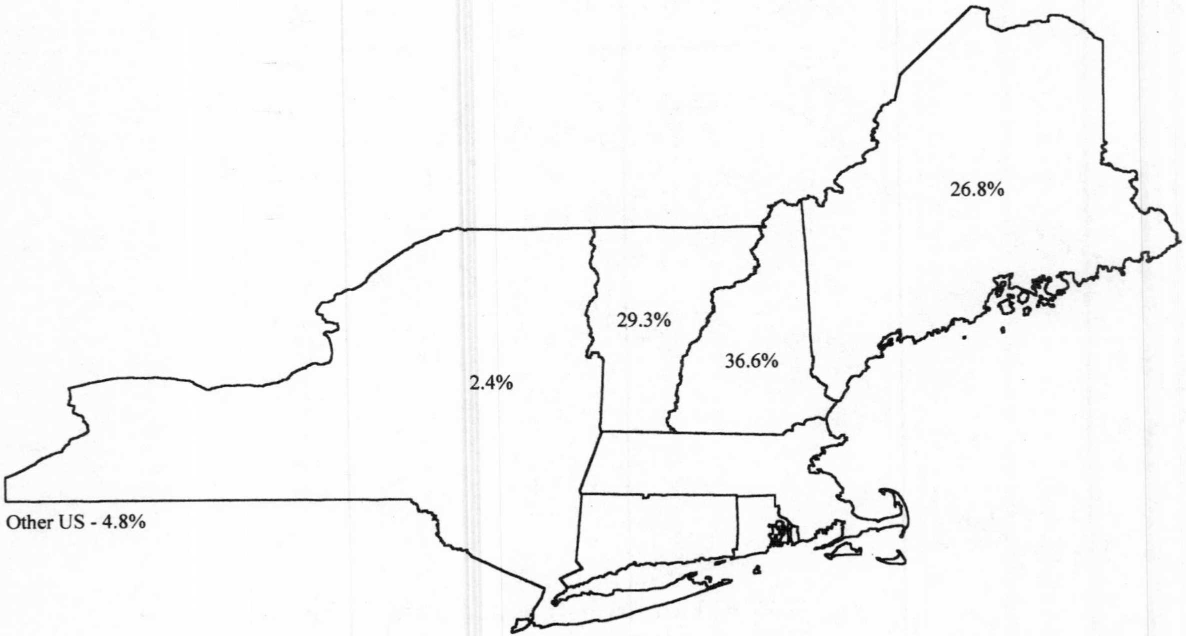

26.8%

36.6%

29.3%

2.4%

Other US - 4.8%

Figure 3.9
Origin of single female migrants to Lowell, 1870.

Figure 3.10
Origin of single female migrants to Lowell, 1880.

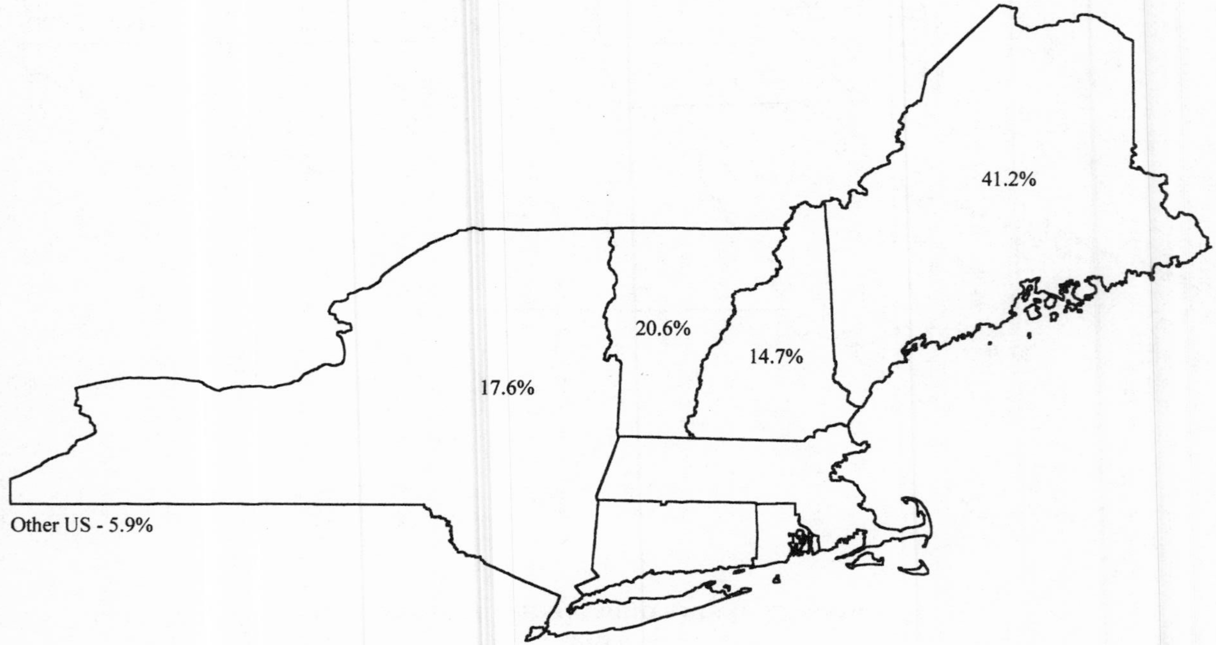

towns, but the workers there, as Emma and her friends showed, were readily enticed to Lowell.[37] There was a substantial drop in the proportion of migrants from Maine immediately following the Civil War, when most of the mills were closed and the migrants returned home. Since the state census day was 1 May 1865, only weeks after the end of the war, and the Maine contingent had rebounded by the time of the 1870 census, their absence in 1865 probably reflects the necessary travel time from Maine while New Hampshire and Vermont migrants were able to return more quickly. New Hampshire, whose southern border is only thirty miles from Lowell, sent approximately 30 percent of the city's migrants until 1870. After that census continuing development within their own state, notably the Amoskeag mills in Manchester, may have created employment opportunities closer to home for potential migrants from New Hampshire and Vermont.[38] At least one of Emma Page's correspondents was encouraged by her family to go to Manchester rather than returning to Lowell for another season.[39]

Vermont contributed from 15 to 24 percent of the female migrants to Lowell, reflecting their greater distance from Lowell as well as the existence of other opportunities in their own state and neighboring New Hampshire. In the last decade of the period, migrants from New York State began to appear in Lowell in considerable numbers. These migrants most likely came not from New York City but from the New York side of the Champlain Valley, which was an easy ferry trip for recruiters from the proven trolling grounds of northwestern Vermont. The Plattsburgh, New York region had sent workers to Lowell as early as 1847, and a large French Canadian community in the area was targeted by Lowell recruiters in the later nineteenth century.[40]

More detailed place-of-birth data might reveal more specific migration streams from particular New England towns to Lowell. Emma Page and her friends show that young women in Kennebec County were ready and willing to move to Lowell; perhaps a recruiter had visited the Readfield woolen mill. Two of Emma's correspondents were from Troy, Vermont, nearly on the Canadian border, which may indicate a connection from that outpost to Lowell. Young women certainly did encourage their friends and relatives to join them wherever they were, be it Readfield, Lowell, or Lawrence, which would encourage women from certain communities to cluster in particular cities.[41]

Like Emma Page and her friends, young women from all over New England were attracted to Lowell after midcentury. Although overall numbers of migrants fell between 1850 and 1880, the migrants continued to come from the same areas: most from northern New England, a few from southern New England and New York. Almost all of the independent migrants to Lowell were within two or three days' travel of their families, which made it relatively simple to return home in times of illness or unemployment. Similar to the internal migrants in England, female migrants to eastern cities in the nineteenth century tended to move relatively short distances, in contrast to the men's preference for continent-spanning reaches of the western migrations or emigration overseas.[42] At the same time, some migrants moved quite long distances and bypassed potentially appropriate cities. The young women from Troy, for example, traveled the length of Vermont to Lowell, passing up available employment in New Hampshire.[43] Lowell had particularly attractive qualities that drew some migrants to it in preference to similar cities.

Migrants and the Textile Industry in Lowell

While the places supplying migrants to Lowell remained the same, what did change in the third quarter of the nineteenth century was the demand for the migrants' labor. As in Preston, employers' needs were a strong, though not the only, influence on single women's migration in New England. After the Potato Famine encouraged large-scale Irish immigration to Lowell, textile mills in the city came to rely more and more heavily on immigrant, family-based workers rather than on independent Yankee women who required lodging in supervised boardinghouses. As domestic service illustrated the influence of employers' needs on the fluctuations of single women's migration to Preston, so industrial textile work serves in Lowell. Changes in the volume of single female migrants to Lowell were heavily influenced by changes in the textile industry that employed them.

The 1850 census did not record women's occupations, so it is difficult to estimate from it what proportion of textile employees in the city were migrants. According to Hamilton Corporation records, 61 percent of the company's workforce in 1850 was "native born," which included both Massachusetts-born and migrant workers.[44] Given that fewer than 20 percent of all adults in Lowell were born in Massachusetts in 1850, it is reasonable to guess that approximately half of the mill's workers were internal migrants in that year. It is logical, in the absence of other data, to extend that estimate to the rest of the city's mills.[45]

It is easier to estimate what proportion of the unmarried female migrants were employed in the mills, due to the requirement (still in effect in 1850) that unmarried employees live either in the company-owned boardinghouses or with their families.[46] In 1850 more than 86 percent of the independent female migrant population in Lowell lived in boardinghouses and thus most likely worked in the city's textile mills.

The volume of independent female migrants in Lowell in 1850, the high proportion of those migrants who worked in the mills, and the estimate of what percentage of the textile workforce they represented all indicate how closely Yankee migration and the textile industry were entwined at midcentury. The migrants were crucial to the success of Lowell's corporations, a dependence reflected in the corporations' maintenance of the boardinghouse system and rules that ensured the mill girls' respectability and thus their migration. The 1850s saw a decline in all of these features. In the 1860 census the number of independent recent female migrants had fallen by more than a thousand, and those women represented not quite 32 percent of all the women recorded as textile workers. While 87 percent of the migrants were still employed in textile mills, they were no longer the dominant supply of labor for those mills. In their stead the mills employed immigrants (47.5 percent of female mill workers) and Massachusetts natives (13.3 percent). Many of these mill workers also lived in the boardinghouses, but more than a third of them lived in family groups. Lowell's employers were clearly beginning to prefer such family-based labor, which reduced the incentive for single women to come to the city from rural New England. Nevertheless the older migration stream did not end. Though fewer than in the past, some young migrant women continued to seek and find employment and housing in Lowell.

The decline in single women's independent migration to Lowell was also influenced by economic troubles in the 1850s. In 1857, in particular, there was a wide-ranging depression that affected capital throughout the industries of New England and Great Britain. During the emergency, the Lowell corporations took advantage of their operatives' ties to rural New England. The Minister at Large for Lowell, Horatio Wood, reported, "Many [operatives] were urged by the Corporations to return to distant homes, with the promise

that they should be individually sent for when business revived."[47]
Workers were also prompted to leave work by a general reduction
in wages of 8 to 30 percent in all but one of the city's twelve major
mills.[48] Those who did not (or could not) return to a rural family
were therefore faced with the possibility of unemployment and
poverty. These migrants were generally refused aid from institutions in the city, instead being "sent back to the places where they
belong, or handed over to the State or city that the charge of them
fall where it should."[49] There is an irony here that once unemployed
the migrants did not "belong" to Lowell. Although the city was dependent on migrants and actively enticing the poor with promises
of work it clung to an older community ethic favoring stationary citizens when times were hard.

Migration continued after the 1857 crisis, but there was no
longer a sense of security in the industry. Wood credited the slowdown with effecting a change in migration to the city:

> [Before the slowdown] the cry of interested parties to the straight-
> ened was 'plenty of work in the Lowell factories.' . . . Our country
> towns continued to send and often to pay the poor to Lowell. . . .
> Untiring attempts were made to turn aside the superabundant
> streams of men, women and children, but without the desired suc-
> cess. In 1857, the great prostration of manufacturing interests
> cured the evil. The incoming ceased. The outgoing had previously
> commenced, which now became the ascendant, until it was the
> sole current; and into it was turned as much as possible of the
> dependent population likely to continue burdensome. When man-
> ufactures revived in the fall of 1858, the diminished resident pop-
> ulation procured the work. The same tide of immigration will
> probably never return upon us. The spell is broken.[50]

It is hard to tell how Wood defined the "resident population" of
Lowell, since the census of 1860 showed that nearly 80 percent of
the city's adult population had been born outside Massachusetts's
boundaries. Nevertheless, his assessment was correct regarding
young Yankee women's migration to Lowell, for the number of independent female migrants never again neared the volume seen before the 1857 depression. The slowdown the depression caused in
women's migration was minimal, however, compared to the events
of the next decade. In Preston, the Cotton Famine caused by
America's Civil War indirectly affected migration when economic
hardship decreased the demand for domestic servants. In Lowell,
the war and cotton shortage influenced migration by closing down

the industry on which the migrants depended. The cotton supply in the war years was intermittent at best, while rumor and anticipation contributed to the uncertainty. Women continued to work in the early 1860s, but they waited anxiously for the word that would end their jobs and could send them back to their parents' homes.

Just days after the onset of war in 1861 Ellen Frost, a native of Belgrade, Maine, wrote from Lowell to a male friend at a military camp in Hampstead, New Hampshire, "There is lots of Men gone from Lowell. There is great excitement here. There never was such a time known before. We expect the Mills will all stop. I should not be surprised if we got our notices tomorrow. If so I shall be in H[ampstead] soon, but not to stop long."[51] In fact, most of the Lowell mills remained open into late 1862, and some converted to wool to ride out the crisis, but all steadily decreased production.[52] For example, in May 1859 and May 1860, at the Lawrence Manufacturing Company workers in the weaving room of Mill One (all women) worked an average of twenty-nine and twenty-one days, respectively. In May 1862 the *maximum* number of days worked in the month was fourteen. By September of that year, when the Lawrence finally closed down, the average number of days worked had fallen to just six and two-thirds. Also between May 1860 and September 1862 the number of women employed in the weaving room dropped from 58 to 21.[53] As fewer and fewer women were employed in the mills, more and more of the independent migrants left the city.

The 1862 shutdown may mark the real end of the corporations' paternalist outlook toward their operatives. Nine cotton companies in Lowell halted operation in 1862, throwing as many as 10,000 operatives out of work. It is significant that at least one company expelled unemployed operatives from the company boardinghouses for the first time in Lowell's history, recognizing that they did not need to keep migrant laborers on hand when the permanent population of the city was large enough to provide an adequate labor supply.[54] Ironically, the uncertainty of the cotton supply during the conflict and the subsequent dismissal of operatives meant that when there was cotton available there was sometimes a shortage of workers to process it. In addition, the workdays and weeks were increasingly irregular, since overtime was added to process the cotton when it was available yet the total number of workdays was falling. The decision to run into overtime, unlike most decisions regarding hours and wages, was not uniform among the companies, which further unsettled a workforce used to nearly identical conditions in all mills.[55]

Thus the war was a period of significant disruption to the working people of Lowell, particularly to single women. As Horatio Wood noted in his 1862 report, "One of the most striking facts in the present change in the city of Lowell is the large number of females thrown out of employment. Those having husbands have not suffered, because of the demand here and everywhere for male help."[56] Wood left the obvious unsaid: the unmarried women would suffer from their lost wages. Many of the young migrant women returned to country homes, some no doubt to help with farm or shop work in fathers' and brothers' absences. Those who remained in the city, according to Wood, often had substantial bank deposits to draw on, or were able to find work sewing uniforms.[57]

Most of the Yankee migrants, however, did not stay in Lowell to search for work sewing uniforms or using up their precious savings. The 1865 Massachusetts state census, taken on the heels of the war, recorded how very few migrant women weathered out the Civil War in Lowell. Before the war there were close to 8,000 female mill employees recorded in the 1860 census, of whom 28 percent were recent, independent female migrants. In the spring of 1865, the state census found fewer than half as many female mill employees, about 3,200, of whom just 14 percent were recent migrants. There were only about 530 recent female migrants in Lowell in 1865, a decline of more than 61 percent in five years. The closure of most of the city's cotton mills had removed the strongest draw for young women's migration.

During and after the war Lowell's corporations were looking for a less skilled, more dependent and more numerous labor force than the Yankee women provided. As well as hiring ever-increasing numbers of immigrants, the corporations were attracting more whole families, rather than single wage earners. In 1862 Horatio Wood noted a large influx of widows to the city, "driven [there] for work for their children."[58] The 1865 census showed that in fact more than 10 percent of the female mill workers were widows, as were 15 percent of all women in Lowell.[59] Nearly half of all the female mill workers lived in family groups, compared to 31 percent in 1860, showing the corporations' further move away from independent female labor. In November of 1866 an Army veteran looking for employment overseeing a carding room appealed to the Hamilton corporation's preference for low-wage, dependent employees when he wrote:

I have three to work in the mill Besides myself one Girl 18 a good Speeder or Wisper tender one 12 a good Speeder or Spinner one Boy 16 a Good Spinner or a Peaser on Mules or a Good Hand. . . .

Besides my family my Wife's Sister a good Speeder Woman she
has a boy 12.[60]

The shift to workers who lived in families, rather than as boarders, was part of an overall pattern of cost reduction in the face of increased competition. Following the Civil War the Lowell mills also
tended to diversify. Some converted to woolen production, others
branched into knitted goods.[61] In spite of these measures, by
February 1866, all of the Lowell corporations were running on
three-quarter time. The Middlesex Company had already reduced the
wages of all workers by 10 percent, and the Lawrence, Suffolk,
Tremont, Appleton, and Hamilton Companies all intended to cut the
wages of their female workers by the same amount at the end of the
month.[62] Company wage policy and the short hours of available work
in this period favored the employment of young women who could live
on low wages and particularly families who could pool their income.

The years of the Civil War were a period of uncertainty for
the entire nation, and Lowell was no exception. But in spite of
short-term discontinuity, those years did not significantly alter the
overriding pattern of women's migration in New England. Paul
McGouldrick, examining the New England textile industry throughout the nineteenth century, concluded, "The structure of the New
England cotton textile industry was hardly touched by the war."[63]
Women's migration to Lowell was based on the vitality and interests of the city's industry, and when cotton returned to Lowell so
did the women from New England. In 1870 the proportion of female
mill workers living in family groups had fallen again to 37 percent,
reflecting the increased number of migrants in the mills. The migration from New England to Lowell had responded quickly to the
loss of employment during the war, but it was by that time too well
established to simply fade away.

Immediately following the war the Lowell mills were anxious
to reclaim workers who had left during the conflict. Recruiters were
dispatched into New England and Canada, promised bounties for
each experienced hand they could entice to Lowell.[64] January 1866
saw eighteen-year-old Emma Page preparing to make the move
from Maine to Lowell, urged on by her friend Mattie.[65] These young
women and hundreds of others helped to restart the pattern that
had been interrupted by the war.

The revitalization of women's migration to Lowell after
the Civil War was relative, however. The 1870 federal census
recorded some twelve hundred recent female migrants in Lowell,

not approaching the numbers at midcentury but more than twice as many as in 1865. More than three-quarters of those migrants were employed in Lowell's textile mills. In spite of the overall decrease from 1860 to 1870, the fact of the increase following the Civil War shows that the wartime closures did not cause the end of women's migration to Lowell from New England. Rather, it produced a severe and temporary dip in a previously established pattern of decline.for some Yankee women migration continued to be a desirable option, and Lowell a desirable destination, after the Civil War.

Indeed, the most remarkable fact about Yankee women's migration after the Civil War was its similarity to migration *before* the war. For most of the migrant women in the 1860s and 1870s, the experience was practically indistinguishable from that of earlier migrants. Compare for example the following excerpts of letters by two different operatives. The first is from Mary Paul, who migrated to Lowell from Vermont in 1845. The second, Mattie Weymouth's first letter to Emma Page after arriving in Lowell, was written more than twenty years later and across the gulf of the Civil War.

Lowell Nov 20th 1845

Dear Father

An opportunity now presents itself which I improve in writing to you . . . . On Saturday after I got here Luthera Griffith went round with me to find a place but we were unsuccessful. On Monday we started again and were more successful. We found a place in a spinning room and the next morning I went to work. I like [it] very well have 50 cts first payment increasing every payment as I get along in work have a first rate overseer and a very good boarding place.[66]

Lowell Nov 27th [1866]

My Dear Em

I suppose you have been looking for a letter all of the week. . . . Len met me at the Depot and before we got home we met Ella going to the Depot to meet me . . . the next morning I went in to the mill stayed on with Ella that forenoon then I run the loom next to her that is flannel. . . . I don't know how much he will pay me a day but he has not payed eny one less than 80 cts when they first went in and some $1.00. . . . I like [it] very much. Think I shall do well.[67]

With the exception of the difference in wages, Mary and Mattie's experiences were nearly identical, from meeting friends in the city and near-immediate success in finding work to their optimism about their future in Lowell.

Nevertheless, after their initial push to recover a workforce in 1865 and 1866, the Lowell corporations continued to employ more workers with permanent residence in the city. By the 1870 census the independent female migrants were only 19 percent of all the female textile workers in Lowell. In 1880 their proportion fell to 10 percent. Immigrants and women born in Massachusetts dominated the Lowell mills in the decades after the Civil War, and by 1880 more than half of the female mill employees lived in family groups rather than as boarders. While independent female migrants did continue to come to Lowell (in fact their numbers increased by a few hundred between 1870 and 1880), they were no longer courted by the cotton manufacturers.[68] Educational lectures and concerts were a thing of the past, and considering wages and pace of work there was little to choose between Lowell and the Lancashire mill towns it had been created to oppose.[69] That single women were attracted to Lowell as long as they were suggests that something other than conditions in the city and its mills was working to maintain the migration pattern.

As in Preston, Lowell's censuses and the history of the city's economic development allow an analysis of women's independent migration based primarily on quantitative data. The survival of the middecade Massachusetts state census, particularly, illustrates both the sensitivity and the resilience of migration patterns to disrupting influences. However, a direct correlation between economic-industrial developments and the volume of migrant women in a city gives an overly simplistic rendering of the many influences on migration. In Preston, there is little to be done to combat this simplicity. Lowell, on the other hand, is unparalleled in the survival of qualitative materials. Observers' reports, business correspondence and records from the corporations, and materials written by the mill girls themselves exist in abundance. The operatives' letters offer the best possible evidence of young women's personal reasons for migration in the nineteenth century. New migrants continued to be persuaded to come to Lowell even as the overall number of migrant mill girls in the city was falling. The surviving qualitative sources help to explain why.

The Migrants' Society

Employment in the textile mills, as the foregoing has illustrated, was the greatest influence on single women's migration to Lowell, both before and after the Civil War. The mill closures of 1857 and the longer interruption in the war years deterred independent migrants from the city. Mill workers with families in Lowell were less likely to be driven out of the city by unemployment since a family economy with several wage earners could support an unemployed member through hard times.[70] Furthermore, it is clear from the numbers that many migrant mill workers who left Lowell when the mills closed in 1857 and 1862 did not return when the factories reopened.

Potential mill workers based their decisions not to return to Lowell (or travel there for the first time) on more than fear of future shutdowns. Since the 1840s the wages and working conditions in the mills had been in steady decline, decreasing Lowell's attractiveness even when the mills were in full operation. The migrants in Lowell as early as the 1840s noted the changes with displeasure, as Mary Paul wrote to her father in 1848:

> I presume you have heard before this that the wages are to be reduced on the 20th of this month. It is *true* and there seems to be a good deal of excitement on the subject.... The companies pretend they are losing immense sums every *day* and therefore they are obliged to lessen the wages, but this seems perfectly absurd to me for they are constantly making *repairs*.... I expect to be paid about two dollars a week but it will be dearly earned.[71]

In addition to the falling wages, managers gradually required workers to tend more machinery and work at a faster pace. Between 1840 and 1854 the workload of spinners and weavers at the Hamilton Corporation more than doubled, while wages remained essentially level.[72] Horatio Wood reported that wages were reduced "materially" in 1851, and they dropped again in response to the economic crisis of 1857–58.[73] In 1867 there was another 10 percent reduction, while the mills were simultaneously running only three-quarter time.[74] It is clear from the census data that many migrants from New England would not tolerate the deteriorating conditions.

Earlier decades had seen the mill girls turning out in organized protest against falling wages, increasing board rates, a faster pace of work, and overly long hours. Fostered by the close-knit community of the company boarding houses, the strikes demonstrated the migrants' sense of independence and prompted a feminist questioning of women's role in industrial society.[75] Following the Civil War there were scattered protests against particular issues, for example in a Merrimack Company finishing room in 1866, where the management invoked cost-saving measures. They shut off the room's fans, and required the women workers to spread the size on their fabric themselves, rather than having men to do the work. The women engaged in a short sit-down strike and the management gave in, retracting the changes.[76] In spite of their victory, the mill girls did not capitalize on their success by engaging in labor protest on any larger scale.

There is no doubt that in general the working conditions in the mills deteriorated after the Civil War, and there was sufficient willing labor available in Lowell to render wide-scale organized protest by the migrant women useless; any work stoppage by the Yankees could be easily overcome by hiring less demanding immigrant workers in their stead.[77] When the Yankee boardinghouse community was no longer dominant in the mills, unhappy migrant operatives were more likely to leave Lowell than to organize protest.[78] Meanwhile, as in England, employment opportunities for women were expanding, with positions available as store clerks or other white-collar workers. Mill workers' correspondence discussed a range of possible employment, from teaching school to harvest labor to "table work" in a hotel or work in a family-owned printing office. Indeed, Emma Page and Mattie Weymouth left the mills to work as "tailoresses" for some of their time in Lowell, while still living in a boardinghouse with migrant and immigrant mill workers.[79]

Even as the falling wages and faster pace of work were driving the migrants away from Lowell, at least some of the mills tried to maintain a native-born workforce, showing that employer demand in itself was not enough to draw young women to Lowell. The New England women continued to be desirable employees even as the immigrant presence in the mills was rising, perhaps because of their education, prior experience of textile work in mills close to their homes, or employers' ethnic bias, and there is evidence that the mills were not able to get as many Yankee workers as they wanted. Lydia Bixby, whose overseer wanted her to recruit other "Groton girls" in the early 1850s, noted, "there is a great cry for Yankee girls here they cant get them for love nor money hardly."[80] During the 1857 depression, the mills assured the unemployed workers that they would be personally recalled from their country homes when the mills reopened, evidence that the trained Yankee workers were valuable.[81] After the Civil War, when cotton returned to Lowell, the mills dispatched recruiters to reclaim the strayed flock of native-born migrant workers, as well as any new hands they could convince to migrate.

These recruiters received payment based on the number of mill hands that they succeeded in bringing to Lowell. The mill managers, understandably, preferred workers with some experience. Trained power-loom weavers or hand-loom weavers from Canada were worth "$3.00 each if they remain a month, and the same for new hands (if smart) and the number does not exceed one new hand to two old ones."[82] The bounty for hands recruited from Vermont was set at only two dollars each, and that for women from Maine was probably the same.[83] The agents were also authorized to advance the wages of the female recruits (up to 20 percent of the anticipated first month's wages, or about $4.50) in order to finance the journey from their homes to Lowell.[84]

It was not always easy to find recruits, and once found they did not always stay recruited. In July of 1865 recruiter James Jordan wrote from Belfast, Maine, to his employer at the Hamilton Mills, "I have made a complete failure, and have concluded to throw the thing up." He continued,

> When I last wrote you I was . . . quite hopefull. I had obtained the names of twenty girls who had agreed to meet me Monday at the time of the Boston boat in Searsport. The time came and the boat came and two of the femanines came and eighteen didn't come . . . .
> I thought at first it must be on account of the weather . . . .
> I have assertained the encouraging fact that the storm was just about as much the cause of their delay as their delay was the cause of the storm, in fact, they had all backed out.[85]

The next day Jordan met a grocer in North Searsmont who "thought that he could without any difficulty find me... about twenty five girls" and the two joined forces. Even with the support of the local businessman, however, he was unable to find "any who we could rely upon to go at a set time. They promise to go there when they go but cant tell exactly when they will be ready."[86] Jordan believed, probably justifiably, that recruiting in the area was more difficult that summer than in previous years because "husbands, brothers and lovers are just returning from the war."[87] Another recruiter found that young women were willing to go to Lowell, but not until the harvest was finished.[88]

The recruiters also found that they were redundant in trying to persuade workers to Lowell. Jordan complained that workers were "able to go alone and shure of a job any time. They are well aware of this from advertisments and other sources, and therefore care very little about me."[89] Nevertheless the recruiters may have had some effect; Emma Page and her friends came from precisely the region in which Jordan was working, though six months after the agent left. Recruiters evidently could not replace all the Yankee workers lost to closures and deteriorating conditions, but they were at least an influence on determining a potential migrant's destination.

Individual women's movements were probably more heavily influenced by their friends than by the recruiters, however. Emma's correspondents did not mention being courted by recruiters; rather, they persuaded and teased one another into first coming to Lowell, then returning again after visits home. The same had been true since Lowell's earliest days, when the first generation of workers convinced their friends and relatives to come to the mills.[90] In 1847, when young Florella Farnsworth arrived in Lowell from Danville, Vermont, for her first experience in the mills, she wrote home about the confusion of her initial arrival in the city when the sister she had expected to meet did not appear: "When I got to the depot I was completely bewildered. I expected to see Huldah but there was not a soul that I had ever seen before . . . and I did not know what to do." Luckily, as soon as she arrived at Hulda's boarding house Florella was swept into a circle of acquaintances from home.

> [The boardinghouse mistress] asked if I knew Harriet Hookes and went upstairs and got her . . . . When Frona Willey was going home from the mill [Hulda] called her in and she pounded me and took her bonnet and struck me with it. And after supper we went over to her boarding place and Mance, Beck and Cinth all gave me a regular built shaking . . . .[91]

The presence of these and more friends in the city made Florella's first days in the city an exciting social whirl, barely giving her time for homesickness. By the end of her first letter she was encouraging another friend to join the migration, "tell Sarah Rinsbury she would do first rate here."[92]

The rough physicality of Florella's welcome recalls the same kind of close female friendships that another class of young women found at women's colleges in the same period, and the camaraderie among the mill girls was just as strong more than twenty years after Florella arrived in Lowell. Emma Page and Mattie Weymouth boarded with a Mrs. Kitteridge in Lowell, who was possibly related to Claire Kitteridge, a Readfield coworker. When separated, the women who boarded with Mrs. Kit expressed an affection verging on familial. Ella Hunt, home in Vermont after a stint in Lowell, wrote to Emma,

> Perhaps you think I have forgotten Lowell folks; but I have not I think of you all every day and nearly every day I think I will write

to some of you: I am so anxious to hear and concluded that I would not unless I wrote to *you*. Well how do you all do? Please write to me all about the folks won't you? . . . How I would like to see you all.[93]

In 1870, while Emma was visiting family in Maine, four of the girls with whom she boarded wrote a group letter enticing her to return quickly. Mat Weymouth, who began the letter, wrote bluntly, "write before you come write soon and come as soon as convenient." Ted urged, "we want you to come back just as soon as you can, come is the order of the day & come you must." Another Mattie, who had been helping Ted into her hoopskirts when the letter was begun, added, "We all miss you very much and want you to make the old House ring with your laugh." Finally, Flora's note opened, "I am glad that you are coming back to Lowell again it is so dull here."[94] The letters reveal a network of close friendships and acquaintances that sustained the migrants in all aspects of life in Lowell, from providing company to and from the depot to help finding jobs and boarding places to recreation and information about the latest city fashions.

It was these personal ties to other women that made migrants want to return to Lowell year after year and persuaded their relatives and friends to do the same. After the Civil War most of Lowell's original attractions—uniquely respectable, highly paid factory work and cultural opportunities—had succumbed to economic necessity. When Lowell's employers no longer worked to maintain women's migration to the city the women's own needs and preferences, including joining friends and relatives, continued to encourage them to Lowell. Those young women in New England who needed or wanted to earn their own livings and were willing to migrate to do so certainly knew of Lowell from reputation, advertisements, and impatient recruiters. But in the face of declining wages and deteriorating working conditions, the factor that continued to attract migrants to Lowell in preference to other cities and sustained the migration pattern for decades after the war was the encouraging, supportive network the operatives constructed for themselves.

The young women who decided to go to Lowell in the nineteenth century were not, however, responding inevitably to economic conditions and the pleas of friends. Each of them, as a potential migrant, had her own personal reasons for moving that might or might not be readily understandable to her family or historians. Once again, the qualitative, personal sources that survive in Lowell make it possible to directly address questions concerning reasons for and effects of migration that can only be speculated about in Preston and Paisley. The Lowell letters do not always explicitly state womens' reasons for moving, but the concerns and activities they describe are strong indications of what they hoped to accomplish by migration. Letters and other reports of their actions can also give insight into how migration affected the women's lives and relationships. As Marc Bloch suggested was possible, when all three cities are compared, if the patterns the statistics show are similar then qualitative sources from one city may help to explain behavior evident in all three.[95] Thus the desires and experiences of American migrants can be useful in unraveling the actions of the British.

A Desire to See the City

Money, in the nineteenth century as much as the twenty-first, was a primary motivation to action. The wages to be earned in the Lowell mills were central to the young women's decisions to move, and they continued to be important to migrants throughout the century. In contrast to the common English pattern, mirrored by immigrant families in Lowell, in which mill workers lived in family groups and turned all or most of their wages over to the family, the Lowell girls, like the domestic servants with savings accounts in Preston, had control over their wages.[96] Their letters show that the young women who traveled to the Lowell mills most often were going in search of some personal wealth and adventure before they settled down to anticipated marriage, not in order to support their families.

Thomas Dublin found that female workers in the Hamilton Mill in June 1860 could expect to earn from $0.53 to $0.61 a day.[97] The previous month, women at Lawrence Manufacturing made wages of $8.20 to $17.64, working from twenty to twenty-four days in the pay period.[98] These average to approximately $13.17 per month. At nineteenth century exchange rates this equalled an average yearly wage of £32 18 s. 6 d.—surprisingly close to the servants' wages recorded in 1860 Preston if room and board was indeed valued at £20 ($100.00) annually. It is unclear what proportion of the mill girls' income went to room and board in 1860; boardinghouse keepers were charged $25.00 monthly for keeping a house with thirty-five or more girls, but beyond that there is no indication of what the

boarders themselves paid.[99] Although much has been made of the
earnings potential for migrants in the Lowell mills, by mid-century
their base income does not appear to have differed drastically from
that of migrant domestic servants in Britain. They did, however,
make considerably more than nonmigrant mill workers in Preston.

More important to many girls than the actual money, though,
was what could be purchased with it. Letters often contained some
mention of the wages women expected to earn, especially when
they first arrived in Lowell, and considerations about how to spend
money—especially details of the latest fashions—occurred frequently. For example, an anonymous mill hand wrote to a friend in
1849,

> I wish you would buy me a pen and send it by the next mail, for
> this, I am realy distressed with. I had an excellent opportunity
> yesterday, to buy a gold one, but, I finerly concluded to wait' till
> after pay-day, which will *come* in one week, and than after pur-
> chasing that pen, what, I pray you, shall I do with the ballance? I
> *realy* hope, there will be a way opened for me to spend so *much*
> *money* profitably.[100]

For this operative and many others the wages paid at the Lowell
mills were unprecedented personal wealth. This letter illustrates
both the mill girl's ability to dispose of her wages as she pleased,
and perhaps a propensity for purchasing less-than-essential items.
A local historian in Sutton, New Hampshire alluded to other mill
girls' fiscal independence in her 1890 account:

> The girls began to go to work in the cotton factories of Nashua and
> Lowell. . . . They went in their plain, country-made clothes, and
> after working several months, would come home for a visit, or per-
> haps to be married, in their tasteful city dresses, and with more
> money in their pockets than they had ever owned before.[101]

Lowell continued to be a desirable destination for young women in
spite of worsening conditions because they could still expect to earn
a reasonable living there.

In the early months of the Civil War, Horatio Wood noted that
many of the single women made unemployed by the wartime cotton
shortages "have had deposits in the bank to keep them up for a
while."[102] By 1863 many of the operatives had given up on work in
Lowell for the war's duration, and returned to their country homes.
"Many carried with them a very respectable outfit and means of

subsistence earned and saved."[103] As in Preston, the presence of bank deposits reiterates many women's goals for migration: to earn money for themselves, not to help their parents.

It is very clear that just as the female migration continued (albeit at a much-reduced level) following the Civil War with only minor changes in experience, so did the migrants' financial arrangements. Although after the war mill workers seem more likely to have sent money home, they still controlled the disposition of their own wages.[104] Consider for example this excerpt from a letter written by Addie Holms, a mill worker from New Hampshire, in 1873:

> I am not to come to New Hampton this *spring*, if ever. Almost everyone I have ever talked with about it favor my going to school. I *wish* to go *so* much but Mother does not wish me to. She and my brothers and sister need me .... If I put what money I have saved to go to school with into the farm (and I have already put in over a hundred dollars) and then go home and devote myself to that, Mother would be relieved of care and worry and would probably have a home after a time.
>
> On the other hand—if I take my money and go to school and then live to see my mother taken from me, killed by work, care and anxiety just as I "was going to" be able to help her; and my brothers confirmed in a course of careless unconcern if not in actual "badness;" shall I not then bitterly regret that I had not given up the long-cherished and much loved plan of going to school?[105]

Addie had a more serious financial decision to make than whether or not to buy a gold pen. Nevertheless, her reasons for working in Lowell were similar to those suggested by the anonymous mill worker in 1849. She had gone to Lowell at least in part to earn money *for herself*, to finance her "long-cherished and much loved plan." Her mother's economic distress put a strain on her resources and sense of obligation to her family, but could not change her original motives in migrating to Lowell. This decision was Addie's to make; her mother was asking, not demanding, that she come home to the farm.

It is possible that migrant mill workers were also sending some of their wages home to their families. Addie Holms had in fact contributed more than one hundred dollars to her family farm. Some of the migrants were "poor girls" who required an advance on their wages in order to pay the train fare to Lowell, and they may have hoped to contribute cash to the family concern.[106] It is surely significant, however, that none of the post–Civil War sources suggest family support as a primary motivation for migration. James Jordan, the recruiter in Maine, found it more difficult to convince parents than daughters of the desirability of migration: if those parents were anxious for extra income, they did not see migration as the means to gain it.[107] In all of the letters Emma Page received over nearly ten years, not one mentioned wages sent home, either by Emma or by any of her friends. When her correspondents expressed an eagerness to return to Lowell, it was invariably to see their friends, not to earn more money. Nor were they simply shy about discussing money. Emma's aunt quite understood that her niece would prefer Lowell to Readfield if the wages were higher in Massachusetts: "Do you like in Lowell [better] then in Readfield[?] If not why dont you return[?] Can you make better pay[?]"[108] A few years later, one of Emma's Readfield friends, Ann Packard, was struggling to support a family selling tatted lace collars, for which Emma took orders in Lowell. Ann unfailingly affirmed when money had arrived with a letter, and was unabashed in telling what was owed for the completed collars.[109] It is very unlikely that money was being sent home by migrants and not acknowledged.

Direct references to actual wages earned in letters after the Civil War were generally limited to the first few letters sent from Lowell. There were, however, frequent mentions of the latest fashion, which suggests what the mill girls were immediately concerned about, reminiscent of the English factory girl derided by Mr. Moore, spending her wages on "mere tawdry finery."[110] The migrants exchanged photographs when they were separated, a gesture that was much appreciated by the recipients and was also a good indicator of disposable income.[111] Without denying the likelihood that some migrants were supporting family in New England, the most common experience among the Yankee migrants after the Civil War as well as before it was apparently keeping their wages for their own use.

Money was not the only reason young women wanted to migrate to Lowell, however. The same anonymous operative who wanted the gold pen wrote, "You probably think it strange, that I should come to Lowell in preference to keeping school, but I had a desire to *see the city* and as I once told you, that I never should see anything untill I started out myself."[112] The move to Lowell was an adventure, as well as an economic opportunity, and something that the workers relished being able to do on their own. Yet the journey could also be daunting, for she went on, "I *did* want to go back to your house again almost as soon as I got home, and bargained, partially, for a seat in the *same* carriage that bro't me home. Then it occurred to me, that possibly you *might not* be glad to see [me] back again the same day, so I gave it up."[113] The nervousness and anticipation apparent in this operative's letter shows that the move to Lowell was a daring one for her, just at the edge of what she felt able to complete on her own.

That the migration could be simultaneously exciting and daunting was confirmed by the frustrated recruiter James Jordan, who wrote, "green hands jump at the chance but on a second thought their confidence is shaken."[114] Certainly the move to Lowell took planning, and the journey could turn out to be an adventure in itself. Mattie Weymouth's first letter to Emma, after describing the important matters of her arrival, first day's work, going to a Sabbath School Anniversary in the horse cars, and that she had not seen any newly styled hats, added a postscript that shows her departure from Readfield was possibly as exciting as her arrival in Lowell:

> Em I wish you would see the job man and pay him for taking my trunk over to the Depot I did not have time for the cars started just as I steped on I did not have time to get a ticket please get my cloud out of Libs room and bring it when you come and my comb I left that.[115]

In spite of the haste and anxiety of the trip, Mattie's tone was entirely undaunted, more pleased to be in Lowell than concerned about the dangers of the city.

Another letter writer, Ella Bailey, may have been expressing her boredom with the pace of life back in the country when she wrote to Emma and Mattie, "Do you go to the Theatre often[?] What are you doing for work[?] I am making Clover leaf tatting dont you wish you could[?]"[116] Ella was also impatient with school teaching, her occupation for part of a year she spent away from Lowell, "I would beg from door to door before I'd teach again."[117] Another friend, Ella Sanders, complained on returning home to Maine, "It is very lonesome here all I have to visit with is old women and men. When I think of the folks in Lowell I can hardly contain myself."[118] Both of the Ellas and Mattie valued their time in Lowell not only for the money they could earn but for the friends, diversions and fashions the city offered. Young women moving to Preston, too, would have been exposed to opportunities and diversions unavailable in their home villages, even if they took advantage of them only on rare days off. The number of actors and musicians present in the

Preston census sample suggests shows and music halls in the city, in addition to attractions like religious and temperance meetings that were common (and entertaining) in Preston in the nineteenth century.[119] Moving to any city was a potentially exciting change from life in a rural parental home.

The Migrants' Independence

The comings and goings, cajoling and figuring that are evident in the Lowell mill girls' letters illustrate the transition young women were making in migrating. The adventure of moving to Lowell distanced them from their parents physically and psychologically, as well as economically. In gaining their financial independence, the migrants were also gaining personal independence. Dublin found personal autonomy to be a much-valued effect of migration among the prewar migrants; like control of their own wages, this additional benefit continued to be true in the years following the Civil War.[120]

Yet of course the decision to migrate, especially the first time, was not a unilateral one. Young women in nineteenth-century New England had limited agency at best, enmeshed as they were in a web of protective parents and social mores. Moving to Lowell had to be negotiated, parents or guardians persuaded that their daughters would be safe, respectable, healthy, and well looked after. Such persuasion was the job of recruiters, employers and the girls themselves. After the Civil War securing permission must have become harder as Lowell's reputation for respectability deteriorated. It is likely no accident that many of the postwar letter writers apparently came from single-parent families; widowed fathers might welcome relief from the difficulty of teenaged daughters and widowed mothers needed the economic relief of fewer mouths to feed. Perhaps in two parent families the parents were better able to resist children's exhortations.

Once a daughter had succeeded in once becoming a mill girl, however, her position in the equation was strengthened. The mere possession of personal wealth might not change a young woman's position in her home community, but sources suggest that female migrants were considered and treated differently than their sisters who remained at home. As the "factory girl" was a recognized type in industrial Britain, marked by overly fine clothes, questionable morals, and a disturbing lack of deference, so the New England "mill girl" was a separate type of woman who existed somewhere between dependent daughter and fully mature woman.[121] Like the Preston domestic servants, they were in transition between their parents' and marriage families. The migrants certainly felt they should be able to make decisions not only about how they spent their money but about their actions. While Ella Bailey was convalescing in Vermont her mother forbade her to attend a dance some seven miles away from her home. Ella, feeling somewhat weak, agreed, but reassured Emma and Mattie of her actual autonomy: "Now privately . . . I say unto you if I took a strong notion to attend that same *Hop go I would* in spite of fate. That is settled is it not[?] Echo simply answers Yes."[122]

James Jordan, the Hamilton recruiter, was surprised by the independence former mill girls displayed. Many of those he spoke to planned to return to Lowell eventually, but he and his accomplices, as described above, were unable to convince previous migrants that they should return under the recruiter's escort.[123] Jordan divided the women he sought into two categories, each of which presented its own difficulties. He wrote to his employer, "As for old hands they are mighty independent." Already familiar with Lowell, knowing where to find jobs and boarding places, the women who had migrated before were capable of returning on their own when they were ready. With green hands, conversely, Jordan faced the problem of parents, writing, "It is very hard indeed to talk it into the old folks."[124]

The "old hands" may have been generally older than the green hands, but by his labeling of them the primary difference Jordan saw between the two groups was the old hands' prior experience of migration and their independence from both his and their parents' influence. The mill girls themselves felt they were entitled to make their own decisions about when and where they migrated. Ella Bailey had given in to her mother regarding the dance in South Troy, but she would not give up her right to return to Lowell. After nearly a year away from the city, having progressed from a euchre-playing invalid to a discontented schoolteacher, Ella wrote to her friends,

> Now I shall be in Lowell just one year from the day I left it . . . .
> Mother would rather I should go to Manchester N.H. but I tell her
> I am not acquainted there so well . . . . My dear parient . . . gently
> insists I shall attend the fall term and teach this winter but that
> *peculiar* whim I shall not gratify.[125]

By her own admission, Ella was bored by country living and did not compare favorably to more demure, nonmigrant women in her home town. "I am *minus* any *gentleman* attendant. Em the trouble is I am not quite modest or retiring enough in my ways for the 'fellah's'."[126] Ella felt herself ill suited for small-town life, and she had the ability to move away from it again, to where gentlemen might prefer less retiring women.

Emma Page's younger sister, Eliza, saw migration and the attendant self-support as a way to circumvent her father's objections to a suitor: "Thommy is going to Canida to work in the shop and I shall go away some whare to work. . . . Then we can write and it will be no bodys mat[t]ers."[127] Nevertheless, not all migrants were inclined to defy their parents. A former mill girl, significantly one with both parents living, wrote in 1872,

> I want to go back this fall but I am afraid it is impossible to leave my folks to let me go. Father says that I have got to go to school this fall but I had rather go back I told Mother you gave me from the time I got home untill Sept to stay. She will not hear one word about my going back to stay.[128]

Most of the migrants did not mention their parents' influences on their decisions at all; they simply told their friends when they planned to arrive, and hoped they would be met at the station. The experience of migration and wage earning took some young women out of the traditional nineteenth-century family dynamic, in which they were dependent on and subservient to their parents' wishes. The ability to sustain themselves in the city often brought with it the autonomy to do so when and how they chose.

The Yankee migrants were leaving their families, but they should not be imagined to be wholly on their own. The mill girls can be identified as much by their close friendships as by their independence from their families. The support of this community was crucial to the single women's migration to Lowell and, the next chapter will show, probably existed in Paisley as well.[129] The mill girls often found work through their friends, so even brand new migrants like Florella Farnsworth usually knew someone in Lowell right from the start. Nor did the mill girls work in isolation. Quite the contrary, the textile machinery was arranged in large rooms, and in spite of the pace of work the operatives had ample time to become acquainted with each other. Even more important than the work environment to the girls' social lives was the dormitory-like atmosphere of the Lowell boardinghouses.

In *Women at Work* Dublin referred to the boarding house system as "an instrument of social control" designed to maintain the respectability of the female operatives, as well as helping to keep wages low.[130] Such they certainly were, and Dublin cites evidence of social pressure brought on boarders by fellow residents, as well as by corporate regulations.[131] On the other hand, the letters written to Emma Page emphasize that the boarding house culture and the network of friends it engendered was at least as enjoyable as it was repressive. They reinforce the importance of friendship in explaining why migration to Lowell continued when there was apparently nothing to choose between Lowell and a dozen other New England mill towns. Being reunited with friends was the single most common reason migrants gave for wanting to return to Lowell, and girls away from Lowell relied on their friends for information about current fashions, job openings, and places to board.

The original editor of Emma's letters noted that Lowell "was the college for them in those days," emphasizing both the separation from their parents and the importance of friendships.[132] Dublin also drew a comparison between the Lowell experience and women's colleges, "The close, supportive relations . . . in mill boardinghouses paralleled the experiences of young women in the boarding schools of the period."[133] The friendships formed in the Lowell mills sustained the migrants' independence by providing necessary support without the subordination that was implicit in a parent-daughter relationship.

It is the migrants' autonomy within restrictions that brings this chapter back to the question of influences on single women's migration streams. The census data in the second half of the century shows that while the Lowell migration had been jump-started by the corporations' need for labor, once established it was not so readily halted. The corporations' need for migrant female labor declined after the Civil War as they became more reliant on immigrant, family-based workers. Nevertheless a substantial population of young women from rural New England continued to travel to Lowell for the same reasons that women had migrated in the antebellum decades. Moreover, they continued to have experiences essentially similar to those of the earlier migrants. Boardinghouses, networks of friends, and frequent travel back and forth to family homes remained important aspects of the migrants' experience.

The letters mill girls wrote before and after the Civil War provide the best source available for direct analysis of the migrants' own motives for migration. The opportunity for mill work in Lowell was one reason they came to the city, but it was far from the only reason. From the anonymous mill hand in 1849 who declared she

had "a desire to see the city" to Addie Holms in 1873 working to
fund her education, the migrants to Lowell were looking for income,
independence and adventure, all without trespassing too far outside
the bounds of respectability. The Yankee girls who went to Lowell
could have found work closer to home as domestic or farm help,
teachers, or other, more esoteric jobs. Yet they were drawn to the
city, with its relatively high wages, access to the latest fashions,
good friends and, not least, distance from family. Becoming a mill
girl facilitated the transition from dependent daughter to womanhood, giving the migrants an opportunity to exercise their independence *while being protected* from the moral dangers inherent to
cities. Employers' needs and parents' permission did influence the
mill girls' migration, but the migrants' own needs, desires, and
hopes were a necessary factor.

    The Yankee migrants in Lowell were highly visible, first as a
symbol of the city and later as a reminder of its past. The many
sources that survive from Lowell because of this visibility permit
an analysis of single women's migration from the migrants' point of
view, revealing the complex personal motivations for migration.
Yet there is no reason to believe that the migrants to Lowell actually had more intricate influences in their lives or more variations
in their experiences than migrants in Preston or Paisley. In spite of
broad similarities migration was a highly individual affair to which
each woman was urged by slightly different circumstances and
from which each had a different outcome. Paisley provides information parallel to that from Preston and Lowell, exhibiting the influence of both employers' and migrants' needs on migration choices.
Paisley's data reveal a combination of the migration patterns
demonstrated by Preston and Lowell. Some of the migrants to Paisley were nearly as visible as the Lowell mill girls, coming from a
particular region and clustered in a single occupation. Others more
closely resembled the Preston migrants, going virtually unnoticed
among Paisley's nonmigrant population. Sources from Paisley lend
themselves to exploring the experiences that were beyond the control of either employers or migrants, the pitfalls that could derail a
migrant's attempt to become independent from her parents.
Through their experiences, the migrants to Paisley illuminate a
third major factor in single women's migration experience after
1850: their inordinate vulnerability to the cities' dangers.

CHAPTER 4

Paisley: The Strangers and the Maids

Nineteen-year-old Isabella McNeil fell prey to the city's dangers in May, 1874, and she turned for help to Paisley's Inspector of the Poor. A shoemaker's daughter, Isabella was born in Oban, Argyllshire. She had migrated to Paisley at sixteen, most likely to work as a domestic servant. She changed positions in May the same year, and sometime after 1872 left domestic service to work in one of Paisley's mills. Isabella also met a weaver named James Waddell. Around mid-September of 1873 she may have been living with Waddell, probably expected him to marry her, and certainly became pregnant by him. James, however, had different expectations. While admitting paternity of Isabella's child he married another woman three months before Isabella gave birth in June 1874 at Glasgow's lying-in hospital. McNeil disappeared from the record for the next year, but on 14 October 1875, Isabella's mother arrived from Oban, "saying she wishes to take her home, but requires some assistance." Paisley's Inspector granted Mrs. McNeil four shillings to help bring her daughter and granddaughter back to Argyll.[1]

Despite her ill-fated relationship with Waddell, Isabella McNeil was a typical independent female migrant to Paisley, who began work as a domestic servant but apparently chose mill work when a situation was available. As in Preston and Lowell, migrants chose occupations that met their needs and helped them achieve their own goals. Through migration young women were often able to establish themselves as independent from their parents. However, like Isabella, not all migrants successfully made the transition out of their parents' homes. The end of her migration experience, taken home by her mother with a child in her arms and no husband at her side, illustrates just one of the ways in which a migrant's plans could be derailed. Even when statistics describe a broadly similar pattern of behavior among all migrants, individual outcomes

101

varied as widely as the migrants themselves. Migration was affected by factors neither urban employers nor migrants could control, factors like rural depression and depopulation, disease, crime, and pregnancy. Precisely because the young women were separated from their families they were often unable to weather out setbacks in the cities and maintain their independence.

Migration was a constant in nineteenth-century Scottish life.[2] Industries developed primarily along the Edinburgh-Glasgow axis, drawing migrants from rural areas to the north and south. From the mid-eighteenth to the mid-nineteenth century, the Highland region experienced "a sustained haemorrage of people," due to social, economic and agricultural changes that all but eliminated the margin in which the rural poor existed.[3] In addition to large-scale emigration, primarily to North America, temporary migration was part of the Highlanders' economic survival strategy. Young men and women migrated to the Lowlands for periods of months or years, easing the strain on their families and funneling cash back into the Highlands. The Highlanders were visible migrants in Lowland Scotland, singled out as "strangers" who spoke Gaelic and formed their own filial societies, additionally set apart by popular romantic images of the Highlands in the nineteenth century.[4]

Lowland-born transcounty migrants were less visible but in fact more prevalent in nineteenth-century Scotland. Even before there was industrial employment available Lowlanders as well as Highlanders had migrated in pursuit of agricultural labor. Workers from the rural Lowlands poured into the cities as the country industrialized.[5] In comparison to the Highlanders and Irish immigrants the Lowland migrants were unremarkable, and they went mostly unnoticed by contemporaries.[6] Nevertheless the Lowland migrants were not identical to their neighbors; as in Preston and Lowell they preferred different occupations and chose different housing than nonmigrants.

Single women were common in both groups of migrants, working all over Scotland in domestic service, in the fields at harvest time, and in coastal areas supporting the herring fisheries.[7] The female migrants in Paisley between 1851 and 1881 followed a well-established pattern of behavior, one which, unlike Lowell's migrants, did not excite much comment from their contemporaries. The presence of the Gaelic-speaking Highland strangers made single female migrants in Paisley more visible than the English migrants in Preston, but there were also many Lowland-born maids of all work who went as unseen as their English counterparts.

Paisley, about ten miles west of Glasgow in Renfrewshire, Scotland, was neither as diverse an economy as Preston nor so highly specialized as Lowell (see maps, Figures 4.1a and 4.1b). Paisley was born as a minor burgh with fair waterways and an abbey, but it grew to historical importance on the basis of two specialized products: fancy shawls and cotton thread. Manufacturers in Paisley were among the first to copy the brightly patterned cotton fabrics imported to Britain from India, forever attaching the city's name to the popular fish-shaped "pine" pattern. For as long as the fashion lasted—through the 1860s—Paisley was one of two shawl centers of Britain, producing them in cotton, wool and silk, with the patterns variously woven, printed or embroidered onto the cloth.[8] Shawl manufacturing employed thousands of men and women in Paisley as hand- and power-loom weavers of plain and fancy shawls. Women employed as "tambourers" hand-embroidered patterns on plain muslin shawls, and shawls with printed patterns required employees of both sexes in printing mills. Hundreds of women found finishing work as "shawl fringers," "shawl sewers," "warehouse sewers," and nondescript "shawl workers." Employing people of all ages and a wide range of skills, the shawl trade was central to Paisley's mid-nineteenth-century economy.

Paisley's thread industry was equally important and better able to withstand the fluctuations of fashion. During the Napoleonic Wars a Paisley manufacturer, Peter Clark, developed cotton sewing thread as a viable substitute for silk and linen. In 1814 the Clark family introduced the practice of selling thread on spools rather than in loose hanks, and an industry was born. By 1857 there were ten thread factories in Paisley with 3000 employees between them. More than three-quarters of those employees were women. Demand for thread grew with the invention of the sewing machine, and thread became the most successful sector of the Scottish textile industry. When the two Paisley giants, Clarks and Coats, merged in 1896 they became the dominant force in the world thread industry.[9]

In addition to these two major fields of textile production Paisley was the national center of a third industry: cotton bleaching and dyeing. From the early eighteenth century bleachers were attracted to the countryside surrounding Paisley, which was an ideal venue for the open-field sun bleaching of linen, wool, and cotton. After the bleaching properties of chlorine were discovered in 1784, cotton bleaching rapidly changed from a long-term, quasi-natural process to a quick chemical one practiced by at least ten different firms in the Paisley area.[10] Cotton bleaching did not employ as many women

Figure 4.1a
Map of Scotland showing county boundaries

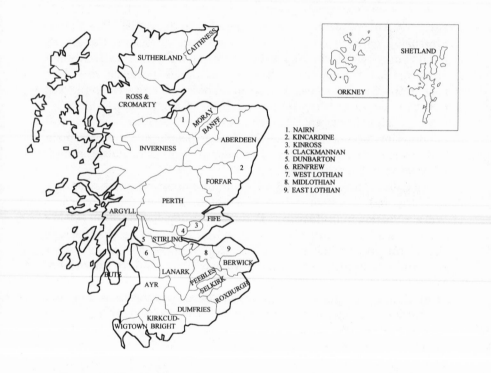

Figure 4.1b
Map of Central Scotland with places mentioned in the text

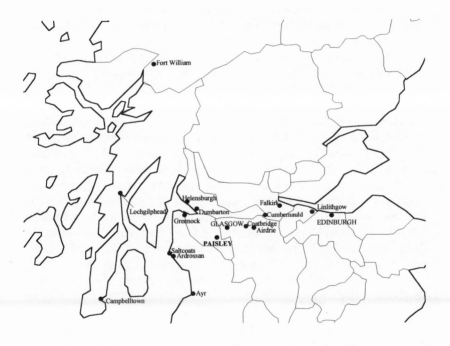

as shawl work or the mills, but in 1851 it was the fifth-most common paid occupation for all women, and the second-most common occupation, after domestic service, for single migrant women.[11]

In the mid-nineteenth century Paisley's economy was based in textiles, but the city also offered young migrant women employment outside the mills. Paisley, like Preston, was a likely destination for migrants because of its location. Very close to Glasgow, it shared many of the same railway lines from the southwest and from the ports on the River Clyde. It was easy, as from London to Preston, to get to Paisley from the west coast and islands without the extra effort of changing trains. Paisley lies close to the Renfrewshire-Lanarkshire border, which made it an easy destination for migrants from the industrialized Glasgow area. Like other industrial Lowland cities, Paisley attracted many types of migrants to its mills and weaving sheds in the nineteenth century.[12]

From 1851 to 1881, approximately 40 percent of Paisley's adult population was born outside Renfrewshire. Between 13 percent and 16 percent were Irish immigrants, whose density in the population peaked, as in Preston and Lowell, after the Potato Famine years, in the 1861 census (Lowell's Irish population continued to grow numerically into the 1880s). There was considerable migration from the neighboring counties of Lanark and Ayr, which together accounted for from 11 to almost 15 percent of the migrants in Paisley. The last substantial group of migrants were Highlanders, primarily from the Western Highland counties of Inverness, Argyll, and Bute.[13] Combined, the Highland counties contributed 5 percent of Paisley's migrants in 1851, and their proportion declined to 3 percent by 1881. The remainder of the city's inhabitants came from all over Scotland, with a few immigrants from England, Europe and North America.[14]

Over the thirty-year period an average of 6.1 percent of independent Scottish women born outside Renfrewshire worked in Paisley's fabric or thread mills (compared to 22 percent of female migrants in Preston), and only 7.6 percent of all women in the city's mills were independent migrants. Although they were more prevalent than in Preston (where just 1.7 percent of female mill workers were independent migrants), migrants in Paisley were still not an important workforce in the city's mills. Most young women who moved to Paisley, unlike those in Lowell, were not recruited by industrialists to fill a labor vacuum in the factories. Nevertheless the large volume of migrants in the city shows that there were employment opportunities for them. Migrants in Scotland, like those in

England and the United States, were most likely to be young, and most likely to be single.[15] In Paisley, as in Lowell and Preston, they were also most likely to be female. From 1851 to 1881 among the current migrant cohort, unmarried independent women ranged from 26.9 to 34 percent, while single independent men averaged 13 percent. Overall, there were usually twice as many independent female migrants in Paisley as male. Figures 4.2 and 4.3 show the estimated proportion among the whole single population and volume of male and female independent migrants to Paisley in each census year.

The two major cultural regions of Scotland—the Highlands and the Lowlands—sent two distinct groups of migrants into Paisley. As in Preston and Lowell, in both groups unmarried young women moved in different patterns than their male counterparts. At mid-century there was good reason to migrate from the Highlands. The potato blight which began in Ireland in 1845 spread to Western Highland and Island potato plots by 1846. The ensuing famine was at its worst in its first two years, but potato crops continued to fail wholly or partially until 1855. The years of the famine saw a substantial rise in temporary migration from the Highlands as life there became less tenable.[16] During the worst years of the crisis, up to 14 percent of the population of some Highland parishes was recorded as "temporarily absent" by census takers.[17] Male Highlanders preferred finding employment with the herring fishers or farmers, both traditional seasonal jobs for Highland men, or on railway construction crews. Very few young Highland men came searching for work in Paisley: only 11 percent of all the male migrants to Paisley 1851 to 1881 were from Highland counties, and they did not cluster in any particular occupation. Highland women, on the other hand, responded to a demand for their labor in Lowland cities, including Paisley.[18] Among the single female migrants, 27 percent overall were Highlanders, and in 1851 and 1861 well over a third of all the independent female migrants were Highland-born.

There were more Lowland than Highland migrant men in Paisley, but they too were heavily outnumbered by women from their home counties. Lanarkshire and Ayrshire, Renfrewshire's neighbors to the south and east and the major Lowland contributors of migrants to Paisley, were very different environments. Lanarkshire was a primarily industrial county, with many opportunities for male laborers. In addition to its famous shipyards and other heavy industries, Glasgow had a thriving textile sector and many smaller

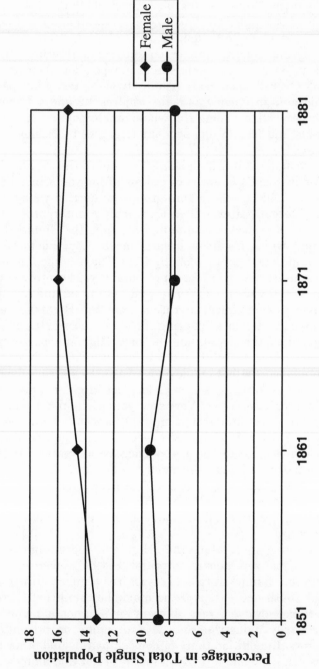

Figure 4.2
Recent independent migrants in the single population.
Paisley, 1851–1881.

Source: Derived from *Census of Great Britain*, 1851 and *Census of Scotland*, 1861–1881, Paisley Parish, Abbey Parish, microfilm, Genealogical Society of the Church of Jesus Christ of Latter Day Saints, Salt Lake City, Utah.

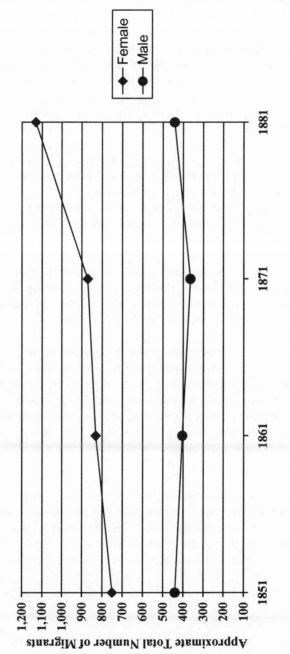

Figure 4.3
Volume of independent migrants to Paisley, 1851–1881.

Source: Derived from *Census of Great Britain*, 1851 and *Census of Scotland*, 1861–1881, Paisley Parish, Abbey Parish, microfilm, Genealogical Society of the Church of Jesus Christ of Latter Day Saints, Salt Lake City, Utah.

industries. Mining districts, especially Airdrie and Coatbridge, also provided work for young men while sending numbers of young women across the county line in search of employment. Ayrshire, in contrast, was predominantly rural, with mining and fishing interests that employed many young men. Ayr's dairy industry provided some employment for women, but there were few other openings for them.[19] Like Westmorland in comparison to Preston, Ayr had few industries to compete with those of the Clyde region. Women who came to Paisley from Ayr were very likely as unfamiliar with the bustle and noise of an industrial city as the Highlanders. Nevertheless the needs of the city and the lack of opportunity at home urged Lowland women toward Paisley, while their brothers were more likely to remain at home or migrate elsewhere.

When Isabella McNeil arrived in Paisley in 1871 she was one of an increasingly rare breed of independent female migrant: the Highland domestic servant. While Lowland female migration increased steadily throughout the period, the number of young women from the Highlands in Paisley decreased dramatically after 1861. Apparently conditions in the Highlands, not in Paisley, caused this shift. Figures 4.4 through 4.7 show in more detail the changing composition of Paisley's recent, independent female migrants from 1851 to 1881.

As these maps show, while the proportion of migrants from Lanarkshire and Ayrshire grew steadily the migration of Highland women slowed dramatically after 1861. In part this was because the population in the Scottish Highlands was falling throughout the nineteenth century. The Famine, added to the collapse of the kelp industry in the 1820s, convinced landlords and charitable groups that there was no way to improve conditions in the Highlands without removing the "redundant population."[20] Between 1847 and 1856 some 16,000 people from the Highlands emigrated to North America and Australia, most of them assisted by their landlords or public institutions. After 1861 conditions in the Highlands did begin to stabalize, as much from a changed economic situation as the calculated depopulation, which may have made Highland women's migration less necessary.[21] In the 1870s and 1880s, Highland women began to migrate seasonally in large numbers to work as gutters in Scotland's herring fisheries.[22] The rise of the new occupation may also explain the decline in Highland women's migration to Paisley, where migrants' primary occupation remained domestic service.

In 1881 there were more independent Scottish-born female migrants in Paisley than for any earlier census, and most of those

Figure 4.4
Origin of single female migrants to Paisley 1851.

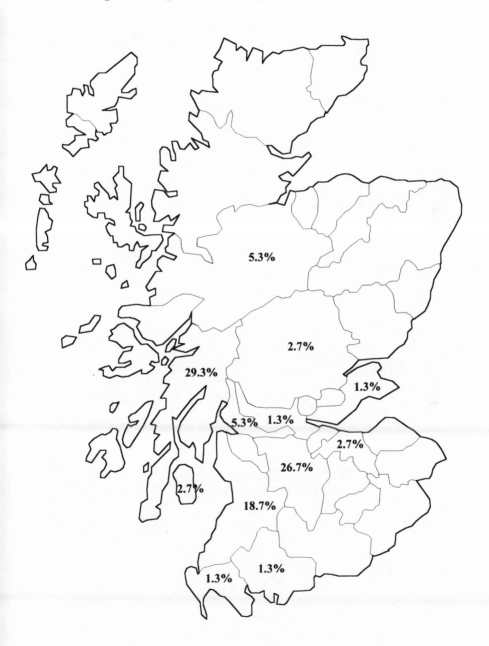

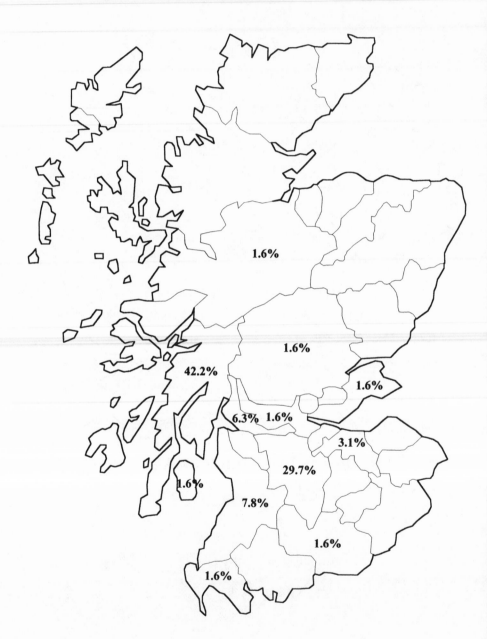

Figure 4.5
Origin of single female migrants to Paisley, 1861.

Figure 4.6
Origin of single female migrants to Paisley, 1871.

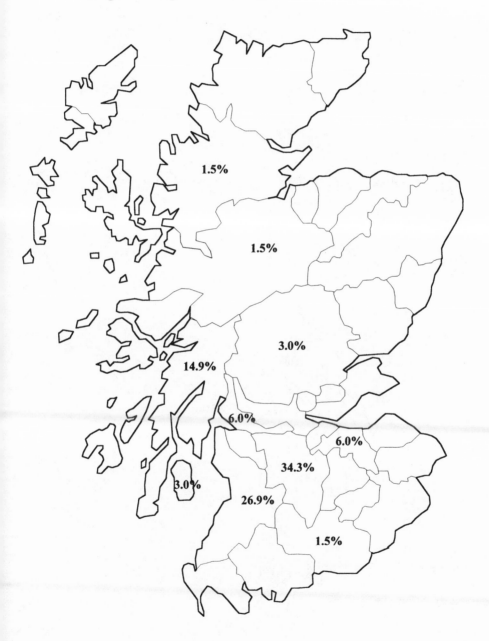

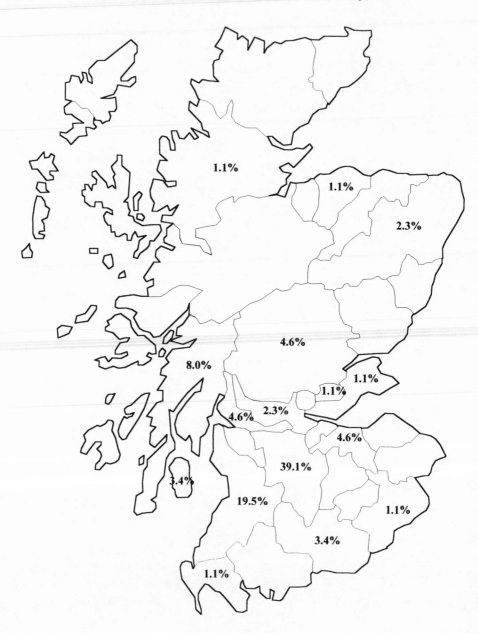

Figure 4.7
Origin of single female migrants to Paisley, 1881.

migrants (87 percent) were Lowland natives. While the Highlanders were trending away from Paisley, ever-increasing numbers
of Lowland women moved to the city, especially in the 1870s. The
agricultural depression that affected women's migration to Preston
in that decade may also have influenced migration to Paisley by
eliminating roles for women in the Lowland rural areas. Contemporaries, however, saw that there was still a demand for female labor
in the fields that the young women were unwilling to fill. A Royal
Commission on Labour concluded in 1893,

> the chief cause of the abstention of women from farm work would
> seem to be the growing dislike to the work itself, coupled with a keen
> desire to enjoy the animation and variety of town life. . . . Young
> women feel ill-disposed to follow in the steps of their predecessors
> and engage in the rather rough . . . requirements of Scottish farms.
> They prefer domestic service and town life to farm labour.[23]

It was probably a combination of changing agricultural requirements, especially the trend away from year-round employment for
women, and the allure of the city that drew Lowland women to
Paisley in increasing numbers.[24] This concurs with Malcolm Gray's
finding that reformed agriculture in Lowland Scotland "squeez[ed]
out those who exceeded the needs of the new farming system" and
the displaced workers flocked to the western cities of Glasgow,
Greenock and Paisley.[25]

Although Highland and Lowland female migration to Paisley
increased and decreased at different times in response to different
conditions in their home counties, the two groups of migrants followed similar behavioral patterns once they were in the city. Figure
4.8 shows that averaged over the entire period the participation of
current Highland and Lowland migrants in various occupational
groups bore more resemblance to one another than to nonmigrants
in the city. As in Preston, domestic service was the most common
occupation for independent migrant women in Paisley. They also
clustered in the city's bleachworks, which like the Lowell mills provided housing for their unmarried female employees. Women born
in Renfrewshire, however, much preferred work in the textile mills
or, as the high percentage in the "other" category shows, occupations connected with the production of Paisley shawls. Figure 4.8 is
an effective illustration of general tendencies, but migrants' employment patterns in Paisley were not actually as uniform as the
figure implies, particularly in the years after the Cotton Famine
sparked by the American Civil War.

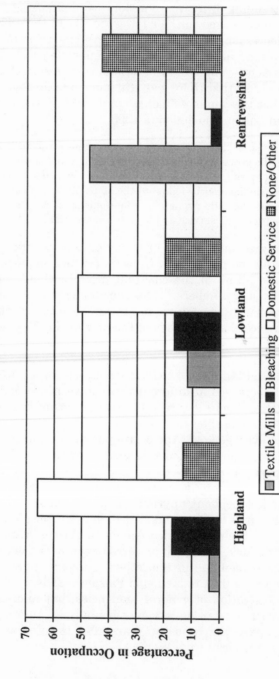

**Figure 4.8
Single women's occupations by place of birth.
Paisley, 1851–1881.**

Percentage in Occupation

70 60 50 40 30 20 10 0

Highland   Lowland   Renfrewshire

⬜ Textile Mills ⬛ Bleaching ⬜ Domestic Service ⬛ None/Other

"Renfrewshire": includes all unmarried Refrew-born women under thirty years old.
"None/other": includes handloom workers and needle trades, both of which were connected to shawl production.

Source: Derived from *Census of Great Britain*, 1851 and *Census of Scotland*, 1861–1881, Paisley Parish, Abbey Parish, microfilm, Genealog-ical Society of the Church of Jesus Christ of Latter Day Saints, Salt Lake City, Utah.

Although Highland migration to Paisley was declining when Isabella McNeil arrived in 1871, she followed a typical pattern; 71 percent of all the recent Highland-born migrants in Paisley chose domestic service that year.[26] McNeil and the other Highland migrants still strongly tended toward domestic service, but in 1871 Lowland migrant participation in the field fell to not quite 40 percent, down from 65 percent ten years earlier. As in Preston, the migrants made their strongest showing in the textile mills in the 1871 census, with almost 25 percent of the Lowland migrants and 14 percent of the Highlanders working in either thread or fabric production. Paisley's thread mills were actively competing for workers in the 1870s, creating positions for migrants that would in most years have been filled by Paisley residents.[27] The bleachfields were also more active, attracting a full 20 percent of the city's Lowland migrants. However, the proportion of Highlanders who went into bleaching fell in spite of the demand for workers there.

In 1871 there were also 25 percent fewer resident domestic servants captured in the sample than in any other census year. Combined with the information on migrants' employment, the statistics suggest that the outcry by the middle class over the shortage of servants in the 1860s was not unfounded, at least in Paisley. As James Colston of Edinburgh remarked in 1864,

> Fifty years ago there were not so many branches of industry accessible to females. *Then* for example, the daughter of a working man in a rural district thought of no other occupation than domestic service, and had no higher ambition than to work her way up until she could become one of the servants in the 'big house.'

But in recent times, "There seems to be a desire abroad among the working classes … to make their daughters something better than domestic servants." Colston also believed that Highland depopulation had had an impact on the availability of servants. As he explained, "emigration [to North America and Australia] has done much to take from us many who would have proved valuable treasure in a household."[28]

In the 1860s, at least, Colston was correct. More independent Lowland migrants were attracted to industrial employment than in other decades, and there were fewer Highlanders in the city overall. There were actually a few more independent female migrants in Paisley in 1871 than in 1861, but employers' demand for domestic servants was apparently not what caused the increase. Migrants' personal preferences combined with increased demand from industrial employers to draw them to work in the mills. Isabella McNeil may have started out in Paisley as a domestic servant, but within two years she shifted to mill work. Her story and the census data illustrate that some of the migrants to Paisley in the 1860s and early 1870s were willing to leave domestic service and bleaching when work was available in the city's mills.

In addition to the fluctuations fostered by the Cotton Famine, Figure 4.8 masks a change in the migrant workforce at the bleachfields near Paisley. In 1851, a full quarter of the recent Highland migrant women in Paisley worked at the city's bleachfields. Seventeen percent of the new Highlanders sampled from the 1861 census were bleachers, but by 1881 none of the most recently arrived Highlanders in the sample went there.[29] Presumably young women had not stopped migrating from the Highlands entirely—economic conditions there did not improve throughout the nineteenth century. Rather, young Highland women had found preferable occupations and destinations. The bleachfields were certainly not turning away from using a migrant workforce. While the number of recent Highland migrants who worked for the bleachers was declining, the number of Lowland migrants in the bleachworks was rising.

The 1851 census showed 15 percent of the recent Lowland migrants employed in the bleachfields. That percentage peaked in 1871 at 20 percent, concurrent with the increased textile production of the period, then fell slightly in the next decade. Numerically, there were approximately seventy recent Lowland migrants in the bleachfields in 1851, and one hundred and seventy in 1881, which left almost exactly the same total number of workers living in the bleachers' boardinghouses.[30] If Highlanders had continued to move to Paisley in large numbers, there is no conspicuous reason why they would not have worked for the bleachers. In spite of its deceptively pastoral name work in the bleachfields was indoors, primarily moving fabric through a series of chemical baths. The workday was an industrial schedule, modified by slack times or pushes in response to orders. The change in the Highland women's migration pattern was apparently *not* related to changes in bleaching in the same way Yankee women responded to altered conditions in Lowell's mills; if so I would expect to see a similar reduction in the number of Lowland migrants in Paisley bleachfields. Nor was the dramatic increase in the number of Lowlanders in Paisley connected to increased demand from either bleachers or the employers of servants, since both occupations continued to employ about the same total number of women.

Single women's independent migration to Paisley was arguably more heavily influenced by developments in their home counties than by the needs of employers in Paisley. The decline in the number of Highlanders in Paisley was in part due to the massive emigrations of the 1840s and 1850s—there were fewer Highlanders in Scotland as a whole. There was also less distress among the Highlanders who remained, hence less reason for young women to migrate. In addition, the growth of an alternative to domestic service, seasonal herring gutting, which allowed young women to support a family fishing business, may have pulled Highland migrants away from Paisley. Lowlanders, on the other hand, came to Paisley in ever-increasing numbers, though there was little growth in the occupations in which they were primarily employed. Agricultural depression and change, perhaps combined with a growing distaste for farmwork in general, helped to push young women from Lowland rural areas toward the cities. Paisley was for them, as Preston was for Westmorland-born migrants, a city relatively nearby that was conveniently located on a major rail line.

Although they did not migrate in direct response to employment opportunities, occupation was important to the migrants in Paisley. They restricted themselves to only a few types of work and were noticeably underrepresented in the most common female jobs in the city, in textile mills and shawl production. The two occupations that employed the largest number of migrants in the third quarter of the nineteenth century (72.3 percent in the two combined, over the entire period) did so because they had particular attractions for migrants. It was easy for strangers to find work in either domestic service or muslin bleaching, and both jobs provided adequate respectable housing.

Migrants and Domestic Service in Paisley

Domestic service was a natural choice for migrants, as it was across Britain, providing housing, family-like supervision, and undeniably gender-appropriate labor. Middle-class families in Scotland and England preferred country-born women as their servants, and James Colston's comments showed that some were quite offended when rural women preferred other forms of employment. In 1851 two-thirds of all the domestic servants in Paisley were migrants from outside Renfrewshire. As in Preston most of these migrants were maids of all work, responsible for everything from scrubbing the front stoop in the morning to banking the fires at night. Employers with varying expectations subjected their servants to long hours and difficult work, making the job easier or harder with the manner of their day-to-day contact.

A few points do distinguish service in western Scotland from similar jobs elsewhere in Britain. Into the 1870s Paisley sponsored semiannual hiring fairs where aspiring servants and potential employers could meet. In conjunction with this tradition a six-month term of service continued to be the rule for Paisley area servants long after other parts of Britain had shifted to a month-to-month system.[31] The fair and six-month term were particularly useful to migrants. The hiring fairs, held each Whitsunday (around May 15) and Martinmas (November 11), allowed strangers in the town to find an employer without having friendly contacts or being able to read newspaper advertisements.

The six-month term, a contract which neither party could break without good cause, gave the migrant servant a degree of security that could not be found with a month-to-month arrangement. Indeed, when it was suggested in 1864 that the six-month term be abolished opponents of the bill argued,

[we] particularly doubt the propriety of that portion of the bill which seems to make it possible at common law, and without sufficient cause, to dismiss female servants at a moment's notice, at any time, as having a tendency to throw young women defenseless upon the world, and thus, in [our] opinion, greatly to swell the amount of female immorality.[32]

With the legal term in place, however, "the natural dependence of the servant on the one hand, and the influence of the master on the other are strengthened."[33] The old system guaranteed servants some stability and kept unmarried women, a potentially volatile segment of the community, controlled.

Wages were not paid until the end of the term, which made it possible (and legal) for the employer to withhold wages in the event of unsatisfactory service.[34] Rather than receiving payments of ten or fifteen shillings monthly, the servant was given a lump-sum of several pounds to take or send home, bank, or spend. There is no data in Paisley comparable to Preston's classified advertisements regarding servants wages for the second half of the century, but an

1860 report on Paisley's Martinmas feeing fair recorded the "better class" of maid servants commanding £5 to £6 per half year, roughly equal to the standard in Preston. By the Whitsun fair of 1872, "first-class" women commanded from £7 10 s. to £9 10 s., a price "ruled high" by hopeful employers, and in the upper range of advertised wages in Preston in 1875.[35] The rise in wages helps to confirm the scarcity of servants recorded in the 1871 census.

Domestic service also provided migrants with food and a place to live, a benefit Colston generously estimated to be worth an additional £20 per year.[36] Though the room might be cramped, cold, or dingy, it was a guaranteed shelter in a strange, potentially dangerous city.[37] With that shelter came constant, parentlike supervision from the employer, which was undoubtedly welcomed by the migrants' parents. In one of the rare surviving comments by a Highlander about Highland women's migration to Paisley, Reverend C. F. Campbell, minister in Tarbut, Argyllshire, commented that he advised migrants from his parish to go to service, "where they would be under the superintendence of masters and mistresses." He felt that their "morals [were] much more exposed in the bleachfield than at service, from their being placed beyond domestic control before their principles [were] duly formed."[38]

Once in service, rural women were expected to abide by middle-class standards. Most important, they were not to engage or admit to previously engaging in sexual conduct. An 1841 pamphlet titled *The Law of Master and Servant Familiarly Explained* clarified a major exception to the six-month term:

> Immoral conduct in a female servant previous to being hired, and concealed at the time of hiring, when the fact was not known to the master; for example, having illegitimate children, is . . . ground for dismissal . . . ; for no man can be bound to keep a strumpet in his family.[39]

Theoretically, the threat of discharge without a reference would keep all but incorrigible girls from transgressing.

The minister's comments and the explicit threat of punishment for misconduct emphasized that young women migrating by themselves in Scotland, like those who migrated to Lowell and presumably to Preston, were considered old enough to be earning a wage, but not quite fit to fend entirely for themselves. The migrants in all three cities were at an ambiguous stage, no longer dependent daughters, but also not adult women capable of managing their own households. They were morally only partially formed, and hence vulnerable to corruption. Domestic service performed the dual role of allowing a young woman distance from her family while providing her with the protective influence of a family setting. As in Preston, middle-class employers expected and often preferred their servants to be migrants, trusting country-bred women more than urban-born.[40] For these reasons migrants in general, not only Highlanders, were overrepresented in domestic service.

Migrants and Bleaching in Paisley

Domestic service was the traditional and most frequently chosen occupation for independent female migrants to Paisley, but not all migrants became servants. A few, who perhaps had exceptional educational, economic, or familial resources, found employment in the city's mills or shawl warehouses, as dressmakers or in later decades as shop assistants or clerks.[41] Paisley's bleachworks, however, were the second-most popular occupation for independent female migrants to the city. From some regions of the Highlands, including Rev. Campbell's parish of Tarbut, Argyllshire, more migrants went to the bleachworks than went to service. The migrants explained to Campbell, "they get rather higher wages than at service, and are also more at liberty."[42] The presence of the bleachworks makes Paisley a prime example of migrants exercising their own freedom of choice within "respectable" restrictions.

There were four bleachworks included in the Paisley sample, all southwest of the burgh proper, clustered around Staneley reservoir. One of the works, Nethercraigs, was tied to the Coats thread factory, and bleached thread exclusively.[43] The other three, Lounsdale, Blackland Mill, and Foxbar, were bleachers of cotton muslin who subcontracted work from various manufacturers in the city. In the 1851 census, almost 43 percent of the single women who worked in the bleachworks were Irish, and about 20 percent were born in Renfrewshire. The remaining 37 percent were Scottish-born migrants, split nearly equally between Highlanders and Lowlanders. Highlanders had been more prevalent in earlier decades, when they were described as "monopolizing" the Paisley bleaching trade.[44] The Highland migrants in the bleachworks stood out as an anomalous group to observers who were not familiar with Paisley. In the 1840s

a Parliamentary investigator into children's employment in the
west of Scotland, Thomas Tancred, discovered the bleachfield workers and included them in his report, even though most of them were
too old to be technically considered "children":

> The circumstance of this employment being followed by young fe-
> males thus separated from their country and parents, placed in a
> strange land, the language of which many of them scarcely under-
> stand, and living within the premises of their employers, natu-
> rally attracted my attention, and inspired interest in their lot, and
> a desire to investigate their condition even more narrowly than
> had they been living like ordinary operatives under the care of
> their parents, and surrounded by their kinsfolk and countrymen.[45]

While it is extraordinarily useful, Tancred's report must be
used with caution, as he clearly approached his work with a strong
middle-class bias, expressing his belief that young women required
protection. Investigating children's employment, he was prone to
overemphasize the migrants' youth and need for supervision. Time
is also a consideration, as the demographics of the bleachfield employees had changed substantially by 1851, particularly with the
addition of the Irish contingent. Nevertheless, Tancred's report and
the evidence he collected is invaluable in describing life and work
in the Paisley bleachfields, and revealing why the occupation appealed to independent female migrants.

Work at the bleachworks was relatively easy, but in hours,
repetitive nature of the work, and work with a group of peers it bore
more resemblance to industrial factory labor than to domestic service. This casts doubt on suggestions that the Highland migrants
avoided the mills from a cultural aversion to factory labor.[46] The
women's work consisted primarily of transferring fabric from one
stage of the bleaching process to another (like a series of giant wash-
ing machines) and of tending the bleached cloth while it dried in
room-sized stoves. Tancred recorded that the occupation appeared
"light and graceful" at first glance, but that the young women were
exhausted by long hours of standing, "never sitting down, and this in
a temperature of from 80 to 100 and 110 degrees."[47] The great temperature was of continuing concern to those who were interested in
controlling women's employment in the bleachworks.[48] The girls
wore lightweight clothing while working in the stoves; wet from handling the damp fabric or simply overwarm, they were subject to
abrupt chills when moving between buildings or dipping their feet in
cool water. Local physicians and the bleach workers themselves

noted a tendency in newcomers to headache, sore, swollen, even ulcerated feet and legs and a danger of feverish "inflammation."[49]

For this work young women over age fifteen were paid from 4 s. to 6 s. 6 d. or even 7 s. per week, paid monthly or every six weeks. Assuming year-round employment, 6 s 6 d. per week totaled nearly £17 a year (about £5 more in cash each year than domestic servants were paid though only about half of what Lowell mill girls would make two decades later—but bleachers paid only a few pence for rent).[50] The long interval between pay packets was intended to repress intemperance among the bleachers, but surgeons to the works nevertheless reported an increased number of calls to treat the effects of overindulgence after each payday. Some of the bleachworks had company stores at which the workers could buy food (but not spirits or clothes) at slightly inflated prices; other works gave "lines" to allow their workers to buy on credit at Paisley shops.[51]

What intrigued Tancred most about the bleachfields, however, was the womanhouses (the local term for the bleachworks' female-only boardinghouses) in which the migrants clustered. Bleaching was a subcontracting operation, dependent on the needs of textile manufacturers and merchants. During the busy seasons of the year merchants were anxious to have their fabric bleached in time to meet shipping schedules. Since the bleachers could not readily control when they received orders, they were subject to "pushes" when workers were needed up to eighteen or more hours a day. Because chemical bleaching required tremendous amounts of clean, pure water, bleachers located themselves well outside the city, clustering around reservoirs that allowed impurities to settle out of the water. Although the four bleachworks included in this sample were the closest to Paisley, about a mile away from the city, others in the area ranged up to six or seven miles away from a town center.[52] The upshot of this combination of necessities was a need for the bleachers to have at least some of their workers living on-site, where they would be available for long hours when required.

Some of the houses at the bleachworks were single- or multi-family houses, as might be found near any British factory. The bleachers also built boardinghouses like the Lowell corporations' that were intended to house single female employees. It was these that caught Thomas Tancred's attention. He described the Lounsdale womanhouse as typical:

This is a building of two or three stories, the lower having an earthen or bricked floor, fireplace, and some tables, the boxes in

which provisions are kept generally serving for seats, and [it] is
sometimes very dimly lighted. Above stairs are the dormitories, in
some of which I have found from 30 to 40 beds ranged in four
rows, having two and often three women in each. If there is room,
a large chest stands at the foot of each bed, in which are stowed
the articles of dress, and a few books belonging to the inmates.[53]

In spite of this rather dismal description, life in the womanhouse did have benefits for the occupants. In addition to living close
to work, rent in the womanhouses was minimal or nonexistent, and
the women were relieved of major housekeeping chores including
cooking for themselves. All of the bleachworks owners hired married or widowed women to keep the common areas clean and to boil
water for the girls' tea and oatmeal.[54] Although they may have
acted as advisers or comforters to younger women, these house-
keepers apparently did not have the formal supervisory role as-
signed to matrons in Lowell boardinghouses. The womanhouses
also provided a community of fellow migrants, which eased the
transition from rural homes to urban labor. Between 1851 and
1881, 44 percent of Paisley's single female bleachers—including
two-thirds of those who were born in Scotland—lived in the womanhouses.[55] On balance, 63 percent of the womanhouse residents
were migrants from Highland or Lowland Scottish counties and another 25 percent were Irish-born.[56]

Prior to the 1840s, the muslin bleachers in Paisley exhibited a
definite preference for migrants from particular regions of the Highlands. Matthew Arthur, manager of Foxbar, explained to Tancred,

> The women come wholly from the Highlands, with the single ex-
> ception of one Irish girl. The employers find the Highland girls
> stouter for the work and healthy, and also they have few acquain-
> tances about the town. It is the general rule in the work to take
> only such girls as are known or recommended by some of the rest.[57]

The other bleachers were apparently not so strict in their hiring,
but their womanhouses were nevertheless dominated by Highland
migrants until the Highland migration patterns shifted away from
Paisley. As Figure 4.9 illustrates, when the Highland migration to
Paisley slowed migrants from the Lowlands replaced the Highlanders in the womanhouses.

The few Highlanders who remained in Paisley's womanhouses
after the 1861 census were not recent migrants. Eighty-seven percent of them were older than forty in 1881 and all were unmarried;

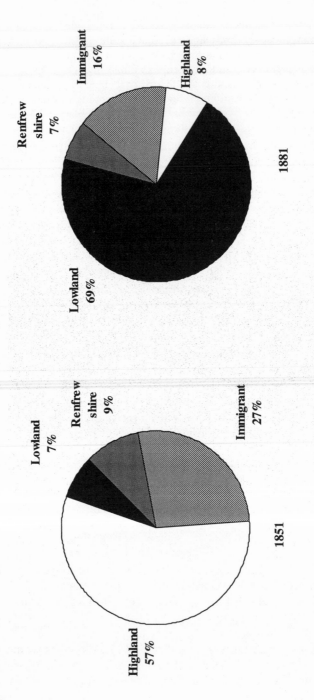

Figure 4.9
Birthplaces of womanhouse residents.
Paisley, 1851 and 1881.

1851

Highland
57%

Immigrant
27%

Renfrew
shire
9%

Lowland
7%

Total Womanhouse Population: 234

1881

Lowland
69%

Immigrant
16%

Highland
8%

Renfrew
shire
7%

Total Womanhouse Population: 210

Source: Derived from *Census of Great Britain*, 1851 and 1881, Paisley Parish, Abbey Parish, microfilm, Genealogical Society of the Church of Jesus Christ of Latter Day Saints, Salt Lake City, Utah.

assuming sixteen years as an average age for first migration, these Highlanders had first come to Paisley in the 1850s.[58] They were the remnants of a migration stream that had not extended much beyond the 1861 census. The Lowland migrants in the womanhouses, on the other hand, were current migrants, of whom almost 90 percent were aged between fifteen and thirty years. When the Highland migration stream turned away from Paisley's bleachfields, Scottish Lowland migrants, not Renfrewshire natives or immigrants, filled the gap. Like domestic service, the bleachfields attracted all migrants, not Highlanders in particular.

From 1851 to 1881, Scottish migrants, like those in Lowell and Preston, demonstrated remarkable uniformity of occupational behavior. With the exception of a slight move toward mill work around the early 1870s (which had disappeared by 1881), the migrants remained rooted in domestic service and secondarily bleaching for the entire period. Lowland migrants followed a different migration pattern than the Highlanders, coming to Paisley in ever-greater numbers as the Highland numbers decreased, but overall there were more similarities between the two groups than differences. The key to this uniformity was only coincidentally connected to the conditions of the occupations themselves, however. Both domestic service and the Paisley bleachworks provided migrant workers with secure accommodations. In Paisley—indeed, in all three cities—the common factor in what occupation the largest number of migrants would prefer was the availability of housing connected with the job.

Accommodating Independent Migrants

It is obvious that independent migrants, defined by their separation from their families of birth, would need to find lodgings in the city. Housing options in Paisley, as in Lowell and Preston, were various. In addition to living with or visiting a family member, migrants could board with a family or in a small or large boardinghouse.[59] There were also small inns and, less desirably, poorhouses, hospitals, and prisons that housed some migrants in every census year. The bleachers' womanhouses were the only single-sex boarding houses in Paisley, and the only type of boardinghouse that Scottish migrants chose in considerable numbers.

All young Scottish women, migrants and nonmigrants alike, avoided living in boardinghouses other than those owned by the bleachworks (Figure 4.10). Young women more commonly boarded with families that kept only one to three boarders: about one-third of independent nonmigrant Scots and close to half of the single female Irish immigrants in Paisley boarded with unrelated families. In contrast, only 14 percent of the migrants boarded with such families.[60] These boarders filled the whole range of female occupations in the city, most clustered in the textile mills and needle trades. Relatively few independent nonmigrants and immigrants, under 20 percent, lived with their employers either as domestic servants or at the bleachfields.[61] Even for those who did not live with their parents or relatives, finding a job and housing at the same location was apparently not terribly important to women born in or near the city or to immigrants. As Figure 4.10 illustrates, however, it was important to migrants.

Most migrants from outside Renfrewshire did not join family members in the city: only 12 percent over the whole period lived with relatives or headed their own households. When single migrant women went into hired lodgings other than the womanhouses they usually did so with families that took only one or at the most two other lodgers, usually also female. Even under these conditions lodgers were a small minority of the migrant population. Sixty-eight percent of the migrants, whether they went into domestic service or the bleachfield womanhouses, whether they were from Lowland counties or Highland, chose occupations that meant they would not have to search for separate accommodations.

Respectability, supervision, and perceived safety were key for the vulnerable migrant population. As in Preston, those migrants who were able to join relatives in Paisley were the best able to recreate their premigration familial role. For those who did not have relatives in the city, domestic service, which so closely resembled a daughter's role in the family, was an obvious and preferred choice. However, while domestic service did mimic family life in terms of environment and supervision, it assured a fundamentally economic, not familial, relationship. Domestic servants were economically independent while sisters, nieces, and heads of households were more likely to contribute their earnings to a family economy. By migrating and controlling their own wages, young women were starting the transition away from their parents' families. They made that transition, though, within a narrow framework of respectable options. Those respectable options, in turn,

Figure 4.10
Independent single women's relationship to head of household. Paisley, 1851–1881.

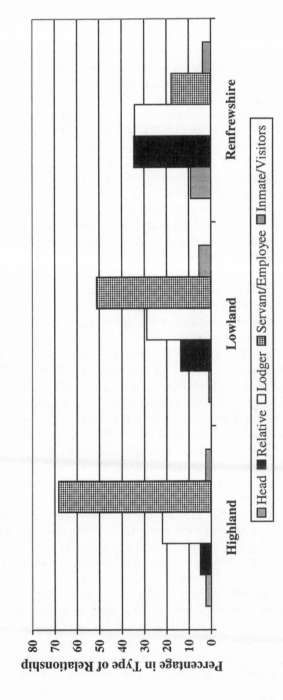

"Renfrewshire": includes single women less than thirty years old not living with their parents.
Head: includes head of household and persons living alone.
Relative: includes any specified relationship other than child.
Lodger: includes boarders and lodgers unrelated to head.
Servant/Employee: includes domestic servants, apprentices, assistants, and other employees.
Inmate/Visitors: includes visitors, boarding school students, prisoners and patients in prisons, hospitals, and poorhouses.

Source: Derived from *Census of Great Britain*, 1851 and *Census of Scotland*, 1861–1881, Paisley Parish, Abbey Parish, microfilm, Genealogical Society of the Church of Jesus Christ of Latter Day Saints, Salt Lake City, Utah.

were defined by employer demand: if an employer needed workers located at a particular place (such as in a home or at a bleachfield, hospital or school) and so provided accommodations, he or she was far more likely to find migrants interested in the position.

Precisely because most independent female migrants to Paisley chose within that framework of respectable options, they were nearly as invisible as migrants in Preston. Nearly all of the surviving sources that refer to the Highland migrants in Paisley as a distinct group were created by men who were themselves outsiders in Paisley. Thomas Tancred in particular was surprised by the cluster of migrants he found "separated from their country and parents."[62] Paisley residents, on the other hand, were remarkably silent on the subject of independent female migrants to their city. Domestic servants, as the case of Preston also illustrated, were expected to be migrants; incorporated into a family setting, they aroused no concern. By the 1840s the migrants in the bleachfields were also of little concern to the people of Paisley. When asked, observers admitted some suspicion of the bleachworkers' moral state and fears that young women would be corrupted by "bad characters" in the womanhouses.[63] Yet from reading the city's newspapers one would be hard pressed to discover that there were independent migrant women in Paisley at all. Only in 1853, when the bleachworkers were agitating for a shorter workday, did the *Glasgow Saturday Post* refer to the migrants in the bleachfields in passing: "We did not hear of many deaths among them [due to long hours]; but this arose from the fact that no sooner were they taken ill, than they . . . return to their houses in Ireland or in the Highlands."[64] Their migration was stated as a simple fact; there was no suggestion that the bleachfield workers were young women, separated from their families and potentially vulnerable to exploitation and corruption. The "strangers" so surprised Tancred that he felt justified in writing a report "disproportionate to the number employed," but they were no more a source of anxiety for Paisley residents than were their domestic servants.[65] The strangers were safely contained.

As in Preston and Lowell, the statistical record provides important information about migrants in Paisley. The census sample shows a striking conformity in the migrants' behavior, notable even within the generally restricted options available to unmarried Victorian women. However, while statistics answer generalities about single women's migration they do not reveal individual experiences. Isabella McNeil, for example, began her migration experience in conformity with the statistical pattern; even her transition to mill work in the early 1870s is accommodated in the census data. But the census does not explain why Isabella left Argyllshire in the first place or why she chose to stop in Paisley rather than continue on to Glasgow, Stirling, or Edinburgh. Neither does it hint why she chose to leave a presumably safe home as a domestic servant in favor of cohabiting with James Waddell. Migrants to Paisley did not leave any letters comparable to the Lowell migrants. Nevertheless, they did leave more traces in the historical record than the Preston migrants, and from those records some of the same questions that were introduced by the Lowell migrants can be addressed. The migrants' actions, revealed through contemporary reports and court and civil records, suggest the young women's motivations for migration. They hint at migrants' decisions of where and when they would move and how they found jobs when they got there. Although in the late 1830s observers of Highland migrants to Glasgow reported that the migrants' income helped their families at home, the evidence from Paisley after midcentury indicates that migration was primarily focused on the young women's needs as individuals, rather than their families'.[66]

The Migrants' Economy

Asserting independence could begin with the choice of occupation. Domestic service required obedience and extremely long hours, factors that prompted complaints from servants all over Britain and the United States.[67] In Paisley, where migrants had an alternative to domestic service, some women took that alternative even in the face of disapproval from their home community, as evidenced by their comments to Reverend Campbell about higher wages and more liberty.[68] On the other hand, desires for more free time, while significant, do not necessarily translate to a desire for independence from family. More indicative of the migrants' goals in migration was their use of the wages they earned.

In the 1840s Thomas Tancred was assured by Foxbar's manager, "More than half of the girls here send home from 15 s. to £1 a year to their parents." This was evidence of the migrants' participation in the Highland economy, in the traditional function of temporary migrants.[69] But that sum must be considered in comparison to what the migrants were earning in the bleachfields. Tancred was told the women earned from 4 s. to 6 s. 6 d. per week (most in the higher range), paid at four- or six-week intervals. The frugal-living Highlanders reportedly owed 10–12 s. at the Foxbar store at every pay period, giving them a remaining total, at a 6 s./week wage, of £1 4 s. to £1 6 s. every six weeks. Another witness estimated a monthly net income of only 8 s. Still other estimates set each bleachworker's net income per pay period from 7 s. to more than a full pound. At least one bleachworks, Blackland Mill, required all workers to contribute 1 s. 6 d. per six weeks to a night school, though they were not required to attend and few did. At Foxbar, each worker was expected to pay 1 s. per year toward a doctor's fee. Other young women probably paid into friendly societies, or had other small expenses in addition to their shop purchases. Though Tancred thought living in the womanhouses was free, later witnesses asserted the residents paid a nominal rent of a few pence a week.[70]

Considering all of this information, an estimate of about 18 s. per six weeks free and clear seems conservative for a bleacher earning 6 s. per week. That estimate, multiplied over an entire year and allowing for two full months off work, gives the bleachers in the womanhouses almost £7 cash each year over and above their room and board. Yet by the estimate of a decidedly positive witness, the Foxbar manager, only a small fraction of that amount found its way back to the Highlands (Figure 4.11).[71]

When Tancred asked what the bleachworkers did with their wages, two migrants from Argyll, Margaret M'Intyre (age 23) and Grace Campbell (18), informed him that "some save a little money to send home to their people, but 'the maist part' spend it all in clothes." The theme of clothes reappeared in other testimony. Fifteen-year-old Margaret M'Kellar, a very recent arrival from Tarbut, Argyllshire, specifically mentioned that the bleachers got "their clothes made in the town," a significant change from sewing clothes oneself. At a bleacher's in Barrhead, west and south of Paisley, the owner noted to the migrants' credit that "the Highland ones will not run into debt though very fond of dress." The surgeon in charge of Foxbar (who received all those one-shilling payments) added that the migrants did not stay in the Lowlands long, "their great object being to amass some clothing and articles for a house." Tancred's conclusion, reported to Parliament, was not that the migrants supported destitute families in the Highlands, but that "the purchase of articles of dress is the great ambition of the Highland females, and to this all the savings they can economise from their scanty earnings are usually applied."[72]

Figure 4.11
Bleachers' yearly expenses (estimated), c. 1843.

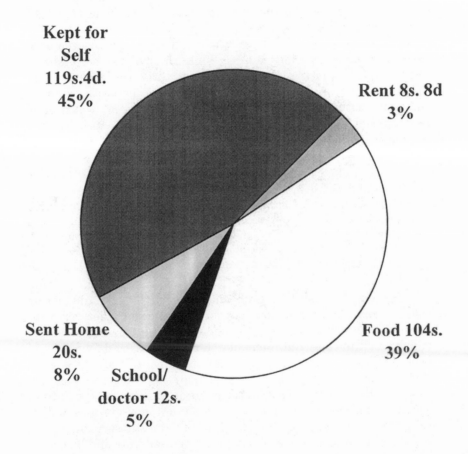

Kept for
Self
119s.4d.
45%

Rent 8s. 8d
3%

Sent Home
20s.
8%

School/
doctor 12s.
5%

Food 104s.
39%

Source: Derived from *P.P.* Appendix to Employment of Children, *passim*; *P.P.* Bleach and Dye, 169.

Nor were the bleachers in Paisley alone in their fascination with dress and household goods. Nineteenth-century domestic servants were notorious among the middle class for their showy clothes when out of uniform.[73] The Lowell mill girls also enjoyed spending money on fashionable clothes that were not available in their home villages.[74] Hard data regarding the spending habits of migrant servants like those in Paisley, however, is hard to come by. What is available suggests that they, like the other migrants, were "fond of dress." For example, in December 1853 a servant named Jane Dunbar, from Forfarshire in eastern Scotland, was admitted to the Glasgow lock hospital for an unspecified illness. While Dunbar was hospitalized, another young woman, Jane Lindsay, reportedly used a forged note to convince the mistress of the house to entrust her with Dunbar's chest and basket. Lindsay absconded with the goods, which Jane Dunbar later itemized for the Paisley Sheriff's Court. In addition to the chest and basket themselves, Dunbar owned

> seven gowns, eight pairs of stockings, two plaids [large tartan shawls], a shawl, five petticoats, twelve cotton caps, two lace caps, thirteen shifts, two parasols, four pairs of boots, two pairs of slippers, five handkerchiefs, a cravat, a net, three towels, a bonnet, a pair of stays, a boa, an apron, four chemisettes, a purse, a bank or banker's note for one Pound sterling, a comb, and a box, some ribbons, night caps, and other small articles.[75]

Dunbar's extensive wardrobe may be partially accounted for by clothes required for her position, for example, an older gown for morning cleaning and a newer dress for serving tea, and an ample supply of clean caps. But items like thirteen shifts and four pairs of boots, not to mention eight pairs of stockings (all of which were items unlikely to go quickly out of fashion) suggest she was using a good portion of her wages to stock up on clothes for the future. Though this evidence is from only one servant, not a representative sample, it does support the stereotype of domestic servants devoting the bulk of their wages to clothes. Some servants and bleachers also ran into debt purchasing clothes. In December 1852 Alexander Wilson, a Paisley-area draper, sued five female bleachers for debts ranging from £0 10 s. 7½ d. to £5 2 s. 5 d; two and a half years later another draper, Walter Menzie, went to court to collect debts of under a pound each from several bleachers and a domestic servant.[76] These debts are clear evidence of anticipated surplus income that for whatever reason did not materialize. That the debts were contracted at all shows that the chance to earn money for their personal use was a major reason for single women's migration in Paisley, whichever occupation they chose.

The evidence provided to Tancred by the Foxbar surgeon showed the logic behind the women's purchases. The women usually only stayed at the bleachworks a few years, he said, "Their great object being to amass some clothing and *articles for a house*."[77] In realizing the migrants were not wholly fixated on clothes, he revealed the women were planning ahead, to the assembly of their own independent households. Though some women did stockpile money in a savings bank or in their chests, perhaps to be used as a traditional dowry, more migrant women in Paisley preferred the objects their wages could buy over the cash itself.[78]

If many migrants spent the bulk of their wages on clothes, the decision was not a frivolous one. Clothing and goods represented a more secure form of wealth than cash. In a city rife with pawnbrokers, clothes could be exchanged for money in times of need, and redeemed after payday.[79] When Jean Watson, an out-of-work farm servant from Largs, Ayrshire, applied for Poor Relief in July 1854, the examiner recorded under "means and resources of applicant" the fact that she had "been living on her clothes since coming to Paisley." The portable wealth of her wardrobe had supported Watson for nearly three months.[80] Thirty years later, when a chest was stolen from the womanhouse at Blackland Mill, the clothes among its contents were scanty, comprising only one short gown and a shawl in addition to various accessories such as collars and cuffs. Tellingly, the chest also contained eight pawn tickets, which probably represented the bulk of the owner's possessions at the time.[81]

Incidentally, clothes-as-wealth also provided the owner with a degree of security from theft. While they were in the owner's possession gowns or plaids were more specifically identifiable than a banker's note. Jane Lindsay pawned Jane Dunbar's belongings after her theft, and the pawn tickets and the pawnbrokers themselves were presented as evidence and witnesses in the trial. Those tickets and testimony, combined with Dunbar's identification of her own belongings, provided a more conclusive chain of evidence than could a relatively nondescript pile of banker's notes or coins. Cash could only be spent once and was easy to steal, but clothes and household goods were useful in and of themselves, identifiable, and readily exchangeable for other forms of wealth when necessary. Migrants who were primarily interested in supporting themselves, not their families, yet who were not solvent enough for the luxury of a bank account, were making a logical choice in spending their wages on "silk and other expensive dresses."[82]

Fine clothes ultimately, however, served a primarily social function. Like the Lowell mill girls who promptly shed their "plain, country-made clothes" for "tasteful city dresses," the young Scottish women must have been eager for their first visit to Paisley's dressmakers.[83] With them a migrant could illustrate her own taste and status to her peers and—it is important to note—to her male friends, perhaps improving her chances of finding a husband. Indeed, nice clothes were important enough that migrants were willing to go into debt, as discussed earlier, in order to have them. A silk dress, even if it was locked away in a trunk or held by a pawn broker, may have been as strong a statement of autonomy as the act of migration itself.

To Prosecute Her Claim

Tancred's witnesses generally expected the Highland migrants in Paisley to be sojourners in the Lowlands, planning an ultimate return to their parents' communities. That implied the migrants were more closely connected to their places of birth than to their Lowland destinations, emphasizing the integration of the migrants into the Highland economy. As the nineteenth century progressed, however, what had begun as seasonal migration evolved to temporary migration of several years or longer between visits home.[84] Exploring to what extent the families left at home expected the migrants to return suggests how thoroughly the Highland migrants actually remained integrated with their home communities.[85] One indication is the number of individuals reported to census takers in the Highlands as "temporarily absent," figures T. M. Devine used as estimates for the growth of temporary migration from the Highlands during the Potato Famine and its aftermath. In Kilmichael-Glassary, the Argyll parish that contained Lochgilphead, a major source of Foxbar bleachworkers, the census takers recorded forty-three individuals temporarily absent in 1851.[86] In Paisley alone (not accounting for any other potential destinations) there were sixty-three women from Kilmichael-Glassary under thirty years old in the bleachers' womanhouses and eight more who were older than the current migrant cohort. Even if all of those recorded as temporarily absent from Lochgilphead were women, there were still twenty or more women unaccounted for in the census.

There are several possible explanations for this disparity. Conceivably, only men away from home were counted by the census takers, or the enumerators were lax in obtaining answers to the question from every household. It is also possible that many of the women at the Paisley bleachworks were not considered temporary migrants by their home community at all, but permanent ones. More than a statement on the women's likelihood of returning to the Highlands, though, I suspect it was a comment on economic relationships. The assumption of the census takers and other observers during and after the famine was that workers in the South would transmit a substantial portion of their wages home.[87] In a Famine-era (1847) census of the Island of Mull, enumerators were specifically instructed to discover (in addition to each family's available food supply) how many members of the family were "south at work."[88] The implication was that the "temporarily absent" members of the household could be counted as potential income. It seems apparent that when it came to the distribution of work or relief, it was in the interests of the Highlanders not to claim as temporary migrants any workers in the South who were not actually remitting regular amounts home (and perhaps some of those that were). If this were the case, the bleachers and servants in Paisley who were saving and investing for their own futures would not be included in the home community's definition of temporary migrants. Although they were not necessarily permanent residents of the Lowlands, the independent Highland migrants were also not necessarily vital support for their families.

Most of the young female migrants, however successfully they were able to support themselves, were in transition between their birth families and anticipated marriage. The second major goal of migration that is evident in the Paisley migrants' actions was the search for a partner. Isabella McNeil lived with the father of her child and probably hoped to marry him right up to the moment when he announced he would wed someone else. Other women, like Agnes Cameron of Kilmonivaig, Inverness-shire, came to Paisley looking for a specific man.

Cameron was twenty-seven years old in July 1851, when she came to Paisley for the first time. She found work at Lounsdale bleachfield and probably lived in the womanhouse there. Within a few months she was on intimate terms with Dan Murphy, who worked at nearby Foxbar. In October 1851 Cameron returned to her home parish, where on 5 June 1852, she was delivered of a baby girl she named Isabella Murphy. Just a month after Isabella was born

Cameron returned to Paisley "to prosecute her claim against the father."[89] The Investigator of the Poor heard a similar tale from Margaret Docherty in November of 1868 when the migrant applied for help with a sick infant. A Dundee native raised in Perth, the young woman had recently come to Paisley "looking for John Cunningham a sailor who she says is the father of her child."[90] Men directly influenced these women's migration plans, and coming to Paisley was a literal attempt to complete their families.

Most of Paisley's migrant women were not migrating because of a specific man. They were looking for men in general, perhaps seeking broader options than they could find at home. A sexual relationship was a normal part of nineteenth-century European and British rural courtship and it often led to marriage or at the very least a steady allowance from the father. A prenuptial pregnancy was possibly even welcomed as incentive and a guarantee to marriage for the young woman, not a shameful liability.[91] Yet expectations of marriage were all too often not met, as a domestic servant from Stirling, Elisabeth Rough, discovered in 1851. She reported to the Inspector of the Poor that her marriage banns had actually been proclaimed when her fiancé (and father of her nine-month-old child) "absconded to evade the marriage."[92] Many migrant women found that a promise of marriage (which at home could be enforced by family pressure) held little meaning in the city.[93] The failure of men to meet their obligations, real or imagined, did not change the women's beliefs and desires in entering into a sexual relationship; finding a husband was probably a strong impetus behind the migration of many Scottish women.

Agnes Cameron's story was particularly suggestive of this motive. Agnes did not leave the Highlands until she was twenty-seven, some eleven or twelve years older than the usual age of first migration. She went directly to work at Lounsdale bleachfield, shunning the greater supervision of domestic service. She probably found work through a friend or acquaintance at Lounsdale; most of the bleachers from Inverness were employed there or at Blackland Mill. By the closest possible estimate she had been in the Lowlands for just two months when she became pregnant. About six weeks later—the earliest she could be certain she was pregnant—Cameron went home to the Highlands and did not return to seek compensation from Murphy until after her child was born. The speed of Cameron's progress may point to a determination to secure a husband for herself, and she may have believed she had: since well before the Union of 1707 there had been an active tradition in

Scotland of irregular marriage, for which the only requirement was the free consent of both parties.[94] However, a consent declared in private could be rescinded in public, and Murphy's refusal to marry Agnes (whether or not he had declared such an intention) must have come as a shock to her; without a well-established network of support in the Lowlands she retreated to her family, which was the usual practice of the Highland migrants in times of illness or trouble, including pregnancies.[95]

The Paisley Poor Law record is riddled with appeals from unmarried migrant women who needed help to get through their confinement or to support a child. A small sample includes Catherine Martin, a country servant from Colonsay who was robbed and abandoned by her fellow servant/lover a month before their child was born in June 1858. Catherine Begley, an unmarried bleacher from Airdrie was herself in good health but, November 1863 being a slack time at the Lounsdale bleachworks thanks to the Cotton Famine, was unable to support her six-month-old daughter. Finally, Mary Livingstone, from Tobermoray, was unable to continue her work as a farm servant as she neared her confinement in November 1871.[96] The women who resorted to parish relief must have represented only a fraction of those who engaged in sexual activity with an eye toward marriage. Many more must have either evaded pregnancy, convinced their partners to marry them, or both.

Migrant domestic servants were more likely to appear in the Poor Law records than bleachers, both because they outnumbered the bleachers and because they were more likely to be thrown out of their jobs and their homes when their pregnancies were discovered. The bleachers were apparently no less interested than the servants in meeting eligible young men, however. Paisley's middle classes widely believed the bleachers to be "an immoral set, and illegitimate births [were] frequently occurring, more so, comparatively, than in any other class of female workers."[97] Young men were known to hang around the womanhouses, and even the owners of some bleachworks were suspected of immoral designs on the inhabitants, to the extent that Tancred reported "the term seraglio has been applied to the woman-house."[98] The migrants may have been contained by the womanhouses, but they were not isolated. The reports of pregnancies are evidence enough that the bleachers were spending some of their free time with men, almost certainly expecting to marry.

Young women may very well have engaged in the same behavior as a marriage strategy whether they were migrants or not. Finding a man was a less direct, less easily identified reason for migration than wage earning, but marriage was the logical, desirable, endpoint of the transitional period marked by young women's independent migration. If finding a husband was not a primary reason for fifteen-year-old girls' initial migration, it was a vital component of the adult womanhood that girls sought through migration. By spending time with eligible men, even taking the risk of being left with a child and no husband, migrants were planning for their futures.

Personal Migration Patterns

Simple desire for a husband or an independent income was not enough to complete a migration. Young women had to negotiate with their parents or guardians, convince them that a migration was in all of their best interests and, above all, safe. The letters of Lowell mill girls suggest compromises (to choose a mill closer to home, to finish school rather than migrate) that must have been universal in the homes of single female migrants, that was hinted at by the Reverend Campbell's recommendation that his parishioners go to service rather than the bleachfields.

Once migration had been agreed to, further decisions loomed. Where—to what place, and what job—should a migrant go? When—at what age, what time of year—was the best time to move? Answers to these questions were again influenced by the young woman's parents and her "personal information field," the knowledge she had of her options from friends, acquaintances, and other sources.[99] To a great extent the personal information fields came from a *female* network. Migrants to Lowell were encouraged by recruiters but often convinced by their friends. In Paisley, word-of-mouth among women was equally important. The Foxbar manager told Tancred, "On a busy time coming on the girls are anxious to send for some friends and relatives from home to get them into the work." Mary M'Ewen, from Argyllshire, had come to Blackland Mill at age fourteen; she "kenned the place because she had a friend here before." Thirteen-year-old Margaret Muir from Lochgilphead "came with her aunty."[100] At the Foxbar bleachfield women's recommendations were favored over any other—the managers preferred to hire Highlanders recommended by those they already employed. The result in 1851 was that more than half of the womanhouse residents were Highlanders from just a few parishes. There were seventy-one women from Kilmichael-Glassary, almost all of whom worked at Foxbar. Other clusters of women came from Tarbut and Campbelltown, Argyllshire, and the Ft. William/Lochaber area of Inverness from which Agnes Cameron came. As girls from a given area succeeded in Paisley they encouraged their friends and relatives at home to come, and their examples no doubt helped convince parents.

Domestic servants could also rely on informal, female networks to find work. For instance, the Poor Law Inspector recorded in 1872 that Catherine McKimon, a native of the Island of Mull, "left Mull about 15 years ago [at about age fifteen] and was taken to Edinburgh by a friend."[101] Using personal connections to find jobs (and hence housing) eased migrants' stress in the transition from life in their parents' houses to the world of work. It also helped to perpetuate the patterns of migrant behavior so apparent in the census statistics. While migrating, young women were ready, willing, and expected to take advantage of all the help offered. That help could determine the decisions about when and to where migration would take place.

While reading was a common skill among the Scottish migrants, writing was rare. Unlike the migrants in Lowell, who often urged their friends to join them in letters, the migrants to Paisley were probably persuaded to migrate through face-to-face conversations with women who had been there before and would go again.[102] Like the Lowell mill girls young Scottish female migrants were actively migrating for a period of years, moving frequently between their parents' homes and various positions, a fact obscured by the "snapshot" census data. During those mobile years they must have made friends and acquaintances, learning about possibilities farther afield and, in turn, telling friends and sisters at home about opportunities in the city.

Migrants' personal patterns of mobility varied depending on the occupation they chose, revealing another difference between the bleachers and the domestic servants in Paisley. Catherine Ferguson from Islay applied for Poor Relief in February 1870, when she was stricken with a fever. "Since leaving Kilchomen 10 years ago [about seventeen years old] [she had] been employed with farmers in various parishes as domestic servant but not in one parish more than one year" (a crucial fact for determining settlement). Ferguson had last been in Dumbarton, across the Firth of Clyde from Paisley, and had worked in Paisley since the previous year.[103] Servants moved to where the work was, not only in a single city but across parish and county boundaries.

The term system divided the Scottish servants' usual migration experience into six-month segments. Jesse Ruthven, a twenty-one-year-old farm servant born in Linlithgow, west of Edinburgh, applied for relief in February 1863. She had first left her mother's house at age sixteen, spent a term in Cumbernauld, midway between Glasgow and Edinburgh, then a full year at one position in Falkirk. She returned to her mother's house for a six-month visit, then went to the Glasgow area for a term and a half. There is no indication of why that term was cut short, but Jesse went from Glasgow to Paisley, where she worked until the term was out in November. Her next move was into rural Renfrewshire, to the aptly named village of Risk, where she worked for two terms. At the end of the second term she was four months pregnant by a servant on a neighboring farm.[104] Of the eight moves Ruthven made before becoming pregnant, seven were made in May or November, in conjunction with the change of terms.[105]

Migrants who did not have connections in Paisley would also be likely to move at term time, when they would be most able to find work. For those planning to work as farm or domestic servants, semiannual "feeing fairs" provided an easy way for strangers in the town to find a position, though the fairs became less popular as the century progressed. By the late 1860s many servants apparently made commitments prior to the fair, a change that reflected the growing scarcity of household help.[106] The hiring fairs were reported in the Paisley newspapers, letting potential employers know what the going wage was for house and farm servants. Unlike the market for domestic servants in Preston, newspaper advertisements seeking servants (or servants seeking positions) were rare. Only in the 1870s, when attendance at the feeing fairs was dwindling, did servants' registries appear in Paisley.[107] Until that time servants' positions were negotiated personally, between the migrant and the employer, with possibly a mutual acquaintance—not a hired mediator—as a go-between. Each May and November "flitting day" saw a flurry of activity as some new servants arrived from out of town, some moved from one position to another, and still more left for home or a position in another city.

Unlike domestic servants, migrants who preferred the bleachfields were not able to search for work in any city or village around the country. The Poor Law record shows that the women who worked at the bleachworks were unlikely to change positions frequently, and when they did it was often just across the reservoir from one works to another. For example, Sarah McGilp from

Kilmichael, Argyllshire spent fifteen years at Paisley's bleachworks with a sister, moving between Foxbar and Blackland Mill woman-houses, as well as spending time in private lodgings.[108] The bleach-workers, like domestic servants, made periodic visits home. Unlike the servants, whose visits were usually for an entire six-month term, the bleachworkers' visits varied from a few weeks to several months. Two of the migrant bleachers, Mary M'Intyre and Grace Campbell, reported to Tancred that they had been in Paisley for ten and four years, respectively. "The first has been at home several times, the latter not at all; but thinks of going in a short time to come again." Eighteen-year-old Bell Murray, from Tarbut, told the investigator it had been "five years past since she came to work here, and [she had] been three times home, for from three to six weeks, and last time six months."[109] Lowland migrants might re-turn home more frequently. Mary Jane Sefton, from Coatbridge, La-narkshire, started at Lounsdale bleachworks when she was very young, and over an eight-year period moved from Lounsdale's to Foxbar's to Blackland Mill's womanhouse. During that time she "went home ... once a quarter and stayed sometimes 2 weeks."[110] The personal migration patterns of women in the bleachfields were more governed by the fluctuations of the textile industry and their individ-ual desires than by a predictable calendar. In both occupations, how-ever, there were ample opportunities for migrants to return home where they helped maintain the migration stream through personal contacts. Although migrants were economically independent of their families, intangible family ties remained important.

Not all migrants left home to assert their independence. The Poor Law recorded that some female migrants, especially those who first moved before they were fifteen, went into service after one or both parents died.[111] Elisabeth Grant, from Airdrie, Lanarkshire, had a typical story. Her father died when she was six years old, and she, her mother, and two siblings went into the parish poorhouse there. Both her mother and a grandmother died by the time the girl was eleven years old. "Soon after the parish sent her out to service in Glasgow 4 mos., then returned to Airdrie [for two years]. Then Lounsdale 2 yrs., then Foxbar 12 mos. Then Lounsdale 3 yrs." Forced to earn her own living at an early age, Grant was one of those who clearly preferred the bleachworks to domestic service.[112]

Many of the other migrants who applied for relief stated that their parents were dead, but their deaths did not immediately cause the daughters' migration. Rather, the death of the parents damaged the migrant's support network. Jean McDougal, born on Mull and raised in Oban, lost her mother when she was nine, and went into service at about age fourteen. Her father died when she was nineteen, and five years later McDougal applied for relief with a six-month-old child to support. The examiner's telling statement was, "no near friends older than self."[113] The young migrants were entirely capable of caring for themselves when times were good. Their position in the community could be painfully marginal, though, and any unexpected misfortune could be disastrous. It is here that the bleachworks showed an advantage over domestic service. In the womanhouses there was a built-in surrogate family, a support network that readily forgave transgressions of middle-class mores.

Marginality was the curse of most independent female migrants, whether they were in Scotland, England, or Massachusetts. Without a family home guaranteeing food and a roof within easy reach, the migrants were vulnerable. Contrarily, some women used marginality to their advantage, manipulating a community that expected to see some strangers in town. Census data provide general behavioral characteristics of migrants, and information about migrants' actions gives an idea of goals and motivations, but neither adequately describes the wide variation of experience within and outside those patterns. It is impossible to detail every variation possible, but the sources from Paisley lend themselves to exploring the obstacles that migrants faced that could prevent or delay them from achieving independent adulthood.

Migrants at Risk

Isabella McNeil's period as a migrant in Paisley lasted five years, longer than some, but she ultimately had a child but no husband and, more significantly, relied on public charity and returned to her parents' home. She neither saved enough money to support herself nor sent enough to her parents to give them the financial means to fetch her home, nor was she able to marry and establish a family of her own. Her story, like others recorded in Paisley's Poor Law records, is not necessarily typical; there is no data at present to show what proportion of migrants ultimately resorted to parish relief. Each story, on the other hand, represents a possibility for every migrant, a treacherous path of which they must surely have been aware. Young migrants who lived and worked in Paisley had to wend their ways through various dangers, any one of which could send askew their attempts to move from their parents' homes to adult homes of their own.

After young women left their parents' homes, work took up most of their time. They had left home, after all, to earn wages, whether to fill their chests or bank accounts or to send money back to their families. While they were working migrants were relatively safe from destitution. Wages were low, but since most of the jobs they took provided housing, they were guaranteed a place to live and adequate food just so long as they remained healthy and employed.

It was not always so easy to remain healthy, however. The bleachfield owners recognized the possibility of epidemic in the crowded womanhouses and were often concerned about smallpox, but fevers and inflammatory bronchial diseases were more common problems.[114] Illness from a fever, an injury, tuberculosis, or other causes could all too easily render a migrant unable to work and hence unable to support herself.[115] Nor was this problem limited to Paisley; migrants to Lowell were frequently forced home to recover their health, and by 1850 Preston's growth had outpaced its water and sanitation systems, creating a danger of cholera and other diseases even for those who lived and worked in private homes.[116] Disease and injury were perhaps the most unpredictable of the obstacles that could keep migrants from their goals: a young woman could through abstinence avoid pregnancy (except in cases of rape), and when work in one occupation was slack she could turn to other forms of employment to get by. But a migrant could rarely control whom she would work beside, whether the water she drank was pure, or whether she would burn herself on an unfamiliar stove. Simply by being in the city and working toward their own support, there was a chance that migrants would fail. Nevertheless it seems it was not at work but during their leisure time that most migrants faltered on the path that led to independent adulthood.

Women at the bleachworks had several hours of liberty for meals and every night after work, and domestic servants were generally given a free half day every two weeks as well as whatever leisure they could slip into odd moments free from the mistresses' eyes.[117] Some free time was inevitably devoted to household chores and shopping. The bleachworkers were specifically expected to make their beds during their breakfast hour, though a woman was employed by the bleachers to do most of the housework. More interesting, no doubt, were the hours after work and before the ten o'clock curfew.[118] Then, bleachers could walk into Paisley to order or be fitted for the dresses that filled their chests. Domestic servants, too, could relish deciding how to spend their wages when the end of the term finally arrived. Newspaper advertisements proclaimed "A Word to Servant Maids" and offered "term boots" with "goat side lacing, plain fronts, a good wearing boot" for 3 s. 10 d. or calf kid boots with elastic sides for 8 s. 6 d. The migrant women, with money in their pockets and few immediate obligations, were a ready clientele for Paisley's merchants.[119]

It does seem, however, that the migrants spent a great deal of time either in company with men or figuring out how to be in company with men. Spending time with suitors, even having sex with them, was potentially an important part of the migrant's transition to adulthood, but it was also fraught with danger. Independent migrant women were by definition separated from family members who could help coerce a man into marriage or provide financial support. Should a child be conceived, they were entirely dependent on the good intentions of the father of the child. Domestic servants were especially vulnerable, since unmarried pregnancies were grounds for immediate dismissal, regardless of how much of the term had been served.[120] Paisley's Poor Law record shows that all too often the trust servants had in their paramours was betrayed.

The first priority of the Poor Law Guardians was to discover who was legally responsible for the migrants' support. The statements carefully recorded the "putative father" of the child, and whether or not he had given the mother money, but there seems to have been relatively little effort expended in searching for him. When Janet McAullay, born in Islay, applied for help supporting her four-month-old son, the Inspector made the simple note, "putative father William Fairlie farm labourer and collier she does not know where he is." No further evidence of Fairlie appeared, and Janet, like most such disgraced servants, was settled on her parents' parish of residence, the place she had left in the first place.[121] Indeed, applying to the Poor Law was a nearly guaranteed way for a migrant to get home, if she was willing to go, without having to find the money for the fares herself.

Bearing a child altered a migrant woman's plans for the future, but it did not necessarily lead to an immediate return to her parents' home. Some applicants for aid were "settled" on their home parish but did not leave, as is evidenced by their re-application several months later. Janet McAullay, in fact, applied again to the Paisley Guardians four years later with a second infant, the father of whom had "gone out of the way and had only said that he never would do a thing for the child."[122] The sisters Flora and Isabella Dow also defied a settlement that could have returned them to Islay. Both unmarried, they bore children two months apart and applied for Poor Relief together. The settlement for both was determined to be Islay, their birthplace. But nine months later, when Flora's infant died, she applied again to the Paisley Poor Inspector for money to bury the child.[123] The parish on Islay may have decided to pay Paisley for the support of these migrants, hoping the women would find work eventually and cease to be a burden on either parish. It is also possible that the sisters themselves refused to return to Islay, knowing there was no means for them to earn a living there.

Migrants who were refused Poor Relief or who themselves refused a removal to their home parish had to find alternate means to survive. Credit extended by merchants could be a lifeline for desperate migrants who were not able to qualify for local Poor Relief. Agnes Cameron—likely but not necessarily the same introduced earlier—was sued in 1854 by the grocer John Colrun for an outstanding bill of £2 8 s. 6 d. At the same court session Colrun also sued one of Cameron's coworkers at Lounsdale and two bleachers from other works.[124] Debts to grocers carry a different connotation than those to drapers; these bleachers were going into debt for survival rather than indulgence. Cameron's situation in Paisley two years after being settled in Kilmonivaig suggests both defiance of the Poor Law and the difficulty of supporting herself and a child whether in Paisley or her home parish.

Though Dan Murphy denied paternity, Agnes Cameron had no doubts about who the father of her child was. Like Murphy, the putative father of a pregnant migrant's child in most cases was a fellow servant or laborer who lived close to the migrant's place of work. These were men that domestic servants could reasonably see as marriage prospects, which supports the theory proposed earlier that servants engaged in sex as a prelude to expected marriage. Servants could also be seduced or raped by employers, which might have been either an attempt at social climbing or outright sexual exploitation.[125] Margaret Campbell was a twenty-two-year-old domestic servant from Islay whose migration was cut short by an employer crossing the bounds of propriety. She reported to the Poor Law Inspector, "the father of her child is John Gardener aged about 20 years, son of Archibald Gardener writer with whom she served 2 years prior to May 1856 and who went to America 6 months ago." Campbell was not yet three months pregnant when she left the Gardeners' service. The next month the putative father of her child emigrated, safely out of reach of any attempt to collect support from him. She was lucky enough to find a position in Glasgow for the next term, but by November, obviously pregnant, she was unable to get another place. The Poor Law granted Margaret a four-shilling one-time payment, which either paid her way home or saw her through until she was able to get another job.[126]

Given the general employers' policy on "immoral conduct," Campbell likely would not have been able to retain her position even if the father of her child had not been her employer's son.[127] Becoming pregnant while in service was grounds for immediate dismissal, and so propriety resulted in the destitution of young migrants just when they most needed income and a warm place to sleep. Some migrants applying for Poor Relief reported they had been through several short-term positions in the months prior to applying for relief; these may be cases of servants trying to work while concealing their pregnancies. Jesse Ruthven, who earlier illustrated the effect of the term system on domestic servants' migration patterns, went through two short-term positions (one for one month, one for two) after leaving Risk before she finally turned to parish relief when she was seven months pregnant and unemployable.[128]

Many middle-class employers believed young women were tainted and dishonored by premarital sex, especially by bearing a child without a husband.[129] They were no longer girls, but "strumpets," unfit to be kept in one's house. As the Poor Law cases show, this belief caused a great deal of trouble for migrant domestic servants, depriving them at least temporarily of their livelihood and sometimes forcing them back to a parental household. The migrants in the bleachfields, however, were apparently much less handicapped by pregnancy. Thomas Tancred was told by a disapproving witness, "the masters of the fields usually . . . make no difference in their treatment of a virtuous girl or one who is the contrary . . . . Certain it is that they are received again into the work a very short time after having a child." Another informed him, "a number of illegitimate births occur every year amongst the girls employed in bleaching, most of whom go to their homes to be delivered and most return again to the works, it being considered nothing against a girl to have been with child."[130]

The Poor Law records also give evidence of the bleachers' tolerance. Elisabeth Grant from Airdrie applied to the parish even as she was earning 9 s./week at a dye works, needing more money to pay her child's nurse. Grant had previously been in Lounsdale and Foxbar works for a total of six years. Just three months after Elisabeth made the initial application, the woman caring for her child came to the Poor Law looking for support for the baby, the "mother [of whom was] supposed to be in Lounsdale."[131] One of Grant's unmarried coworkers at Lounsdale, Mary McKechnie, also from Airdrie, had two children whom she was normally able to support on her wages.[132] Although the presence of unwed mothers in the womanhouses fostered middle-class fears that "corruption . . . must naturally result to the other workers," the bleachfields were ultimately a more secure occupation for some migrants than domestic service because they were not cast out for "immoral" behavior.[133]

Some women faced with the problem of supporting an infant took a third way out. Rather than returning to their parents' home or asking for Poor Relief, they simply abandoned the baby. Mary McPhee from Strontian, Argyllshire, first went to service in Glasgow when she was about twenty years old. She worked several terms in Glasgow, then went back to Strontian for six months, but in November of 1851 she traveled hastily to Glasgow again. "She came direct from Strontian to bear her child which was born in the Lying In Hospital [in] St. Andrews Square Glasgow." On her journey back to Strontian, she left the infant girl in a Paisley alley, where the baby was discovered by a letter carrier.[134] Mary, unlike some migrants, had a potential support system—two living parents—to whom she could return. Nevertheless, her circumstances made her unwilling to cope with the problem of a child. Attempting to abandon her baby is clear evidence that her plans had gone awry.

Pregnancy was not the only danger women faced in spending time with men. Sexually transmitted disease was rampant in Victorian Britain, and migrants were not immune.[135] The Poor Law recorded, for example, the case of Margaret McLean, who was a sixteen-year-old prostitute from Kilsyth, in the Stirling area. She was admitted first to Paisley's House of Refuge (a residential reform program for prostitutes and suspected prostitutes) and then to the Paisley infirmary with advanced syphilis, where she subsequently became insane.[136] Women who contracted less severe infections were treated in the infirmary, then transferred to the House of Refuge if appropriate, or sent back to their parents. At the time of the 1871 census, 39 percent of the inmates in the House of Refuge were migrants from elsewhere in Scotland.[137] None of them gave their occupations as prostitute—most were mill workers, domestic servants or seamstresses. They had nevertheless somehow transgressed middle-class ideas of morality and were placed in the strict care of strangers.[138] In 1881, 67.7 percent of the House of

Refuge's inmates were Scottish migrants (35 percent from Lanarkshire alone) while in the general single female population only 8.5 percent were migrants.[139] The high proportion of migrants in the House of Refuge may indicate their lack of a support system: with no one to help them find a respectable position or to come to their defense or protection, they were open targets to police or other authorities who disapproved of their behavior.

Some migrant prostitutes, however, may have been actively choosing prostitution over a return to their parents. Ellen McAllum, from Ayrshire, was twenty-five years old when she applied for Poor Relief, where her occupation was recorded as "domestic servant now prostitute." McAllum, who had come to Paisley five years earlier, provided some vague information about her sisters in Glasgow and claimed she had "not heard anything about her parents since she left Ayr." Within two weeks, however, the Inspector recorded, "This woman's mother writes... [and] states that her daughter's baptized name is *Janet*." It is hard to avoid the conclusion that McAllum, who had been in Paisley without any fixed residence for nearly a year, had turned to public charity in preference to contacting her family. There is no way to know what McAllum was avoiding, whether she had escaped from a bad situation at home or in an employers' house, or if she did not want to face her family with the shame of prostitution against her name.[140] Nevertheless she was disconnected from her birth family, and struggling to maintain her independence from them.

Isabella McNeil was not alone in her failure to support herself successfully in Paisley. Indeed, she seems to have been one of the lucky ones in that she was able to return to her parents' home instead of turning to prostitution or abandoning her infant in an alleyway. Most of the independent female migrants to Paisley, however, never turned up in the Poor Law record at all. They were generally successful in supporting themselves until they established a home of their own. Most were also able to find marriage partners. From 1851 to 1881 84.5 percent of female Scottish migrants over fourty who had probably migrated as single women were married or widowed. Half of those whose husbands' place of birth was known had married Renfrewshire natives—that is, men they had most likely met in Paisley.[141] Furthermore, more than 80 percent of married female migrants had no occupation recorded in the census, suggesting that their families were well enough off that the migrants did not need to earn regular wages. In spite of their vulnerability, most migrants evaded the pitfalls and managed to meet their original goals.

Migrants as a class were not victims. Based on information available to them, they made choices about their lives. They decided where they would move, what sort of job they would search for, what they would do with their wages and how they would spend their leisure time. In some cases, when they contracted a disease or were abandoned by a lover, those choices ran out of control and landed them in the hospital, the hands of the Poor Law or the matrons at the House of Refuge. In most cases, the migrants were ultimately successful in finding a husband and creating their own adult family, or at least in supporting themselves respectably. Some unusual women even used migration to their distinct advantage, manipulating poor communication and a general lack of suspicion to meet their own ends. As a case in point, in December 1871 the *Paisley and Renfrewshire Gazette* reported a "Singular Case of a Woman Dressing and Working as a Man." Marie Campbell, an Inverness-shire native, was orphaned at age thirteen and had traveled through the country, living in, at least, Edinburgh, Tranent, and Renfrew. She "commenced to wear male attire to enable her better to maintain herself." Campbell was "short, but stout, and...about thirty-two years of age." Calling herself John, she worked as a railway surfaceman and in a shipbuilding yard. She also swore in order to keep up her disguise, and had a "Highland sweetheart" named Kate Martin.

In later issues, the "Extraordinary Disclosures" stretched readers' credulity: Campbell was reportedly married in Edinburgh to a woman who swore she did not know the truth until several days after the ceremony, though Campbell claimed the sham was prearranged. According to the *Gazette*, "John Campbell" was being sought by the Edinburgh Parochial Board on charges of desertion.[142] This story was good for a titillated Victorian chuckle, and it is clearly not representative, but it also reveals advantages that women could find in migration. It would be easier for a woman to pass herself as a man in an area where she was not known from birth, and migration offered an escape when her secret was found out. Barring an embarrassing disclosure in the newspaper, there was little chance of people in a new city being on the lookout for a cross-dressing surfaceman. As Janet "Ellen" McAllum also demonstrated, if less dramatically, migration could be an escape, whether from an overbearing family or the handicap of being a young woman alone.

Migration, or a story of migration, could also provide a means to swindle innocent parties. Paisley's Sheriff's Court did not record where Mary Henderson was born, but she was accused of telling Mrs. Margaret Turnbull in October of 1873 that she had recently

been at service in Ness-bank, Inverness-shire, and currently lived
with an aunt in Helensburgh, Dumbartonshire. Henderson had
come to Paisley to apply for a position as a domestic servant with
Turnbull but had, she said, accidentally left her purse at her aunt's
house, and would Mrs. Turnbull please give her a shilling for her
fare home? Later on the same day Henderson used the same ruse to
gain 2 s. 6 d. from Elizabeth Robertson, and another shilling from
Ellen Geddes. Mary Henderson apparently did have an aunt in
Helensburgh (a Marjory Henderson of Helensburgh testified at
Mary's trial), but it came out in court that the Ness-bank reference
was entirely fictional.[143] Whether she was an actual migrant or not
Henderson was exploiting the well-known migratory propensities of
young women and domestic servants in particular. It was entirely
plausible to the three swindled women that a young woman whose
last position had been in Inverness would be searching for work in
Renfrewshire, and apparently no less probable that the same young
woman had forgotten her purse in another county. Knowing that
there was no ready way for her victims to check, Henderson could be
confident in making up a story of migration for her own personal
gain.

Like Marie "John" Campbell's story, Henderson's exploits were
likely unique, rarely if ever repeated by other migrants. Yet these
stories point out that not all migrants who deviated from the path
of approved, sheltered occupation to eventual marriage were derailed by mere chance or bad judgment. Whether a migrant was a
Gaelic-speaking Highlander in a bleacher's womanhouse at midcentury or a collier's daughter from Lanarkshire, she was thought-
ful and active in solving problems she encountered, not passively
accepting what fate threw at her. Leaving domestic service for mill
work, abandoning an infant, turning to prostitution, hiding a pregnancy to secure a position, even applying for Poor Relief were all
active responses to problems in the migrants' lives, choices that
they made about how to cope with life when they were no longer
fully integrated into their parents' families.

Migrants in Paisley were able to make decisions about their
lives and actions, but that ability should not be confused with complete control. Women's nineteenth-century migration was influenced by myriad factors, from regional and extraregional economic,
social, and political developments to the fashion in women's clothes
or middle-class beliefs about the sanctity of the family. Female migrants' plans could be altered by other people's actions, as when a
lover refused marriage or support for a child or an employer refused

to provide a character reference. They could also be affected by events entirely beyond their control such as disease, famine, or war. Migration was most directly affected by the needs of employers in potential destinations and the needs and desires of the migrants themselves. After migration individuals found particular, personal dangers that could prevent them from meeting their goals. Like the variety among migrants, Preston, Lowell, and Paisley were each individual cities with unique influences on women's migration. As many migrants' stories give a rounded picture of their experience, direct comparison allows the construction of a multidimensional description of nineteenth-century single women's migration.

CHAPTER 5

Comparisons: The Migrants Beside Themselves

Isabella McNeil, Emma Page, and the anonymous rural servant native hired by R. Hignet migrated in different decades to different cities in response to different immediate influences. Each migrant and the population to which she belonged left traces that
emphasize a different factor in single women's industrial migration
in the third quarter of the nineteenth century. Although there were
clear differences in experience among the three cities, especially in
terms of migrants' economic need, there were also similarities that
beg comparison and justify the use of sources from one city to make
suggestions about experience in another. Such an analysis adds
much-needed complexity to the basic model of single women's migration and helps to explain why characteristic patterns emerged.

Migrant women in all three cities were at an age when they
were moving from their parents' home toward adulthood. As subordinate members of the community, separated from the protection of
their family, their parents' and employers' morals limited them to
"respectable" employment that also provided accommodation, a
limitation reflected in the census data of all three cities. Correlat-
ing the census data with changes in each city's economic climate
confirms the common-sense assessment that migration fluctuated
with the demand for labor. The migrants generally were more concerned with their independence than with providing economic aid
to their families. Evidence from the Preston Savings Bank and
observers' reports in Paisley suggest that women in the cities had
control of their own wages, a control that also appears and is
expanded on in letters from Lowell mill girls.

Yet the migrants' very independence from their families neces-
sitated the creation of supportive networks. The Lowell migrants'
high literacy rate gave them a means to maintain social and familial networks that was not open to most of the migrants in Britain,

and gives the historian special insight into the nature of those connections. Nevertheless, evidence from Preston and Paisley suggests similar ties among migrants in those cities. Both British cities had concentrations of young women from particular areas, which in the absence of targeted recruitment by employers argues for migration streams maintained by personal contact between friends and family. In Paisley the bleach workers in particular fostered a social network similar to that in Lowell's boardinghouses. The affectionate ties evident between migrants in the United States can well be supposed between British migrants.

In spite of such affective networks, independent female migrants were among the most vulnerable members of the urban population. As the letters from Lowell migrants give a uniquely personal perspective, the Poor Law records from Paisley are unique in the bureaucratic perspective they give on independent female migrants. Nevertheless the problems the migrants encountered in Paisley were far from unusual. Domestic servants in Preston were as vulnerable to seduction and abandonment, disease, and unemployment as were maids and bleachworkers in Paisley. Mill girls in Lowell were perhaps more protected from men than were domestic servants, but they were still open to injury, disease, and loss of their jobs. The evidence of migrants' distress in Paisley is unique to that city, but the potential problems were universal.

Despite differences in origin, occupation, and accommodation, single white women's experiences of independent internal migration seem to have been strikingly similar whatever country they were in. It is possible, therefore, to postulate generalizations about migrants to Preston or Paisley using sentiments articulated by migrants to Lowell. Yet even in the face of the apparent similarities between the migrant groups the historian must use great care in applying sources from one place to people in another. Marc Bloch's idea of historical analogy is not a complete solution to a lack of documentation, since there will always be differences between communities that this process by its nature does not reveal. Nevertheless the conclusions drawn through these comparisons are suggestive, in the absence of more definitive evidence, of how young women in general experienced migration to nineteenth-century textile cities.

One of the most uniform characteristics of the female migrants was their youth: even when all independent single migrant women were included (not only the "recent" cohort), their average age was still from twenty-six to twenty-eight years in all three cities. The fifteen-to-thirty-year-olds most likely to be recent migrants (at least

70 percent of all the independent female migrants in the samples) averaged twenty-one years old in every city, in nearly every census.[1] This age profile confirms that women were most likely to be independent migrants in their late teens and early twenties, while they were in transition between their parents' families and their families of marriage. Not all migrants married, not all migrants *wanted* to marry, and certainly not all marriages were happy ones. Nevertheless, the small number of unmarried migrant women older than their mid-twenties shows that the migrants tended to either marry or remigrate, whether to another city or back to their parents' home. Being an independent migrant was most often a temporary state.

The majority of migrants in this study were also from similar origins. Only in Paisley did a large number of migrants come from an urban region, Lanarkshire, and even many of those had come from mining areas where industrial textile work was relatively unfamiliar. Some migrants to Preston from the combined urban/rural county of Yorkshire, and some migrants to Lowell after the Civil War came with prior experiences of textile work, even familiarity with a factory setting, but rarely from large cities. Most independent migrants to all three cities came from rural or small-town backgrounds. They were liable to be unfamiliar with the noise, smoke, and bustle of the cities to which they moved, the smallest of which (Paisley) had more than 48,000 residents in 1851. Often migration was a transition not only out of the family home but into industrial urban life.

Because migrants were predominantly young and inexperienced with limited connections in the city, they usually moved to protected positions. In Lowell 79 percent of recent migrants worked in the mills, and in Paisley 72 percent were in domestic service and bleaching. Migrants to Preston were the most likely to deviate from the common path, and even there 52 percent of all recent migrants followed a single occupation, domestic service. Migrants in general clearly preferred particular occupations in each city, and their migration was therefore dependent in part on employer needs and employers' requirements.

Nevertheless in each city there was a substantial proportion of single female migrants (in Preston nearly half) who did not conform to the other migrants' behavior. Some of these young women had family in the city, which affected both their housing and occupation choices. Others were barred from domestic service or respectable boardinghouses due to a pregnancy or bad reputation. Still others may simply have chosen to take an alternate path for reasons beyond the reach of the historian.

The volume of migrants in any particular city was determined by a constantly shifting balance between the demand in that city for labor in the migrants' preferred occupations and circumstances in home communities. The broadest correlation evident is volume of migrants to employers' demand: Yankee migration into Lowell was initially very high, because employers in that city made careful arrangements to attract a migrant labor force. As the city's population grew the corporations had less need to retain the migrants, and the volume fell rapidly. In Preston, the volume of migrants fluctuated with the city's economic health, rising when there was increased demand for their labor in middle-class homes, falling when fewer families could afford to keep servants. Single female migrants did not pour thoughtlessly into textile cities when conditions deteriorated in their places of origin; the Lowell girls' letters and clusters of Highlanders in Paisley bleachworks show that young women learned about possibilities in accessible cities through networks of prior migrants and chose their destinations in response.

Yet employer demand alone does not do justice to the complexity of influences on single women's migration. The presence of appropriate employment was perhaps a necessary condition for migration, but it was not in itself sufficient. The number of migrants into Paisley and Preston rose substantially during the 1870s, when agricultural depression reduced opportunities in rural areas and, coincidentally, when improvement to the railways further eased transportation to the cities.[2] In Paisley patterns of migration changed without obvious influence from the migrants' major employers there, as the bleachfields demanded a migrant labor force after the 1860s but the Highland migration to the city nevertheless declined. In Lowell, some Yankee women continued to migrate to the city in the 1870s even after the corporations, content with their family-based immigrant labor supply, had effectively stopped recruiting in New England. The conditions in places of origin and in other potential destinations also had an important effect on how many young women chose to migrate to a particular city, as did the women's individual situations, personal desires, and even their circle of acquaintances.

The conditions of the jobs available were extremely important to migrants, though the jobs themselves varied from city to city. As the standard historical model suggested, domestic service was the single most common occupation for independent female migrants in both British cities. But the important factor in domestic service was not the domestic, gender-appropriate labor it required. Service,

like the industrial textile work undertaken by most migrants to
Lowell and a quarter of the migrants to Paisley, provided housing
in conjunction with the employment, either as part of the wage or
heavily subsidized. Even many of the alternate occupations migrants pursued, such as dressmaking, nursing, or school teaching, offered accommodations as part of the package. Over all, 64.6 percent
of the 1,231 migrants in the census samples chose occupations that
furnished shelter as well as a regular wage. If migrants who lived
with relatives in the city are included, the percentage who found
protected accommodation is even higher. Although migrants were
leaving their parent's homes, it was extremely important to most of
them to be able to move to into a safe housing arrangement.

These distinctive occupational patterns were based in the young
women's status as *migrants*, not in an ethnic or cultural prejudice
regarding appropriate occupations for women. With the possible exception of Highland migrants in Paisley the internal migrants were
culturally identical to the nonmigrant women in every city who
worked happily in the many occupations that did not provide accommodations. Even the Highlanders proved perfectly willing to
take on an industrial occupation when appropriate housing was
assured. Ethnic bias in fact worked in favor of the English and
Scottish migrants, who found they were preferred over Irish immigrants as household employees.

Their numbers were often small, but single female migrants
were in demand in nineteenth-century textile cities. Their tremendous advantage over nonmigrant single women was their mobility:
when employers needed inexpensive workers in a specific location,
be it next to a reservoir outside the burgh, in the factories of a newly
constructed model city, or in their own homes, they turned to a
migrant workforce. When the occupation was believed especially
suited for young women, such as domestic service or light factory
work, employer demand tended to draw young women to the cities.
Rural, native-born migrants were particularly favored for domestic
service. In Britain, at least, by the third quarter of the nineteenth
century there was growing suspicion of the urban working classes
among middle-class residents, and disdain for the urban "factory
girl" that could describe most nonmigrant single women in the city.[3]
The "country girls" preferred as domestic servants were, in popular
perceptions, healthier both physically and morally, more docile, and
less inclined to change positions frequently. In the United States
the demand for urban domestic servants was filled primarily by the
nation's immigrant population, but the potential mobility of single

women was still valued. When Lowell's corporations closed during the Civil War, the city's unemployed permanent residents were a potentially disruptive population, but the migrants at some mills were simply turned out of their boardinghouses and expected to return to their families, eliminating a potential burden on the employers and the city. Considering the clamor for servants that continued into the 1880s, and the presence of Lowell's corporate recruiters in New England until the point when they were clearly ineffectual, it was apparently not a lack of employer demand that limited single women's migration into textile cities. Rather, it was the disinclination of the potential migrants themselves to embark on a possibly dangerous adventure that was less appealing or less profitable than remaining at home. Although employer needs could strongly influence where and when a young woman migrated, they did not cause the need or desire to migrate.

Young women who did decide to migrate after midcentury primarily did so as part of a transition to adulthood, not in order to support their parents' families financially. However, the family economy model of single women's migration does have a degree validity for this period. Migrant daughters were more likely to be net contributors to their parents than daughters who remained at home and could not earn a wage, simply by finding their own food and sending home a few shillings or dollars a year. While the real value of wages paid to migrant women varied across time and place, most migrants found themselves with personally unprecedented surplus income. In extreme cases, such as a Lowell mill girl with an impoverished mother struggling on the family farm or a Highland migrant during the Potato Famine, a migrant daughter's contribution to her family could be crucial. Yet by far the bulk of the evidence points to independent migrants using their wages to meet their personal needs, not their families'.

However, migrants' economic independence does not translate to either complete autonomy or total separation from the family. Even the generally independent-minded migrants to Lowell usually consulted with their parents before making migration decisions, and some were persuaded not to move by their parents. Migrants in Paisley who were able relied on their families for emotional and physical support when they were ill or unemployed, or when they simply wanted a rest from taking complete care of themselves. Migration was a transition period in which young women gained experience, confidence, and possibly financial independence for adulthood, but migrants also maintained ties with home and family.

Indeed, Ella Bailey, who so emphatically declared her hatred of teaching and rejoiced in her planned return to Lowell after a long hiatus, was recorded in the 1870 census at home in North Troy again, teaching school.[4]

Migrants to the city were connected to their country homes by a web of relatives, friends and acquaintances, never fully leaving that community. Mill girls already in Lowell wrote to their friends, persuading them make the journey to the city. The large number of migrants to Paisley's bleachfields from particular Highland parishes argues strongly for personal connections that maintained the stream of migrants. It is more difficult to discern direct lines of communication among migrant domestic servants, but many servants traveled back and forth between the city and their parents' home during the years they were independent migrants. Those visits home familiarized friends and sisters with migration, showing potential migrants where and when and how jobs might be found. Those few migrant servants who recorded their entry into service often recounted being "taken ... by a friend."[5] Newspaper advertisements and professional recruiters could be influential in determining where young women would migrate and what jobs they would take, but much more important were personal contacts between current and potential migrants.

Migration was also a crucial step in creating young women's adult families. British domestic servants and bleachfield workers spent a good portion of their leisure time with single men, engaging in sexual relationships most probably expecting marriage. Even in Lowell, where the migrant textile workers' propriety was closely guarded by motherly boardinghouse keepers, a mill worker could report to an absent friend, "Mat & George are down keeping the sitting room warm they do considerable of that now."[6] Even when they were in closely supervised living situations migrants found ways to spend time with young men.

Especially in areas where rural populations were small or falling, migration could be part of a strategy to find a marriage partner. For example, in 1851 there were approximately 400 unmarried female migrants under thirty years old in Preston. The next census found more than 300 female migrants aged from twenty-five to thirty-nine years who had married men born in Lancashire. (Some of these married migrants had certainly migrated as children with their families, but there is no way with the available data to determine how many.) In 1881, ten years after the dip in migration to Preston following the Cotton Famine, the number of female migrants married to nonmigrants had fallen as well. While not conclusive without further research or documentary evidence, this suggests that many migrants did find husbands in the city.

Independent female migrants might also return to their home communities for marriage. In Lowell, although there were close to 4,000 recent single female migrants in the city in 1850, in the 1860 census there were only about 830 women who had probably migrated prior to 1850 and married after their migration.[7] Among the letter writers in "Grandmothers' Friends," none are known to have married in Lowell, and some definitely returned to their home states at the time of their marriage.[8] For these migrants, the savings they could accumulate from their work in the city was probably more important to their future lives than the men they could meet in Lowell.

The differences among migrants' marriage patterns in the cities was partly related to the presence of eligible marriage partners in the city. The immigrant population in Lowell was growing steadily after midcentury, and many Yankee migrants apparently did not find foreign immigrants suitable partners (from 1860 to 1880, only about 20 percent or fewer of the Yankee migrants who married in Lowell married immigrant men).[9] Even if an American migrant was willing to marry an immigrant she was in a competitive marriage market. From 1850 to 1880 on average there was one single man for every 1.9 single women in Lowell, and about one-third of those single men were immigrants. In Preston and Paisley migrants also avoided marriage with immigrants, but they found there were much larger populations of native-born men from which they could choose.[10] The American women may also have seen better prospects in leaving the city. Land ownership (through their husbands) and farm life continued to be feasible in the United States, either in New England or farther west. In Britain even year-round agricultural employment, not to mention running one's own farm, was becoming difficult to achieve.[11] While most migrants to textile cities were interested in their future marriages, where those marriages would take place depended on conditions in the places of origin and the cities themselves.

Employer demand, potential migrants' desire, repeated communication between the origin and destination points leading to eventual marriage and an end to migration broadly outline an ideal course of single women's migration into textile cities. Not all migrants, however, could move from the status of daughter to migrant to wife without misfortune. Paisley's Poor Law records give ample evidence of the disasters that could befall migrants, but Scottish migrants were not the only ones in danger. In Lowell, poor health was frequently an issue. The letter writers in "Grandmother's Friends" were often separated because a mill girl left Lowell to recover her health, weakened from long months of hectic work and rushed meals.[12] Florella Farnsworth, who arrived in Lowell to a flurry of friends in 1847, died there the next year of typhoid.[13] No comparable evidence of the hazards migrants faced survived in Preston, but the domestic servants in England were not protected by even the six-month term that gave Scottish servants some security in their positions. Migrants in that city were not exempt from the dangers of unemployment, disease, and pregnancy that plagued migrants in others.

In the face of these dangers, female independent migrants in textile cities were potentially more vulnerable than any other group of workers. Separated physically from their families, unable legally to claim local charity (though many tried and some were successful), and counting on their employers for housing and often food as well as a wage, the migrants were immediately dependent on the goodwill of their employers and their own resources. Yet migrants were not so vulnerable as they may seem. They maintained emotional ties to their families, and many could retreat to their parents' homes in times of trouble. Migration patterns recorded in Paisley showed both domestic servants and bleachfield workers making regular visits home. Highlanders returned home to recover from illness and confinements in a pattern similar to the Lowell mill girls returning home periodically for their health, or when the mills closed. Even Janet "Ellen" McAllum, apparently avoiding her parents, found them willing to correspond on her behalf when she was in need. Individual migration patterns into Preston are obscured in the record, and further research, perhaps through record linking, would be necessary to determine if movement from rural areas to Preston was one-way or often repeated. Evidence from migrants in the other two cities, however, argues that those in Preston did indeed maintain contact with their families.

Migrants also developed support systems in the cities. The same lines of communication that facilitated single women's migration gave migrants contacts in their new homes. The boardinghouses of the Lowell mills are the most obvious case, where migrants helped new arrivals find jobs and lodging and carried them into a raucous community of young women. The Paisley bleachfields also relied on word of mouth to fill their womanhouses, encouraging clusters of friends and relatives to develop. Ironically the domestic servants in Scotland and England, who at first appear the most protected, were the most marginal of independent migrants, largely isolated in their employers' houses and subject to their employers' conceptions of morality as well as long work hours. Occasional visits home could not substitute for a ready source of support close at hand. However, I suspect that one of the domestic servants' reasons for frequently spending their leisure time with men was to build a support system in the city. Although the women for whom there are records were for the most part abandoned by their lovers it is possible, even likely, that others were able to count on men they met for company, an occasional treat and eventual marriage.

In part because they worked in isolation in private homes, independent female migrant servants were rarely a visible population. Domestic servants were expected, even preferred, to be migrants. Although servants were a source of frequent exasperation for their employers, they did not usually arouse anxiety because they were a population of unsupervised, potentially disruptive women. Quite the contrary, this largest group of independent female migrants in England and Scotland were well controlled and incorporated into their employers' households. Not only subject to their mistresses' orders, domestic servants were also expected to conform with middle-class ideals of morality. Servants who transgressed these ideals, through theft, pregnancy, or defiance, were likely to be dismissed without a character reference, one of the hazards that could send a migrant servant back to her parents' home.

The ability to return to a parents' home also contributed to the invisibility of migrants in Paisley's bleachfields. The migrants in the bleachfields were safely contained in the supervised accommodations of the womanhouses. When the migrants were ill or pregnant and a potential public burden they were likely to return home, out of sight. Although there were some voices raised about the immorality of the womanhouse residents, those worries were not an ongoing public concern.[14]

The migrants to Lowell, on the other hand, were a public concern from the moment the first mill girls arrived in the city. They had been recruited to a city built in explicit contrast to the English factory system, and the migrants themselves differed from the working-class factory girls of Britain. Primarily the daughters of small landowners, the Lowell migrants were not only literate but educated, and endowed with the virtue that nineteenth-century Americans associated with the countryside.[15] There were many times more independent female migrants in Lowell than in other textile cities and, significantly, they were put on display by the city's promoters. Even after conditions deteriorated in the mills and most of the Yankees were replaced with immigrant workers the myth of the Lowell mill girl remained, echoed in the remaining boarding- houses and the slow trickle of New England natives who continued to come to Lowell to earn some money for themselves and see something of the city. When the volume of internal migration to Lowell had fallen to approximately the same levels as migration into Preston and Paisley, the origin of the migration continued to affect the mill girls' experience. Life in a boardinghouse and textile mill was the rule for Yankee women, rather than the exception it was for English and Scottish migrants.

Independent female migrants were a minority of the single women in textile cities from 1850 to 1881, but examining their experiences in comparative perspective is nevertheless useful to understanding both nineteenth-century migration and the structure of the textile cities themselves. Parallels are immediately apparent, both between the cities and among the migrants. Yet in spite of the similarities of influence, restriction and hazards, it is impossible to specify one "typical" migration experience for single women. Women came to textile cities from experiences as diverse as destitute Highland crofts, prosperous New England villages, and industrial urban areas. A move to the city might be as short as a few months or it might be a permanent transition, and the migrant's intentions at the beginning were not necessarily manifested in the outcome. Employment probably but did not always provide housing, the quality and conditions of which varied widely with the occupation and the employer. A migrant might experience illness, injury, crime, pregnancy, or none of these. A young woman's migration could end satisfactorily in marriage, tragically in premature death, or with mixed emotions in a return to parental oversight. From beginning to end the individual experience of migration turned on individual circumstance.

Viewed in a wider perspective, however, patterns of behavior emerge, such as the tendency for young migrant women to find occupations that provided supervised, respectable accommodations or to be independent for only a few years before marriage. Rural migrants held an important place in the urban economy, working in textile mills and the homes of middle-class employers. A population in transition, single female migrants required little commitment from their employers. These women moved to new positions at will, returned to their home communities during illness or trouble, and most eventually married and blended in with the larger population in either their home or host communities. Although individual women moved on, the migrant streams continued, attracting successive generations of rural daughters to the opportunities in the city. Their individual lives and the different contexts in which their migration occurred reveal both the intricate complexity and broad patterns of the single female migration phenomenon, showing that in addition to being a transformative stage in individuals' lives, single female migration contributed a small but crucial element to the nineteenth-century textile city.

Appendix: The Statistical Methodology

Statistics must be at the root of large-scale migration history. Qualitative sources give more immediate access to the personal experience of migration, but only statistics can provide a hint of how representative those experiences were. The statistics I used in *Mill Girls and Strangers* came from a random/systematic sample drawn from the manuscript censuses of Preston, Lowell, and Paisley for the years 1850/1 through 1880/1. The census data were originally collected over a period of months, but they represented the population of the city as it was constituted on a particular night in the Spring of each census year. In this period, only 1851 was a composite "Census of Great Britain"; afterward the Scottish and English and Wales censuses were separate endeavors, which requested different information in addition to the basic demographics.

The samples used for this study were 10 percent samples of people over fifteen within the city or borough boundaries of each city in 1850/1, and 7.7 percent samples (every thirteenth person) in all other years. Table A.I shows the total sample size for each of the cities in each of the four census years.

The samples were initially randomized by choosing the first individual to be recorded in each census year through the use of a random number generated by a pocket calculator. Further randomization was incorporated by the practice of only counting people over age fourteen. The number of resident children in families varied widely, which guaranteed I was not favoring persons, such as household heads, who were more likely to be recorded on particular lines of the census forms. The samples do vary greatly in size, which is one reason I have relied on percentages, rather than gross numbers, for making comparisons. Although Preston was considerably larger than either Paisley or Lowell, the large size resulted in a useful number of migrants in the sample, in spite of their small proportion in the population. The variation in sample size does not

Table A-I
Sample Sizes, Preston, Lowell, and Paisley
1850–1881

	1850/1 (10%)	1860/1 (7.7%)	1865 (7.7%)	1870/1 (7.7%)	1880/1 (7.7%)
Preston	4465	4114	n/a	4004	4613
Lowell	2364	2076	1691	2307	3341
Paisley	3196	2427	n/a	2484	2861

affect the validity of my conclusions. The proportions derived from the samples do not differ substantially from other statistics available for the cities, such as those collected by Michael Anderson about Preston in 1851 for *Family Structure in Nineteenth Century Lancashire* or those that can be derived from the published census reports.[1]

As I briefly discussed in the Introduction, I limited the data I recorded to that which was either explicit in or could be accurately deduced from the censuses throughout the entire series of data (with the exception of female occupation, which was not recorded in the United States in 1850). Although the United States requested information on personal wealth in 1850 and 1860 and Scotland inquired on the number of windowed rooms in the house in 1860 and 1870 and recorded native Gaelic speakers in 1880, all information that would be useful in studying migrants, I did not include those data in the statistical sample. To identify each case, I recorded the census year and enumeration district, page number and line number. Data recorded for each individual case included sex; age; marital status (single, married, widowed, divorced); occupation (as it was recorded); type of household (based on ages and surnames of the individuals resident in the house); relationship to the head of household (see below); place of birth; spouse's, mother's, and father's place of birth when available. In the United States census, marital status (except in 1865) and relationship to head of household were inferred from other data until the 1880 census. The 1880 United States census was also the only one in the series to record the parents' place of birth for every individual. For the English and Scottish censuses and the United States 1850 to 1870 censuses, parents' place of birth data was only recorded when an individual resided in a household with one or both parents.

Throughout the study, certain terms were used with specific definitions, all of which were derived from the census data. An adult was any person whose recorded age was fifteen years or greater on the day of the census. A "migrant" was an individual whose place of birth was recorded as a place outside the county or state in which the census was taken, but within the same country. An "immigrant" was a person born outside the country in which the census was taken. An "independent migrant" was any unmarried migrant who did not live with his or her parents or parent. A "recent migrant," also called a "current migrant" was any independent migrant under thirty years old.

Relationships within households and marital status (when they were not recorded) were determined based on the surnames and ages of the individuals, and the order in which they were recorded. My method for identifying relationships was based on that used by Thomas Dublin in *Women at Work*, and similar to that used by Alan Armstrong regarding York in 1841.[2] Individuals who lived alone were not given a relationship, but in practice they were grouped with household heads. The first individual in a household was assumed to be the head and if the person following had the same surname, was of the opposite sex, and was aged within five years of the head, he or she was assumed to be the head's spouse. Residents who followed, if they were sixteen to fifty years younger than the head, spouse, or both and shared the same surname, were categorized as children. If they shared the same surname but were outside the appropriate age group they were categorized as "other relatives." Individuals who did not have the same surname as the head, and who followed any children in the schedule, were assumed to be boarders or lodgers. Two adult boarders with the same surname were assumed to be married, and any children who followed with the same surname were assumed to be theirs. In the 1850 United States census only, a single female with a different surname than the head, who was the last person listed in the household, was assumed to be a resident domestic servant. In all other years, the occupation category was used to identify resident domestic servants. All residents of hospitals, poorhouses, or other institutions were assumed to be inmates, unless their occupation was specifically listed as an employee of the institution.

Household types were defined by the number of unrelated boarders living in them. Families were any group with three or fewer adult boarders, including households made up of a head and up to three unrelated adults. Small boardinghouses were those with between four and seven adult boarders, and large boardinghouses were those with more than seven.[3] Boardinghouses were categorized as "single sex" if they held one or no married men. They were considered coed if they contained any single men or more than one married man. Institutions were identified when they were listed as such in the census.

Occupational categories were the most widely varied, and the most difficult to describe briefly. In the original data collection, occupations were copied verbatim from the enumerators' books. When they were entered into the database they were combined into categories based on the type of occupation. The categories most often used in the text were textile work, domestic service, other, and none, but the data was actually categorized in much finer detail. The Occupations used varied somewhat from city to city, depending on the terms common in the country (e.g., "carter" in Britain versus "teamster" in the United States) and the occupations available in the city. These hundreds of categories were then grouped into larger sections, like "craftwork" or "textiles" for manageability.

After the data were collected, numbers were entered into a computerized data base which was also used to manipulate the data. Because of the nature of the data available from the census (primarily descriptive, not numerical) the statistics in this dissertation are simple proportional analyses. Although the technique is quite simple, the mass of data collected from the census has made possible a remarkably detailed description of single women's migration into textile cities in a period when few other sources give such wide-ranging data.

Notes

Chapter 1. Transitions in the City

1. *Parliamentary Papers*, Second Report of the Commissioners for Enquiring into the Employment of Children [Trades and Manufactures], 1843 [430.], XIII. 307, 25. Lawrence Sturtevant, ed., "Grandmother's Friends: Letters of Maine Girls in the Lowell Mills 1864–1876," unpublished typescript and original letters, Special Collections, Colby College Library, Waterville, Maine. Esther Jackson, no account number, Depositors' Ledger (B.2), 1838–1856, Preston Savings Bank Records, DDP 144, Lancashire Record Office, Preston.

2. See for example Deborah Valenze, *The First Industrial Woman* (New York and Oxford: Oxford University Press, 1995), 20–22; Joanne Meyerowitz, *Women Adrift: Independent Wage Earners in Chicago, 1880–1930* (Chicago and London: University of Chicago Press, 1988); and Linda Mahood, *The Magdalenes: Prostitution in the Nineteenth Century* (London and New York: Routledge, 1990).

3. Michael Anderson, *Family Structure in Nineteenth-Century Lancashire* (Cambridge: Cambridge University Press, 1971), 40; James Jackson, Jr., and Leslie Page Moch, "Migration and the Social History of Modern Europe" in *European Migrants: Global and Local Perspectives*, eds. Dirk Hoerder and Leslie Page Moch (Boston: Northeastern University Press, 1996); 56–57; Bruce C. Daniels, "Opportunity and Urbanism: Population Growth in New England's Secondary Cities, 1790–1860," *Canadian Review of American Studies* 22, no. 2 (1991), 185; and Dudley Baines, *Migration in a Mature Economy: Emigration and Internal Migration in England and Wales, 1861–1900* (Cambridge: Cambridge University Press, 1985), 105.

4. Preston was the central focus of Michael Anderson, *Family Structure*, and was identified as one of several important Lancashire textile cities by Duncan Bythell, *The Handloom Weavers: A Study in the English Cotton Industry During the Industrial Revolution* (Cambridge: Cambridge

University Press, 1969); Patrick Joyce, *Work, Society and Politics: The Culture of the Factory in Later Victorian England* (New Brunswick, N.J.: Rutgers University Press, 1980); and Geoffrey Timmins, *The Last Shift: The Decline of Handloom Weaving in Nineteenth-century Lancashire* (Manchester and New York: Manchester University Press, 1993), among others. Lowell was created to be a model in contrast to cities like Preston, as described in Thomas Bender, *Toward an Urban Vision: Ideas and Institutions in Nineteenth-Century America* (Lexington: University Press of Kentucky, 1975); and John F. Kasson, *Civilizing the Machine: Technology and Republican Values in America 1776–1900* (New York: Grossman Publishers, 1976). Its creation and development have been the subject of many histories, including Thomas Dublin, *Women at Work: The Transformation of Work and Community in Lowell, Massachusetts, 1826–1860* (New York: Columbia University Press, 1979); and Arthur L. Eno Jr., ed. *Cotton Was King: A History of Lowell, Massachusetts* (Somersworth, NH: New Hampshire Publishing, 1976). Paisley, though less well studied than the other two cities, was singled out by W. W. Knox, *Hanging by a Thread: The Scottish Cotton Industry, c. 1850–1914* (Preston: Carnegie Publishing, 1995) as the center of the most successful sector of Scotland's textile industry in the nineteenth century.

5. Moch, *Moving Europeans*, 132–136. Moch's description was based on Michel Raman, "Mésure de la croissance d'un centre textile: Roubaix de 1789 à 1913," *Revue d'histoire économique et sociale* 51 (1974): 470–501; and George Alter, *Family and the Female Life Course: The Women of Verviers, Belgium, 1849–1880* (Madison: University of Wisconsin Press, 1988).

6. For example, Peter Laslett and Richard Wall, eds., *Household and Family in Past Time* (Cambridge: Cambridge University Press, 1972), Louise Tilly and Joan W. Scott, *Women, Work, and Family* (New York: Holt, Rinehart and Winston, 1978); and Tamara K. Hareven, *Family Time and Industrial Time: The Relationship between the Family and Work in a New England Industrial Community* (Cambridge and New York: Cambridge University Press, 1982); as well as Anderson, *Family Structure*. For critiques of this approach as it concerns single women, see George Alter, *Female Life Course*, 9–13 and Thomas Dublin, *Transforming Women's Work: New England Lives in the Industrial Revolution* (Ithaca and London: Cornell University Press, 1994), Introduction.

7. This model was presented in Tilly and Scott, *Women, Work, and Family*, 106–111; and more recently repeated in Jane Rendall, *Women in an Industrializing Society: England 1750–1880* (London: Basil Blackwell, 1990), 96; and Bridget Hill, "Rural-Urban Migration of Women and their Employment in Towns," *Rural History* 5, no. 2 (1994), 188.

8. Moch, *Moving Europeans*, 136.

9. The best general definition was provided by Everett S. Lee in 1966: A "permanent or semi-permanent change of residence. No restriction is

placed upon the distance of the move or upon the voluntary or involuntary nature of the act, and no distinction is made between external and internal migration." "A Theory of Migration," *Demography* 3, no. 1 (1966): 49.

10. Anderson, *Family Structure*, 39, identified "single men and women in their late teens and early twenties" as some of the most frequent migrants in Lancashire. Dudley Baines, *Mature Economy*, 105, used an upper limit of twenty-five years to identify recent unmarried migrants in England and Wales. Thomas Dublin, *Women at Work*, 31, found that 95 percent of the female migrants to Lowell in the 1830s were under thirty years old when they first migrated. George Alter, *Female Life Course*, 86–88, found single women between the ages of 20 and 34 to be the most likely to migrate independently.

11. In reality, migration did not necessarily end either with marriage or reaching age thirty. However, the census samples returned very few independent migrants in the twenty-seven to twenty-nine-year-old range of the current migrant cohort, and for the sake of practicality unmarried migrants aged thirty or older were assumed to have found permanent settlements in their destination cities and to be unlikely to migrate in the future.

12. Individual migrants might actually move many times in the course of years, completing a move from country to city in a series of short moves. Such steps are obscured by the place-of-birth data available in the census. The most recent destination of the migrants who appear in this study was Preston, Lowell, or Paisley, but they had not necessarily come in a single step from their birthplaces to the city. See C. W. J. Withers and Alexandra J. Watson, "Stepwise Migration and Highland Migration to Glasgow, 1852–1989," *Journal of Historical Geography* 17, no. 1 (1991): 35–55.

13. Nancy L. Green, "The Comparative Method and Poststructural Structuralism—New Perspectives for Migration Studies," *Journal of American Ethnic History* 13, no. 4 (1994), 3. See also James E Cronin, "Neither Exceptional nor Peculiar: Towards the Comparative Study of Labor in Advanced Society," *International Review of Social History* 38 (1993), 59; Raymond Grew, "The Case for Comparing Histories," *American Historical Review* 85, no. 4 (1980), 768.

14. William H. Sewell, "Marc Bloch and the Logic of Comparative History," *History and Theory* 6, no. 2 (1967), 210.

15. George M. Fredrickson, "From Exceptionalism to Variability: Recent Developments in Cross-National Comparative History," *Journal of American History* 82, no. 2 (1995), 604.

16. Marc Bloch, "Toward a Comparative History of European Societies," in *Land and Work in Medieval Europe: Selected Papers by Marc Bloch*, trans. J. E. Anderson (New York: Harper and Row, 1967), 47. Recent scholarly commentary on Bloch has not addressed the question of "hypothesis based on analogy," either in support or critique of it.

17. Christopher A. Whatley, "Women and the Economic Transformation of Scotland c. 1740–1830," *Scottish Economic and Social History* 14 (1994), 19.

18.   Population of Preston, Lowell and Paisley, 1850/51 and 1880/81

	Preston	Lowell	Paisley
1850/1851	69,542	33,383	48,240
1880/81	96,537	59,475	55,638
Percent increase	28%	44%	14%

Parliamentary Papers, Census of Great Britain, 1851, Population Tables II. [vol. LXXXVIII (c. 1691.II), sess. 1852–1853], 664, 1041; Census of England and Wales, 1891, Preliminary Report [vol. XCIV (c. 6422), sess. 1890–1891], 30; Census of Scotland, 1891, Tables of the Number of the Population [vol. XCIV (c. 6390), sess. 1890–1891, 232; *The Seventh Census of the United States: 1850* (1853; reprinted New York: Norman Ross, 1990); *The Tenth Census of the United States: 1880*, vol. 1 (1883; reprinted New York: Norman Ross, 1990).

19. Lowell created in contrast to Manchester, Kasson, *Civilizing the Machine*, 61. Regarding Lowell's rapid industrialization, Bender, *Toward an Urban Vision*, 31–32, 43–44.

20. David Hunt, *A History of Preston* (Preston: Carnegie Publishing, 1992), 145–158; Dublin, *Women at Work*, 19–22; Knox, *Hanging By a Thread*, 27–34.

21. The best work on the Potato Famine in Scotland is T. M. Devine, *The Great Highland Famine: Hunger, Emigration and the Scottish Highlands in the Nineteenth Century* (Edinburgh: John Donald Publishers, 1988). For Ireland, see (among many others) Cormac O'Grada, *The Great Irish Famine* (Basingstoke, Hampshire: Macmillan, 1989).

22. W. J. Lowe, *The Irish in Mid-Victorian Lancashire: The Shaping of a Working Class Community* (New York: Peter Lang, 1989); Lynn Hollen Lees, *Exiles of Erin: Irish Migrants in Victorian London* (Ithaca: Cornell University Press, 1979).

23. Hasia Diner, *Erin's Daughters in America: Irish Immigrant Women in the Nineteenth Century* (Baltimore and London: Johns Hopkins University Press, 1983), especially chapter 4. On native-born American women's distaste for domestic service, see David M. Katzman, *Seven Days a Week: Women and Domestic Service in Industrializing America* (New York: Oxford University Press, 1978), especially chapter 1.

24. For Lowell, see Paul McGouldrick, *New England Textiles in the Nineteenth Century: Profits and Investment* (Cambridge, Mass.: Harvard University Press, 1968), 180. For Lancashire, see W. O. Henderson, *The Lancashire Cotton Famine: 1861–65* (New York: Augustus M. Kelly, 1969). For Scotland, see Knox, *Hanging by a Thread*, 20, 35–36 and Henderson, *Cotton Famine*, chapter VI.

25. E. L. Ravenstein, *The Laws of Migration*, 1885, Reprint ed. (New York: Arno Press, 1976).

26. Oscar Handlin, *Boston's Immigrants: A Study in Acculturation*, rev. ed. (New York: Atheneum, 1972), ix.

27. A few migration historians have done the same regarding international migration. See Nancy Green, *Ready-To-Wear and Ready-To-Work: A Century of Industry and Immigration in Paris and New York* (Durham: Duke University Press, 1997); Christiane Harzig, ed., *Peasant Maids—City Women: From the European Countryside to Urban America* (Ithaca and London: Cornell University Press, 1997); Kathie Friedman-Kasaba's *Memories of Migration: Gender, Ethnicity, and Work in the Lives of Jewish and Italian Women in New York, 1870–1924* (Albany: SUNY Press, 1996).

28. How this process affected women is described historically by, among others, Louise Tilly and Joan W. Scott, *Women, Work, and Family* (New York: Holt Rinehart and Winston, 1978); and Thomas Dublin, *Transforming Women's Work: New England Lives in the Industrial Revolution* (Ithaca and London: Cornell University Press, 1994). I found the change women experienced most effectively described, however, in Ester Boserup's study of modern women in industrializing nations, *Women's Role in Economic Development* (New York: St. Martin's Press, 1970).

29. "Class" is a familiar, if amorphous, term for nineteenth-century British historians. It is more problematic in "classless" New England, where young rural women were usually literate and quite affluent relative to most women in Great Britain. I have found class most useful in terms of "respectability," where it is bound up with gender, and how perceptions of their position in society affected migrants' choices, rather than in extended comparisons of the migrants' economic status.

30. Many of the migrants to Paisley were in fact able to read, thanks to an emphasis on primary education by the Scottish Kirk, but relatively few could write.

31. Dublin, *Women at Work*, 200–202.

32. Highlanders living in the bleachworks' womanhouses were reported to gang together against other groups, especially Irish workers but also against Lowland Scots. *Parliamentary Papers* "First Report from the Select Committee on Bleaching and Dyeing Works; Together with the Minutes of

Evidence" 1857 (151 Sess. II), vol. XI, 169; Second Report of the Commissioners for Enquiring into the Employment of Children [Trades and Manufactures], 26. For bleachers and labor agitation, *Glasgow Saturday Post and Paisley and Renfrewshire Reformer*, "Operative Bleachers' and Scourers' Short-Time Movement," 17 September 1853.

Participation in organized protest is certainly not the only way labor dissatisfaction could be expressed, and there is evidence in Lowell after the Civil War of female operatives engaging in spontaneous sit-downs and other protest activities without formal organization (see chapter 3). The fact no such informal protests were recorded in the surviving sources in Preston and Paisley does not mean they did not occur.

33. I have thought here of "gender" as it was defined by Joan Wallach Scott, *Gender and the Politics of History* (New York: Columbia University Press, 1988), 42, as a "constitutive element of social relationships" that creates certain power relationships and expectations for behavior based on biological sex. The migrants' definition of themselves as women (or girls, a different gender category), what it meant to be a woman, and how that affected their future options are all questions of gender.

34. Again, Thomas Dublin revealed some feminist awareness in the protests at Lowell in the 1840s (*Women at Work*, 123–128), but the sources I have used never directly addressed questions of women's proper role in the community.

35. For a further discussion of "respectability," and gradations of class, see Robert Q. Gray, *The Labour Aristocracy in Victorian Edinburgh* (Oxford: Clarendon, 1976) and Trevor Fisher, "Respectability" *Modern History Review* 5:2 (1993), 17–19.

36. Joan Perkin, *Victorian Women* (New York: New York University Press, 1993), 178.

37. Barbara Littlewood and Linda Mahood, "Prostitutes, Magdalenes and Wayward Girls: Dangerous Sexualities of Working Class Women in Victorian Scotland," *Gender & History* 3, no. 2 (1991), 160–175; Joanne Meyerowitz, "Women and Migration: Autonomous Female Migrants to Chicago, 1880–1930," *Journal of Urban History* 13, no. 2 (1987), 162.

Chapter 2. Preston

1. *Preston Guardian*, 3 July 1858. Hignet actually lived in nearby Blackburn, which was also served by the *Guardian*, but there is no reason to suppose his requirements differed substantially from those of Preston employers.

2. Theresa M. McBride defined domestic servants as migrants throughout the nineteenth century, *The Domestic Revolution: The Modernisation of Household Service in England and France 1820–1920* (New York: Holmes & Meier Publishers, 1976), 34, as did Pamela Horn, *The Rise and Fall of the Victorian Servant* (New York: St. Martin's Press, 1975), 32. Louise Tilly and Joan Scott's model of daughter's participation in the family wage economy includes the migration of young women to, primarily, domestic service, *Women, Work, and Family* (New York: Holt, Rinehart and Winston, 1978), 108.

3. In contrast, historians have determined that domestic servants were likely to contribute to the prostitute population. Barbara Littlewood and Linda Mahood, "Prostitutes, Magdalenes and Wayward Girls: Dangerous Sexualities of Working Class Women in Victorian Scotland," *Gender & History* 3, no. 2 (1991), 165. Unwed mothers in Paris in the same period were frequently migrant domestic servants. Rachel G. Fuchs and Leslie Page Moch, "Pregnant, Single, and Far from Home: Migrant Women in Nineteenth-Century Paris," *American Historical Review* 95, no. 4 (1990), 1019. Nevertheless, the perception of service as an appropriate and protected occupation persisted, as described by Tilly and Scott, *Women, Work, and Family*, 108.

4. Tilly and Scott, *Women, Work, and Family*; George Alter, *Family and the Female Life Course: The Women of Verviers, Belgium, 1849–1880* (Madison: University of Wisconsin Press, 1988).

5. Unless otherwise noted, all statistics regarding Preston and its inhabitants 1851–1881 were compiled by the author from the census enumerators' books. See Appendix for methodological details.

6. See Michael Anderson, *Family Structure in Nineteenth Century Lancashire* (Cambridge: Cambridge University Press, 1971), 22–29 for a more detailed discussion of the occupational structure of Preston's inhabitants in 1851. General historical information regarding Preston from David Hunt, *A History of Preston* (Preston: Carnegie Publishing, 1992).

7. On the irregular work of married women, see Jane Rendall, *Women in an Industrializing Society: England 1750–1880* (London: Basil Blackwell, 1990), 56; Tilly and Scott, *Women, Work, and Family*, 125.

8. The remaining 7 percent were in a variety of occupations such as goldwire worker, shop proprietor, performer, artist, and educator. Regarding numbers of women in various occupations, Rendall, *Industrializing Society*, 56; for the distribution of women's occupations in industrial cities see Ivy Pinchbeck, *Women Workers and the Industrial Revolution, 1750–1850* (1930; reprint London: Frank Cass, 1977), appendix, 317–321; for Preston in particular see Anderson, *Family Structure*, 24–25.

9. Hunt, *History of Preston*, 145–146.

10. Mary B. Rose, "Introduction: The Rise of the Cotton Industry in Lancashire to 1830," in *The Lancashire Cotton Industry: A History Since 1700*, ed. Mary B. Rose, (Preston: Lancashire County Books, 1996), 24.

11. Spinners, doffers (bobbin changers), rovers, and slubbers (both preparatory processes before spinning the cotton) worked in the spinning mills. Weavers, winders (who prepared bobbinsful of yarn), and warpers (threaded warp onto looms) worked in weaving mills. Piecers tied together broken or finished threads in either type of mill. Gender division from Michael Winstanley, "The Factory Workforce," in Rose, *Lancashire Cotton*, 127. Division of occupations between spinning and weaving from enumerator's notes in enumeration district 28, Preston census, 1861.

12. J. Lowe, "An Account of the Strike in the Cotton Trade at Preston, in 1853," in *Trade Societies and Strikes*, presented at the fourth annual meeting of the National Association for the Promotion of Social Science (1860; reprinted New York: Augustus M. Kelly, 1968), 207; William Dobson, *The Story of Proud Preston; Being a Descriptive and Historical Sketch of the Borough of Preston, In Lancashire* (Preston: J. E. Dobson, 1882), 19.

13. Michael Anderson, *Family Structure*, 37–38.

14. I have followed Brinley Thomas, *Migration and Economic Growth: A Study of Great Britain and the Atlantic Economy*, 2nd ed. (Cambridge: Cambridge University Press, 1973) and Baines, *Migration in a Mature Economy: Emigration and Internal Migration in England and Wales, 1862–1900* (Cambridge: Cambridge University Press, 1985) in considering England and Wales a single unit, and Scotland a separate one, as far as internal migration is concerned. A total of six persons born on the Isle of Man were captured in the sample, and they, like the Scots were counted as immigrants.

15. Geoffrey Timmins, *The Last Shift: The Decline of Handloom Weaving in Nineteenth-Century Lancashire* (Manchester and New York: Manchester University Press, 1993), 110, 142.

16. Duncan Bythell, *The Handloom Weavers: A Study in the English Cotton Industry During the Industrial Revolution* (Cambridge: Cambridge University Press, 1969), 44, 48.

17. Arthur Redford, *Labour Migration in England: 1800–1850*, 2nd ed. (Manchester: Manchester University Press, 1964), 186.

18. Michael Anderson, "Household Structure and the Industrial Revolution; Mid-nineteenth-century Preston in Comparative Perspective," in *Household and Family in Past Time*, eds. Peter Laslett and Richard Wall (Cambridge: Cambridge University Press, 1972), 233.

19. Anderson, "Comparative Perspective," 228.

20. "Single adult population" includes all unmarried people over fifteen years, regardless of birthplace or their relationship to the head of their household.

21. E. L. Ravenstein, *The Laws of Migration*, 1885, Reprint ed. (New York: Arno Press, 1976).

22. Baines, *Mature Economy*, 235.

23. Baines found that women's internal migration could act as a substitute for emigration, but "the relationship was not strong enough to confirm our hypothesis that the possibility of finding jobs in the towns reduced female emigration from rural areas." *Mature Economy*, 166. Some young women were able to emigrate by themselves either through sponsored emigration schemes to Canada and Australia or to join family members. In a few cases educated, independent middle-class women like African explorer Mary Kingsley might travel or emigrate without family members. These were rare circumstances, however, and most young women would have found it far easier to move independently within Great Britain.

24. W. O. Henderson, *The Lancashire Cotton Famine, 1861–1865*, 2nd ed. (New York: Augustus M. Kelley, 1969), 11.

25. Hunt, *History of Preston*, 210–211; Joyce, *Work, Society and Politics*, 103–104.

26. Thomas Aspden and Joseph Dearden, *The Preston Guide* (Preston: M. Mather, 1868), 53.

27. Henderson, *Cotton Famine*, 24–25.

28. Henderson, *Cotton Famine*, 115. Preston's total population in 1851 was 69,542; in 1861 it was 82,985; and in 1871 it rose only to 85,427. By 1881 the population had grown again, to 96,537. *Parliamentary Papers*, Census of Great Britain, 1851; Census of England and Wales, 1871, Population Tables III. (LXXI.[c.872.I].1873; Census of England and Wales 1891, Preliminary Report, XCIV [c.6422]. 1890–1891. Baines does not point to the 1860s as a period of either high internal out-migration or emigration from Lancashire, although emigration from all of England's urban counties was higher in the 1860s than in the following decade. *Mature Economy*, 243. Other cities within Lancashire, such as Blackburn and Ulverston, saw considerable growth in the 1860s, and may well have absorbed migrants from Preston.

29. Thirty years was the cutoff age to determine "recent" migrants, but more than three-quarters of the sample were twenty-three years old or younger, making it even more likely that they had migrated after 1871.

30. Baines, *Mature Economy*, 240.

31. Henderson contended that the lean 1860s resulted in a sleeker, more efficient Lancashire cotton industry which was able to compete successfully in subsequent decades. *Cotton Famine*, 26.

32. Alun Howkins, *Reshaping Rural England: A Social History, 1850–1925* (London: HarperCollins Academic, 1991), 138–141.

33. Baines, *Mature Economy*, 221. On the effect of the railway on migration prior to 1850, Redford, *Labour Migration*, 190.

34. Horn, *Victorian Servant*, 23–24.

35. Redford noted, but did not explain, a "large special migration from London" into Lancashire throughout the first half of the century. *Labour Migration*, 183.

36. Baines's "Urban 1" counties included: London and Middlesex (grouped as one unit and described as "London"), Lancashire, Warwickshire, and Staffordshire. "Urban 2" (defined as "urban with significant rural parts") included Yorkshire, Durham, Northumberland, Cheshire, Nottinghamshire, Gloucestershire, Leicestershire, Essex, Kent, Surrey, Hampshire, Sussex, and industrial Wales (Glamorgan and Monmouth). All other counties of England and Wales were designated "rural." Baines, *Mature Economy*, 144. In practice, Preston's census enumerators were erratic in recording county of birth within Wales. When the county was not specified, Welsh migrants were designated as rural.

37. This pattern was consistent with Redford's description of internal migration in the first half of the century.

38. Baines, *Mature Economy*, 235.

39. Vivien Brodsky Elliott found similar young migrant women in early-seventeenth-century London were frequently higher-status girls who lived with relatives after one or both parents died until a suitable marriage could be found. The same is a likely scenario for these young women, whose average was just 17.5 years. "Single Women in the London Marriage Market: Age, Status and Mobility, 1598–1619," in R. B. Outhwaite, ed., *Marriage and Society: Studies in the Social History of Marriage* (New York: St. Martin's Press, 1982): 81–100.

40. Nonresident service, such as laundry work and charring, was included in "other" occupations.

41. Anderson, *Family Structure*, 118.

42. Forty-four percent of all the independent female migrants who lived in households headed by relatives worked in textile mills. See discussion of housing and occupation below.

43. The possibility that urban women scorned domestic service and rural women's reasons for preferring it were forwarded by McBride, *Domestic Revolution*, 48; Horn, *Victorian Servant*, 27–28; Baines, *Mature Economy*, 165.

44. See Deborah Valenze, *The First Industrial Woman* (New York and Oxford: Oxford University Press, 1995), 3, 85–86; Jane Rendall, *Women in*

an Industrializing Society: England 1750–1880 (London: Basil Blackwell, 1991), 3.

45. Preston Penny Bank Minute Book, 4 March 1859, Harris Library, Preston.

46. Linda Mahood, *The Magdalenes: Prostitution in the Nineteenth Century* (London and New York: Routledge, 1990), 120.

47. This very high percentage may very well be due to sampling error: with the general decline in Preston's migrant population in the 1860s, there were only two urban-born migrants in the 1871 sample. Nevertheless, it is significant there were so few urban-born migrants in Preston for the 1871 census, which suggests that those urban-born migrants who could afford to go elsewhere to pursue other occupations in 1871 had done so.

48. Very few women lived in houses with more than three boarders: only 3.5 percent of all the independent single women, migrants and Lancashire-born, sampled lived in such boardinghouses. Even fewer, 0.3 percent, lived in boardinghouses with more than seven boarders.

49. Anderson, "Comparative Perspective," 228.

50. Again, due to the small sample, this should be considered a tendency, not a hard and fast rule.

51. A difference this does not explain, however, is the 6.5 percent of urban/rural migrants who fell into the "inmate" category, when neither the urban nor the rural migrants returned any individuals in that group, and only 1.5 percent of the young Lancashire-born women who lived away from their parents were living in institutions. This statistic is most likely due to sampling error (only three migrants constitute that 6.5 percent), but it may be related to the greater tendency for urban/rural migrants to work in occupations other than domestic service. Without the behavioral restrictions placed on servants and removed physically from hometown support networks, these migrants may have been more likely to fall onto the care of the city, ending up in prisons, poorhouses, or hospitals. See: William Sewell, Jr., *Structure and Mobility: The Men and Women of Marseille, 1820–1870* (Cambridge: Cambridge University Press, 1985), 214–226; Louise Tilly, Joan Scott, and Miriam Cohen, "Women's Work and European Fertility Patterns," *Journal of Interdisciplinary History* 6 no. 3 (1976): 447–476 and Moch, *Moving Europeans*, 143–147.

52. Horn, *Victorian Servant*, 7; McBride, *Domestic Revolution*, 10; Valenze, *Industrial Woman*, 157.

53. Women who had never been married represented 73.3 percent of all the resident domestic servants in Preston in 1851. Married and widowed women accounted for 9.3 percent, and 17.5 percent were single, married, or widowed men. For the remainder of the period, single women made up from 71 percent to 80 percent of Preston's domestic servant population.

54. As Figure 2.9 illustrated, more than 20 percent of the independent single Lancashire-born women in Preston lived with employers, most as domestic servants. Michael Anderson found that most of the domestic servants in Preston in 1851 had been born outside Preston ("Comparative Perspective," 221), a point repeated by Pamela Horn, *Victorian Servant*, 28. It is possible that some of the women recorded as domestic servants were actually kin, even though their surnames differed from the head. Di Cooper and Moira Donald found a number of cases in Exeter, Devonshire, in which women listed as servants were actually related through the female line. "Households and 'Hidden' Kin in Early Nineteenth-century England: Four Case Studies in Suburban Exeter, 1821–1861," *Continuity and Change* 10, no. 2 (1995): 257–278.

55. Pamela Horn estimated that nearly two-thirds of all the domestic servants in England in 1871 were maids of all work, an estimate confirmed by my census analysis. She also detailed the general servants' "daily round" of duties. *Victorian Servant*, 18, 47–53.

56. There were a very few servants even younger, who were excluded from the sample.

57. McBride, *Domestic Revolution*, 72; Valenze, *Industrial Woman*, 172.

58. See note 19 above. On the average, only about 10 percent of the current migrants to Preston lived with relatives. Almost 13 percent, however, lived as boarders and worked in textile mills, showing there were definitely exceptions to the general rule.

59. Olwen Hufton, "Women, Work, and Family," in *A History of Women: Renaissance and Enlightenment Paradoxes*, eds. Natalie Zemon Davis and Arlette Farge (Cambridge, MA: Harvard University Press, 1993), 20–21; Horn, *Victorian Servant*, 37–38.

60. More than thirty years was an unusually long life for a registry; it may have profited by its location on one of the main thoroughfares into Preston from the countryside to the east. No other Preston establishment continued, according to the city directories, for more than ten years. *Oakey's Commercial Directory of Preston* (Preston: Henry Oakey, 1851); P. Mannex, *Preston and District: Being the first volume of the Directory and topography of North Lancashire* (Preston: J. Harkness, 1865); Mannex & Co., *Directory of Preston and District* (Preston: T. Snape & Co., 1877); Mannex & Co., *Directory of Preston and Fylde District* (Preston: P. Mannex & Co., 1880). *New Survey of the Town of Preston* (Preston: Henry Oakey, 1851). Also census record of 107 Church Street, Preston, 1851, 1861, 1871, 1881.

61. Geo. A. Gillett, *Commercial and General Directory of Preston* (Preston: Chas. Greenall, 1869); Mannex, *Preston and Fylde 1880*.

62. McBride, *Domestic Revolution*, 71,77; on suspicions of registries, Horn, *Victorian Servants*, 40–41.

63. McBride, *Domestic Revolution*, 113–114.

64. *Guardian*, 17 January 1857.

65. *Guardian*, 3 July 1858; 29 December 1860; 14 May 1870.

66. Emphasis added. *Guardian*, 4 May 1850.

67. *Guardian*, 7 July 1855.

68. Young men, on the other hand, could in a single month in 1855 respond to advertisements for apprenticeships to drapers, tea dealers, or chemists. There were, however, also more men seeking positions (as carding-room managers, bookkeepers, or other skilled jobs) than positions seeking men. *Guardian*, 7, 21 July, 1855.

69. *Guardian*, 7 July 1860, 1 July 1865.

70. Emphasis added. *Guardian*, 17 July 1875. Also, for example, 15 July 1865, 16 July 1870.

71. *Guardian*, 1 July 1865. There were some fears that registries purposefully overenrolled servants in order to collect fees without finding positions, or to snare the innocent country girls for more sinister purposes. Horn, *Victorian Servants*, 40–41.

72. *Guardian*, 2 July 1870.

73. *Guardian*, 3 July 1875.

74. Between 1861 and 1871 the number of domestic servants in England rose by 23.5 percent. From 1871 to 1881, the figure was only 4.7 percent. McBride, *Domestic Revolution*, 112.

75. *Guardian*, 3, 17 July 1880.

76. *Guardian*, 8 January 1876.

77. *Guardian*, 15 September 1880.

78. *Guardian*, 3 July 1880.

79. Anderson, "Comparative Perspective," 228.

80. Linen drapers were originally merchant-manufacturers who provided raw yarn to hand-loom weavers and sold the finished product. By the mid-nineteenth century, with the decline of hand-loom weaving and the putting-out system, "draper" came to refer to dealers in fabric at either the retail or wholesale level. Some drapers kept dressmakers on staff, but it was more common for women to buy fabric in one shop, and have a dress made up in another. Rose, "Rise of the Cotton Industry," in *Lancashire Cotton*, 3–5.

81. Wendy Gamber, *The Female Economy: The Millinery and Dressmaking Trades, 1860–1930* (Urbana: University of Illinois Press, 1997), 69.

82. Gamber, *Female Economy*, 68.

83. Howkins, *Rural England*, 102.

84. *Guardian*, 4 July 1857; 1 July 1865; 3 July 1880.

85. *Guardian*, 29 September 1880.

86. *Guardian*, 7 July 1860, 15 July 1865.

87. Because wages were irregularly and infrequently recorded in advertisements a structured sampling procedure was not possible. These dates represent all the advertisements that included a wage in each year; in the period 1872–1874 I found no advertisements offering specific wages.

88. Glyn Williams and John Ramsden, *Ruling Britannia: A Political History of Britain 1688–1988* (London and New York: Longman, 1990), 292–293.

89. Throughout the nineteenth century, £1 Sterling was equivalent to $5.00 in United States currency. One pound was equal to twenty shillings, and each shilling was made up of twelve pence. The figure £1 5 s. 6 d. is read, 'One Pound, five shillings six pence.'

90. McBride, *Domestic Revolution*, 62.

91. *Guardian*, 9 October 1880.

92. J. Ginswick, ed., *Labour and the Poor in England and Wales, 1849–1851*, vol. 1 (London: Frank Cass, 1983), Appendix 2. Concrete, general data about women's wages in the nineteenth century is very difficult to come by, due to the wide variability of wages from place to place and year to year. Nevertheless the specific wages reported here give at least an idea of how domestic servants' wages compared to industrial workers'.

93. Pinchbeck, *Women Workers*, 192–193.

94. James Colston, *The Domestic Servant of the Present Day* (Edinburgh: n.p., 1864), 18–19 n. In a few cases the census recorded women as both "boarders" and "domestic servants." They may have had an employment arrangement that did not include their lodging, but they were not at all the rule. The condition and quality of the food and housing provided to servants could be as variable as factory workers' wages. Throughout the period there were stories of servants abused and starved by their employers, and servants' reminiscences often included the dismal attic rooms they occupied. Nevertheless, in many cases the food and room were better than those the servant had enjoyed at home. In any case, servants did not have to spend their wages on day-to-day survival.

95. Across the whole period 74.4 percent of unmarried female textile workers (migrant, immigrant, and nonmigrant alike) under thirty years old lived with their parents or another relative. Among the Lancashire-born women in the group this percentage rose to 78.2.

96. The family wage economy contributions were emphasized by, among others, Tilly and Scott, *Women, Work, and Family*, 115; McBride, *Domestic Revolution*, 37.

97. Catherine Billington, acct. 1535; Esther Jackson, no account number; Maria Craven, no account number; Mercy Clayton, account 1629, Depositors' Ledger (B.2) 1838–1856, DDP 144, Lancashire Record Office, Preston. It is unclear when these accounts are listing a depositor's place of residence and when they list the servants' family home. Given other evidence regarding the origin of servants, odds are good that servants were migrants from rural Lancashire, if not from outside the county.

98. Elizabeth Zoë Lawson, "Working-Class Shopkeeping in Preston, 1860–1890" (Dissertation for Diploma in Local History, Preston Polytechnic, 1989), 26.

99. *Souvenir: Preston Savings Bank, 1816–1907* (Preston: C. W. Whitehead, 1907), 40.

100. When the regular bank created a Penny Savings Bank in 1859 "for the benefit of the working classes," they accepted only deposits between 1 d. and 2 s. More mill workers took advantage of this system than deposited in the regular Savings Bank. In the first year alone, nearly three times as many operatives opened accounts as had had regular accounts in 1845. Only forty-nine domestic servants, on the other hand, opened Penny Bank accounts in the first year, which implies that those who wanted to save part of their wages were depositing amounts greater than two shillings. Preston Penny Bank Minute Book, 12 February 1859, 13 January 1860.

101. Preston Penny Bank Minute Book, 4 March 1859.

102. *Preston Guardian*, 25 September 1858.

Chapter 3. Lowell

1. Mattie Weymouth, Lowell, to Emma Page, Readfield, Maine, 27 May [1866], in "Grandmother's Friends: Letters of Maine Girls in the Lowell Mills 1864–1876," ed. Lawrence Sturtevant, unpublished typescript, Special Collections, Colby College Library, Waterville, Maine, part I, 7. I have left the spelling and punctuation in this letter, and all others in this chapter, uncorrected, except where the meaning was obscured.

2. "Yankee migrant" is used here to designate women born in the New England states of Maine, New Hampshire, Vermont, Connecticut, and Rhode Island. Most Yankee migrants to Lowell came from the first three, northernmost, states.

3. The best history of women in Lowell to 1860, and the one from which I drew this synopsis, is Thomas Dublin, *Women at Work: The Transformation of Work and Community in Lowell, Massachusetts, 1826–1860*, 2nd ed. (New York: Columbia University Press, 1979). See also John F. Kason, *Civilizing the Machine: Technology and Republican Values in America, 1776–1900* (New York: Grossman, 1976). Other histories of the city's early years, which tend to focus on business and industrial developments include Arthur L. Eno, Jr., ed., *Cotton Was King: A History of Lowell, Massachusetts* (Somersworth, NH: New Hampshire Publishing, 1976) and Robert Weible, ed., *The Continuing Revolution: A History of Lowell, Massachusetts* (Lowell: Lowell Historical Society, 1991).

4. Regarding Lowell and American uncertainty about industrialization and the city, see Thomas Bender, *Toward an Urban Vision: Ideas and Institutions in Nineteenth-Century America* (Lexington: University Press of Kentucky, 1975). For a more general discussion of anxieties regarding the city, see James W. Ceaser, "The City and the Country in the American Tradition," *Journal of Political Science* 15, nos. 1–2 (1987): 21–35; John Archer, "Country and City in the American Romantic Suburb, *Journal of the Society of Architectural Historians* 42, no. 2 (1983): 139–156.

5. For labor activism in the mills, see Dublin, *Women at Work*, chapters 6 and 7.

6. Regarding the *Lowell Offering's* value as propaganda, Benita Eisler, ed., *The Lowell Offering: Writings by New England Mill Women, 1840–1845* (New York: Harper Torchbooks, Harper & Row, 1977), 34–35.

7. Eisler declared 1850 "the end of native labor in New England mills." *Offering*, 38. Dublin did not claim Yankee migration to Lowell stopped, but he saw the 1850s as the crucial transition decade between "an educated group of rural Yankee women who wanted to work for economic and social independence" and "immigrant women who had to work for their families' subsistence." *Women at Work*, 197.

8. Eisler, *Offering*, 38.

9. Dublin, *Women at Work*, 199–202.

10. In addition to individual letters from across the period, I make use here of a previously unpublished collection of nearly one hundred letters written to Emma Page, who worked in Lowell from 1866 until 1876. This collection, titled "Grandmother's Friends," includes lengthy epistles and short notes from Emma's friends, family, and business connections, and

gives a broad-ranging picture of a migrant mill girl's life and concerns in the decade after the Civil War. See note 1, above.

11. Dublin, *Women at Work*, 33–35.

12. Lydia Bixby, Nashua, to Mother, 22 May [1852?], Letters Collection, Center for Lowell History, University of Massachusetts at Lowell (hereafter CLH).

13. Eisler, *Offering*, 19.

14. Henry A. Miles, *Lowell, As It Was and As It Is*, 2nd ed., 1846, reprint (New York: Arno Press, 1972), 67.

15. John Aiken, *Labor and Wages, At Home and Abroad: In a Series of Newspaper Articles* (Lowell: D. Bixby & Co., 1849), 9.

16. Dublin, *Women at Work*, 85.

17. Aiken, *Labor and Wages*, 10.

18. Thomas Dublin, ed., *Farm to Factory: Women's Letters, 1830–1860*, 2nd ed. (New York: Columbia University Press, 1993), 11 (figure).

19. Eisler, *Offering*, 29–33.

20. Dublin, *Women at Work*, 26.

21. Brian C. Mitchell, *The Paddy Camps: The Irish of Lowell, 1821–61* (Urbana and Chicago: University of Illinois Press, 1988), 101.

22. It is a chicken-and-egg problem to determine for certain if the Irish immigrants actually pushed Yankee women out of Lowell, or if they simply filled a preexisting vacuum. Declining wages and increased pace of work preceded the arrival of large numbers of Irish immigrants, and were already persuading some Yankees to stay away from the mills (witness the end of *The Lowell Offering* in 1845 due to a loss of readership). The influx of poverty-stricken workers who did not require corporate housing during the Potato Famine, however, made it possible for Lowell's corporations to continue and intensify the cost-saving strategies on which they had already embarked. See Dublin, *Women at Work*, chapter 9, especially 160–164.

23. Women's occupations were not recorded in the 1850 census.

24. As in Preston, migrants under thirty years old were designated "recent" migrants.

25. These and all other statistics regarding Lowell's population, unless otherwise specified, are derived from a sample drawn from the enumerators' books of the Federal censuses of Lowell, 1850 to 1880, and the Massachusetts State Census of 1865. See Appendix.

26. Of 818 migrants in the 1880 sample, only 102 were independent single females under thirty.

27. Independent single men were just 16.2 percent of all the recent migrants in Lowell in 1880.

28. Bruce C. Daniels, "Opportunity and Urbanism: Population Growth in New England's Secondary Cities," *Canadian Review of American Studies* 22, no. 2 (1991), 181. Some single women did make the long journey to the West, but mostly in the later nineteenth century, when railroads had eased the rigors of the journey. Susan A. Hallgarth, "Women Settlers on the Frontier: Unwed, Unreluctant, Unrepentant," *Women's Studies Quarterly* 17, nos. 3–4 (1989): 23–34; Paula M. Bauman, "Single Women Homesteaders in Wyoming, 1880–1930," *Annals of Wyoming* 58, no. 1 (1986): 39–53.

29. Women's occupations were not recorded in the 1850 census. In Figure 3–4 "Yankee migrants" includes only current, independent female migrants. "Mass born" and "Immigrants" include all single women under thirty years old.

30. David M. Katzman, *Seven Days a Week: Women and Domestic Service in Industrializing America* (New York: Oxford University Press, 1978), 240.

31. Unlike migrants to Preston and Paisley, nearly all migrants to Lowell lived in houses headed by people with different surnames, regardless of their occupation, showing that they were most likely independent migrants, but their relationship to the head of the household was not recorded until 1880. It is therefore very difficult to distinguish between relatives with different surnames, a family which took in a few boarders, and domestic servants whose occupations were not specified. For this reason, migrants' housing in Lowell is analyzed here by the type of household in which they lived rather than their relationship to the head of the household.

32. Paul McGouldrick, *New England Textiles in the Nineteenth Century: Profits and Investment* (Cambridge, Mass: Harvard University Press, 1968), 66.

33. Between 1850 and 1880 from 6 to 23 percent of independent female Massachusetts natives lived with same-surname relatives, and from 4 to 13 percent of immigrants did so. Only 2 to 3.5 percent of Yankee migrants lived with same-name relatives until 1870, but in 1880 the proportion leapt to almost 12 percent. At least some of this gain is due to the appearance for the first time of a "relationship to head" category in the U.S. census, resulting in more accurate tabulation.

34. Large and small boardinghouses in Preston housed 6.3 percent of the city's independent single women 1851–1881; just 6.3 percent of those

residents were English or Welsh internal migrants, reflecting about half their density in the independent single female population.

35. Dublin, *Women at Work*, 27–28.

36. James Jordan, Belfast, Maine, to O. H. Moulder, Hamilton Corporation, Lowell, 18 July 1865, "Letters re: Labor Recruitment, 1865" (hereafter "Labor Recruitment"), vol. 717, Hamilton Manufacturing Company Collection (hereafter Hamilton Collection), Baker Library, Harvard Business School (BHC). Correspondents in the Sturtevant "Grandmother's Friends" collection came from, among other towns in Maine, Swanville (near Searsport), North Belfast, Waterville, Somerville, and Gardiner (all within 20 miles of Augusta).

37. "Grandmother's Friends," part I, 1 and 5 (map).

38. Tamara Hareven, *Family Time and Industrial Time: The Relationship Between the family and Work in a New England Industrial Community* (Cambridge & New York: Cambridge University Press, 1982), 10–15.

39. Ella Bailey, North Troy, Vermont to Page, 30 June 1868, "Grandmother's Friends," part I, 52.

40. *Plattsburg Republican*, 31 July 1847.

41. "Grandmother's Friends," contains examples of migrants encouraging friends to move to or looking for work in all three of these cities. Nellie to Emma Page, Readfield, June 1864; [Mattie Weymouth], Lowell to Page, 27 May 1866; Nell Furbush, Lawrence, Mass, to Page, 27 December [1866?].

42. Daniels, "Opportunity and Urbanism," 187; Dublin, "Rural-Urban Migrants," 630.

43. See Ella J. Bailey, North Troy, Vermont to Page, 30 June 1868, "Grandmother's Friends," part I, 52.

44. Dublin, *Women at Work*, 193.

45. The surviving records of Hamilton Corporation are the most complete of any of the Lowell corporations, but that mill is not necessarily representative. Paul F. McGouldrick analyzed the profitability of some of the Lowell mills from 1836 to 1886, and found that the Hamilton was less fiscally sound than some mills (though more profitable than others), especially the Merrimack and Lawrence Corporations. It is possible that some corporations offered more desirable employment than Hamilton, and attracted more of the also desirable native-born workers. McGouldrick, *New England Textiles*, 13–17.

46. Dublin, *Women at Work*, 78; McGouldrick, *New England Textiles*, 65–66. The boardinghouses stand out in the census schedules, with a married couple, or commonly a widowed older woman, listed first, followed by

as few as four or as many as several dozen young women, all with different surnames. Marital status was recorded in the censuses of 1865 and later. See Appendix for a full definition of the categories used in the analysis of the census.

47. Horatio Wood, *Thirteenth Report of the Minister at Large in Lowell to the Missionary Society Connected with the South Parish* (Lowell: Courier Steam Press, 1858), 22. Wood was appointed by the nondenominational, charitable "Ministry at Large" to "minister to the temporal and spiritual wants of all those not reached by any of the existing religious charities." Miles, *Lowell As It Was and Is*, 206. Wood and his successor filed annual reports regarding the state of the poor in Lowell. These reports will hereafter be cited only by number.

48. Wood, *Thirteenth Report*, 22.

49. Wood, *Twelfth Report*, 12.

50. Wood, *Fifteenth Report*, 3–4.

51. Ellen Frost, Lowell, to Charles Grover, Hampstead, New Hampshire, 14 April 1861, Letters Collection, Lowell National Historic Park (hereafter LNHP).

52. McGouldrick, *New England Textiles*, Appendix A, 219–222.

53. For these averages, only those women who were on the payroll for the entire month were included. Lawrence Manufacturing Company Payrolls, Mill 1, "Weaving Room," 14 May 1859, 12 May 1860, and May, 1862, vol. GA-18, Lawrence Manufacturing Company Collection (hereafter Lawrence Collection), BHC.

54. "The Merrimack River Group and the Lawrence Manufacturing Company (1811–1865)," Lawrence Manufacturing Company Finding Aid folder, MSS 442, 1831–1955, BHC, 16.

55. Robert G. Layer, *Earnings of Cotton Mill Operatives, 1825–1914* (Cambridge: Harvard University Press, 1955), 31.

56. Wood, *Seventeenth Report*, 9.

57. Wood did take the opportunity to rid the city of some of its surplus Irish population. More than 500 Irishmen, by his calculation, had left Lowell by the time of his 1863 report for destinations as diverse as California, Australia, and their home country. The Irishwomen thrown out of work, meanwhile, scattered to other manufacturing cities in the region, or filled positions as domestic workers in Lowell. *Eighteenth Report*, 4.

58. Wood, *Seventeenth Report*, 5.

59. The 1865 State census is the first in the series that recorded marital status, allowing an accurate count of the widows in Lowell. Among the

widows whose position in the household could be determined, 60 percent headed their own families and 55 percent reported no waged occupation. These figures suggest that many widows were indeed supported by their children's wages in a family economy.

60. J. A. Sargent, Farmsville, to O. H. Moulder, Lowell, 18 November 1866, "(Incoming Letters) October 1866–December 1866," Hamilton Collection, vol. 717a, BHC.

61. McGouldrick, *New England Textiles*, 39–41, 219–221.

62. Time and wage information from notes for reply on M. F. Forster, Cincinnati, to O. H. Moulder, Lowell, 9 February 1867, "Hamilton Manufacturing Company (Incoming Letters) January 1867–April 1867," Hamilton Collection, vol. 717a, BHC.

63. Paul McGouldrick, *New England Textiles*, 6.

64. Telegram, W. Ratchelder, Burlington, Vermont to O.H. Moulder, Lowell, 29 July 1865, "Labor Recruitment;" Draft letter, O. H. Moulder, Lowell, to Benjamin Fletcher, Canada East, 26 August 1865, Hamilton Collection, vol. 498, BHC.

65. Claire Kittredge, Readfield, Maine, to Emma Page, North Belgrade, Maine, 25 January 1866, "Grandmother's Friends," part II, 4, shows Emma was planning her move to Lowell months before she actually went. Emma's exact age is uncertain; her birthdate is given as 1848 in "Grandmother's Friends," part I, 1, but in the 1870 census her age was recorded as 21—making her sixteen or seventeen in January 1866. Mattie was twenty years old in 1870, so probably was sixteen when she first went to Lowell. *Ninth Census of the United States*, 1870, Lowell, Massachusetts, National Archives.

66. Quoted in Dublin, *Farm to Factory*, 125.

67. [Mattie Weymouth] to Emma Page, 27 May [1866], "Grandmother's Friends," part II, 7.

68. The destruction of the 1890 census makes it impossible to determine if the number of single female migrants in Lowell continued to rise after 1880.

69. Steven Dubnoff, "Gender, the Family, and the Problem of Work Motivation in a Transition to Industrial Capitalism," *Journal of Family History* 4, no. 2 (1979), 124. Mary H. Blewett, ed., *The Last Generation: Work and Life in the Textile Mills of Lowell, Massachusetts, 1910–1960* (Amherst: University of Massachusetts Press, 1990), 5.

70. On the advantages of family wage-earning in poor economic climates, see Dublin, *Women at Work*, 175–176.

71. Quoted in Dublin, *Farm to Factory*, 129.

72. Dublin, *Women at Work*, 110–111.

73. Wood, *Seventh Report*, 1; *Thirteenth Report*, 22.

74. Notes for reply on Foster to Moulder, 9 February 1867.

75. Dublin, *Women at Work*, chapters 3 and 4, esp. 125–131.

76. *The Boston Daily Evening Voice*, 15 July 1866, in *The Factory Girls*, ed. Phillip S. Foner (Urbana, Chicago and London: University of Illinois Press, 1977) 340–341. Size is a gluelike liquid that slightly shrinks and stiffens fabrics, making them easier to work with and visually more appealing.

77. In 1867 a manager at the Williston Mills in East Hampton, Massachusetts, wrote to the superintendent of Lowell's Hamilton mills regarding a recent strike by (male) mule spinners at Hamilton, "glad to know your mule spinners have *succumbed* and hope they will remember that there is plenty of help. If you are short we can send you some from this way." S. Williston, East Hampton, Mass. to O. H. Moulder, 27 April 1867, "Hamilton Manufacturing Company (Incoming Letters) January 1867–April 1867," Hamilton Collection, vol. 717a, BHC.

78. Dublin, *Women at Work*, 200.

79. Ella J. Bailey to Page, 15 April 1868; Mary W. Chick to Page, 19 October 1864, "Grandmother's Friends," part I, 44; part II, 1; *Ninth Census of the United States*, 1870, Lowell, Mass., National Archives, 39.

80. Bixby to Mother, 22 May [1852].

81. Wood, *Thirteenth Report*, 22.

82. Draft Letter, Moulder to Fletcher, 26 August 1865.

83. Telegram, W. Ratchelder, Burlington, Vermont to Moulder, Hamilton Mfg. Co., 29 July 1865; James Jordan, North Searsmont, Maine to Moulder, 19 July 1865, "Labor Recruitment." Jordan promised Searsmont locals a fee of one dollar for each girl who arrived in Lowell, to be paid from Jordan's own bounty. Supposing he would keep some profit for himself, it is probable he was receiving at least the same fee as the Vermont recruiters.

84. F. F. Rattles, Lowell, to Moulder, Lowell, August 1865, "Labor Recruitment." Dollar amount noted in Jordan to Moulder, 19 July 1865.

85. Jordan, Belfast, to Moulder, 18 July 1865, "Labor Recruitment."

86. Jordan, North Searsport, to Moulder, 19 July 1865; Jordan, Portland, to Moulder, [27] July 1865, "Labor Recruitment."

87. Jordan to Moulder, 18 July 1865.

88. H. C. Boardman, East Alburgh, [Vermont] to Moulder, 1 August 1865, "Labor Recruitment."

89. Jordan to Moulder, 18 July 1865.

90. Dublin, *Farm to Factory*, 28–29.

91. Florella E. Farnsworth, Lowell, to Mary Ann Farnsworth, Danville, May 1847, Letters Collection, CLH.

92. F. Farnsworth to M. Farnsworth, May 1847.

93. Ella Y. Hunt, North Troy, to Emma Page, Lowell, 23 August 1874, "Grandmother's Friends," part I, 74.

94. Mat, Ted, Mattie & Flora, Lowell, to Page, No. Belgrade, 9 January 1870, "Grandmother's Friends," part II, 49–51.

95. Marc Bloch, "A Contribution Toward a Comparative History of European Societies," in *Land and Work in Medieval Europe: Selected Papers by Marc Bloch*, trans. J. E. Anderson (New York: Harper and Row, 1967), 47.

96. Dublin, *Farm to Factory*, 24.

97. Dublin, *Women at Work*, 190.

98. Lawrence Manufacturing Company Payrolls, Mill 1, "Weaving Room" and "Carding," 12 May 1860, vol. GA-18, Lawrence Collection, BHC.

99. Eliza Kittredge paid her $25 rent to Hamilton Corporation on 3 July 1860, and was recorded in the census at the head of a house with 38 boarders. Rent book, 1 July 1860, vol. 508, Hamilton Collection, BHC. *Eighth Census of the United States*, Lowell (microfilm), National Archives.

100. Unknown Mill Operative, initials possibly L.B.S., to Mrs. James Fuller, 25 August 1849, Accession 613, LNHP.

101. [Augusta Worthen], *The History of Sutton, New Hampshire* (Concord, N.H: Republican Press Association, 1890), 192; quoted in Dublin, *Farm to Factory*, 34.

102. Horatio Wood, *Seventeenth Report*, 9–10.

103. Horatio Wood, *Eighteenth Report*, 4.

104. Steven Dubnoff, studying 1860 Lowell, found that Irish-born mill workers who lived in boardinghouses, instead of with their parents, "display[ed] an unambiguously calculative orientation to work," that is, they were willing to exchange increased income for leisure time, and were more dedicated to their own leisure than a family's economic welfare. "Work Motivation," 133. Tendencies toward independent economic behavior may very well be typical of all unmarried boarders, not only migrants.

105. Addie Holms, Lowell, to Lillian Abbott, 14 April 1873, Letters Collection, CLH.

106. Boardman to Moulder, 1 August 1865.

107. Jordan to Moulder, 18 July 1865.

108. Clara Morrill Norton, Readfield, to Page, 9 December 1866, "Grandmother's Friends," part I, 23.

109. Ann [Packard], Readfield, to Page, Lowell, twelve letters from 13 March 1870 to March 1872, "Grandmother's Friends," part II, 53–57, 59–63, 65–66, 69–70, 74–76, 81. "Packard" is Sturtevant's interpretation of Ann's name, as she signed herself simply Ann or Ann Pack—. Other letters in the collection do mention an Ann Packard, a former Readfield mill worker.

110. Preston Penny Bank Minute Book, 4 March 1859, Harris Library, Preston.

111. Unknown, Readfield to Page, Lowell, 28 August 1866; Cli, Readfield to Page, Lowell, 21 April 1867, "Grandmother's Friends," part I, 19; part II, 17.

112. Unknown Operative to Fuller, 25 August 1849.

113. Unknown Operative to Fuller, 25 August 1849.

114. Jordan to Moulder, 19 July 1865.

115. Weymouth, Lowell, to Page, Readfield, 27 May [1866], "Grandmother's Friends," part II, 7–8.

116. Ella J. Bailey, North Troy, Vermont, to Page, Lowell, 15 April 1868, "Grandmother's Friends," part I, 44–47.

117. Bailey to Page, 30 June 1868, "Grandmother's Friends," part I, 52–55.

118. Ella F. Sanders, Swanville, Maine, to Page and Weymouth, Lowell, 12 June 1867, "Grandmother's Friends," part II, 23–24.

119. The census sample from Preston yielded at least three performers in each census year, a number that peaked at twelve in 1881—for an estimate of roughly 150 performers in the city. On the temperance and missionary movements in Preston, see David Hunt, *A History of Preston* (Preston: Carnegie Publishing, 1992), 198–202, 205–210.

120. Dublin, *Women at Work*, 54–57.

121. For the English factory girl as archetype, see Deborah Valenze, *The First Industrial Woman* (New York and Oxford: Oxford University Press, 1995), 3, 85–86; Jane Rendall, *Women in an Industrializing Society: England 1750–1880* (London: Basil Blackwell, 1991), 3; and Preston Penny

Bank Minute Book, 4 March 1859, Harris Library, Preston. Dublin described the close-knit community of the Lowell boarding houses prior to the Civil War as fostering a "sisterhood" among the mill workers, which women entered when they migrated to Lowell and tended away from after marriage. *Women at Work*, 83, 130. Ava Baron found the same type of gender divisions within a single sex among male printers of the nineteenth century in "An 'Other' Side of Gender Antagonism at Work: Men, Boys, and the Remasculinization of Printers' Work, 1830–1920," in *Work Engendered: Toward a New History of American Labor*, ed. Ava Baron (Ithaca and London: Cornell University Press, 1991): 1–46.

122. Bailey, North Troy, to Page and Weymouth, Lowell, 8 November [1867], "Grandmother's Friends," part II, 35–39, 47–48.

123. Jordan to Moulder, [27] July 1865.

124. Jordan to Moulder, 18 July 1865.

125. Bailey, East Hill Troy, Vermont to Page, Lowell, 30 June 1868.

126. Bailey to Page, 15 April 1868.

127. Eliza A. Page, West Waterville, Maine, to Page, Lowell, 16 March 1872, "Grandmother's Friends," part I, 68.

128. Ella Y. Hunt, North Troy, to Emma Page, Lowell, 23 August 1874, "Grandmother's Friends II," 74.

129. Studying single women in Chicago at the end of the nineteenth century, Joanne Meyerowitz found a distinct subculture among "women adrift" that helped them to function successfully in the city. "Women and Migration: Autonomous Female Migrants to Chicago, 1880–1930," *Journal of Urban History* 13, no. 2 (1987): 157. Networks of migrants are most evident in the historical record when migrants lived in fairly large groups, where similarities of birthplace or surname suggest personal connections. In Preston, where many migrants lived and worked in isolation as domestic servants such networks are more difficult to perceive, but migrants may nevertheless have helped friends and relatives to find work, loaned money in times of difficulty, or simply spent free Sunday afternoons with other migrant servants.

130. Dublin, *Women at Work*, 77.

131. Dublin, *Women at Work*, 83–84.

132. "Grandmother's Friends," part I, 1.

133. Dublin, *Farm to Factory*, 29. Dublin was referring particularly to Carol Smith-Rosenberg, "The Female World of Love and Ritual: Relations between Women in Nineteenth Century America" in *Disorderly*

Conduct: Visions of Gender in Victorian America, ed. Smith-Rosenberg
(New York and Oxford: Oxford University Press, 1985).

Chapter Four. Paisley

1. *Paisley Poor Law: Statements of Cases*, vol. 11–17, 21 May 1874, case
no. 16890, Paisley Public Library. Scottish Poor (or Parish) Relief was a
local affair, with eligibility founded in the applicant's place of legal residence. A "settlement," or determination of from where an individual was entitled to relief, was endowed first by birth and secondarily by residence and
employment in one area for a specified length of time. Women, when married, took their husbands' settlement, and retained it after being widowed.
Since the funds for poor relief came from the pockets of local taxpayers, the
Poor Law Guardians were anxious to return poverty-stricken migrants to
their proper parishes of residence or, if appropriate, to claim reimburse-
ment from the pauper's home parish. In the search for a proper settlement,
the Guardians conducted extensive interviews with applicants for relief,
often recording to the month or even day the length of the person's stay in
every parish since birth. This collection of data is invaluable in helping to
describe young women's patterns of movement in more detail than the census allows. It can be suspect, however; the applicants no doubt slanted their
stories to what they thought the examiners wanted to hear and the examiners themselves filtered the information they were given through a middle-
class bias. In the absence of any corroborative evidence, rather than adding
another layer of interpretation to the problem I have taken the case histories in most records at face value. Because many of the statements consist
of little more than brief notes, insertions (enclosed in brackets) are sometimes necessary to make quotations understandable. They will hereafter be
cited as Poor Law, by volume, date, and case number.

2. Malcolm Gray, "Migration in the Rural Lowlands of Scotland,
1750–1850," in *Ireland and Scotland: 1650–1850*, eds. T. M. Devine
and David Dickson (Edinburgh: John Donald Publishers, 1983): 104–117.
See also Malcolm Gray, *Scots on the Move: Scots Migrants 1750–1914*
(Edinburgh: The Economic and Social History Society of Scotland, 1990) and
D. F. MacDonald, *Scotland's Shifting Population, 1770–1850* (Glasgow: n.p.,
1937).

3. T. M. Devine, *The Great Highland Famine: Hunger, Emigration and
the Scottish Highlands in the Nineteenth Century* (Edinburgh: John Donald
Publishers Ltd., 1988), 3. See also Eric Richards, *A History of the Highland
Clearances: Agrarian Transformation and the Evictions, 1746–1886*
(London: Croom Helm, Ltd., 1982) for a detailed discussion of the process
of Highland depopulation.

4. Thomas Tancred, who inquired into children's employment in Western Scotland for Parliament in the early 1840s, described the Highland migrants in Paisley as "strangers," more used to "rude and smoky cottages" than urban industrial life. *Parliamentary Papers*, Second Report of the Commissioners for Enquiring into the Employment of Children [Trades and Manufactures], 1843 [430.], XIII.307, 125, 130. (Cited hereafter as *P.P* Employment of Children.) Thirty years later the beneficiaries of a bazaar held to raise funds for Paisley's Gaelic chapel were identified with the romantic image of their homeland when they were lauded in Robert Burns's words as "our friends . . . from the 'land of brown heath and shaggy wood/Land of the mountain and the flood.'" *Paisley Herald and Renfrewshire Advertiser*, 25 March 1871.

5. For Lowland agricultural migration, see T. M. Devine, ed., *Farm Servants and Labour in Lowland Scotland, 1770–1914* (Edinburgh: John Donald Publishers, 1984), 6; Malcolm Gray, "Scottish Emigration: The Social Impact of Agrarian Change in the Rural Lowlands, 1775–1875," *Perspectives in American History* VIII (1973), 95–96, 153.

6. Devine, *Farm Servants*, 56–57; Gray, "Scottish Emigration," 97–98.

7. Devine, *Highland Famine*, 149–150; Withers and Watson, "Stepwise Migration," 49; Devine, *Farm Servants*, 21, 113; Gray, "Scottish Emigration," 160.

8. The other major shawl center was Norwich, England. The shawls were woven originally on hand harness looms, each requiring an adult weaver and at least one "draw boy" to create the pattern. The Jacquard loom, which replaced the draw boy with a series of punch cards, was not accepted by the Paisley shawl industry until the 1830s, and they were not uniformly powered by steam until the 1860s. Because of the demand for shawls, hand-loom weaving survived longer in Paisley than in Britain's other textile centers. Pamela Clabburn, *Shawls: In Imitation of the Indian* (Aylesbury, Buckinghamshire: Shire Publications, Ltd., 1981), 11–12, 15–18.

Even after most shawls were produced by steam, as late as 1871, more than 12 percent of all the adult men in Paisley worked as handloom weavers, a higher percentage than in any other occupational group. Nearly 20 percent of these described themselves as shawl or 'fancy' weavers. In comparison, Geoffrey Timmins estimated that hand-loom weaving employed just 2 percent of Preston's population in 1861, and handlooms were practically nonexistent there by 1871. (It is uncertain if Timmins's statistics refer to Preston's entire population, or men only. When the entire adult population of Paisley is considered, hand-loom weaving employed 7.6 percent of the population, still more than any group except the powered textile and thread mills.) Geoffrey Timmins, *The Last Shift: The Decline of*

Handloom Weaving in Nineteenth-century Lancashire (Manchester: Manchester University Press, 1993), 109.

9. W. W. Knox, *Hanging By a Thread. The Scottish Cotton Industry, c. 1850–1914* (Preston: Carnegie Publishing, 1995), 77–79.

10. S. H. Higgins, *A History of Bleaching* (London: Longmans, Green and Co., 1924), 37; *P.P.* Employment of Children, 26 Linen, which did not respond as well to chemical treatment, was bleached by the older "Irish" method on the eastern side of Scotland much longer than cotton in the west. Enid Gauldie, "Scottish Bleachworks 1718–1862" (Bachelor of Philosophy thesis, Social Science Faculty, Queen's College, University of St. Andrews, 1966).

11. All of the statistics regarding Paisley in this chapter, unless otherwise indicated, come from the samples drawn from census enumerators' books, 1851–1881.

12. Gray, *Scots on the Move*, 16–17.

13. The "Highland Line" has been traditionally bounded by the reach of the Gaelic language, used as an indicator of a dominant Highland culture. As such, it has fluctuated considerably over time. Caroline Bingham provides both a cultural and geographic definition of the Highlands in *Beyond the Highland Line: Highland History and Culture* (London: Constable, 1991), 13–16. For this study, the counties of Argyll, Bute, Inverness, Ross, Cromarty, Sutherland, and Caithness and the Orkney and Shetland Islands have been considered "Highland." These are the counties Malcolm Gray excluded from his study of Lowland migration ("Migration in the Rural Lowlands," 104). Those counties with only a few Gaelic-speaking parishes, such as Perth and Aberdeen, have been classed as "Lowland." Since they contributed relatively few migrants to Paisley, this simplification of Scotland's Highland region has little effect on the statistical outcome.

14. Over the course of the four censuses, at least one migrant (not necessarily female or independent) from each of Scotland's counties, with the exception of the Orkney Islands, was captured by the sampling process.

15. Withers and Watson estimated the average age of first migration for women from the Highlands to be in the late teens or early twenties, and for men a little older. "Stepwise Migration," 49.

16. Devine, *Highland Famine*, 156–157.

17. Devine, *Highland Famine*, 147.

18. Devine, "Temporary Migration and the Scottish Highlands in the Nineteenth Century," *Economic Historical Review* 39, no. 3 (1979), 353.

19. Devine, *Farm Servants*, 59–60.

20. James Hunter, *The Making of the Crofting Community* (Edinburgh: John Donald Publishers, 1976), 38–39.

21. Hunter, *Crofting Community*, 107.

22. Hunter, *Crofting Community*, 110.

23. Quoted in Devine, "Temporary Migration," 350.

24. On changes in agriculture after midcentury, see Devine, *Farm Servants*, 102, 106, 109–111.

25. Gray, *Scots on the Move*, 15–16.

26. McNeil moved from Oban in January, 1871, which was not the usual time of year to begin a term of domestic service (see discussion of domestic service in Paisley, below), but she moved from one house in Paisley to another in May 1871, and again in May 1872, which was the usual month for a servant to change positions. Considering the statistics of Argyllshire-born women in the census sample, it is most likely that Isabella spent her first year and a half in Paisley in service.

27. Knox, *Hanging by a Thread*, 107.

28. James Colston, *The Domestic Servant of the Present Day*, Presented to the National Association for the Promotion of Social Sciences at York (Edinburgh: n.p., 1864), 7–9, 15.

29. A person-by-person examination of the bleachfield womanhouses in the 1881 census actually revealed two female Highland migrants under thirty years old residing there. Compared to more than eighty recent Highland migrants recorded in the woman houses in the 1851 census, this shows a substantial reduction in Highlanders in the bleachworks, in addition to their overall decline in Paisley's general population.

30. The Lounsdale bleachworks closed in the 1870s, which eliminated two womanhouses with about fifty residents combined. Nevertheless, there were still a few more women living in Paisley's womanhouses in 1881 than there had been in 1851.

31. The term system was described in *The Law of Master and Servant Familiarly Explained: So Far as Applicable to Domestic and Farm Servants, etc.* (Glasgow: n.p., 1841), 8. The author specified that English servants were hired with no set term of service, only the requirement that a month's wages or a month's warning be given if either side terminated the appointment, 35. The last notice of a hiring fair I found was in the *Paisley and Renfrewshire Gazette*, 18 May 1872.

32. *Glasgow Saturday Post and Paisley and Renfrewshire Reformer*, 25 June, 1864.

33. *Saturday Post*, 11 June 1864. The same article objected to the change on more than moral grounds. The author feared that instating "a system of monthly hiring would end in nothing but time-serving, irritation, and bickering for increase of wages, with threats of quitting the service if ungratified."

34. *Master and Servant*, 19.

35. *Saturday Post*, 10 November 1860; *Gazette*, 18 May 1872.

36. Colston, *The Domestic Servant*, 18–19n.

37. In spite of the perception, domestic servants in Scotland, as in the rest of Europe and the United States, were exposed to the risk of sexual advances from their employers or other servants. Domestic and farm servants with illegitimate children to support were the most common type of single woman to appear in the Paisley Parish Poor Law records in the second half of the nineteenth century.

38. *Parliamentary Papers*, Appendix to the Second Report of the Commissioners for Enquiring into the Employment of Children [Trades and Manufactures], part II, 1843[432.]XV.I., 24. Hereafter cited as *P.P.* Appendix to Employment of Children.

39. *Law of Master and Servant*, 35. Apparently, if employers knew of illegitimate children at the time of hiring, that fact could not be used later to break the contract.

40. Rev. Norman Mcleod, D.D., specifically asked about Highland migrants, reported to a Parliamentary Select Committee in 1841 that the people of Glasgow "generally prefer the Highland females in their families, as they are better acquainted with the management of cows," in comparison to Irish immigrants. *Parliamentary Papers*, Report from the Select Committee Appointed to Inquire into the Condition of the Population of the Islands and Highlands of Scotland, and into the Practice of Affording the Proper Relief by Means of Emigration, 1841[182.]VI.1. (hereafter *P.P.* Islands and Highlands) One of the few newspaper advertisements for a servant in Paisley, however, mentioned only "one from the country preferred," not specifying what part of the country. *Gazette*, 27 October 1866. I have found little evidence to support a middle-class preference for Highlanders, except that they preferred them over Irish servants, not other Scottish migrants. For the opposite view, see Denis Docherty, "The Migration of Highlanders into Lowland Scotland 1780/1850 with Particular Reference to Paisley" (BA Thesis [Honours], University of Strathclyde, 1977), 68.

41. Forty-four percent of the recent independent female migrants in Paisley, 1851–1881, who did not work as domestic servants or in the bleachfields either had no occupation, suggesting another form of support, or worked in an occupation such as dressmaker, store clerk, teacher, or grocer that implied either financial or educational investment.

42. *P.P.* Appendix to Employment of Children, 24.

43. Bleachers' location: *Renfrewshire 12: Abbey Parish* (Ordnance Survey, 1858). Nethercraigs employed many fewer migrants than the other three bleachworks, possibly because, being connected to the thread mill, they were better able to predict demand and so had less need for a residential workforce. The thread bleachers may also have been more closely connected to kin-based employment practices that encouraged hiring non-migrants. I am indebted to Bruce Nye for suggesting the significance of Nethercraigs's close ties to Coats.

44. *P.P.* Employment of Children, 25.

45. *P.P.* Employment of Children, 25. Tancred's report, the Highland bleachers and Highland female migration to Paisley are discussed in more detail in Wendy Gordon, "Highland Daughters, Lowland Wage: The Migration of Single Highland Women to Abbey Parish, Paisley, c. 1851" (Dissertation for Postgraduate Diploma, University of Strathclyde and Central Michigan University, 1995).

46. The "cultural aversion" explanation for the dearth of Highland women in Lowland mills was put forward by R. D. Lobban, "The Migration of Highlanders into Lowland Scotland (c. 1750–1890) with Particular Reference to Greenock," (Ph.D. Thesis, University of Edinburgh, 1969), 148–149; Denis Docherty, "The Migration of Highlanders ... Paisley," 67; and Joan MacKenzie, "The Highland Community in Glasgow in the Nineteenth Century: A Study of Non-Assimilation," (Ph.D. Thesis, University of Stirling, 1987), 124–125.

47. *P.P.* Employment of Children, 26.

48. Fifteen years after Tancred's report, a Paisley surgeon listed the artificial heat in the stoves and the transition from the stoves to cold outdoor weather as two of the "four evils" faced by bleachfield workers (the other two were constant standing and overly long hours). *Parliamentary Papers*, First Report from the Select Committee on Bleaching and Dyeing Works; Together with the Minutes of Evidence, 1857(151 Sess. II) XI, 155. Cited hereafter as *P.P.* Bleach and Dye.

49. *P.P.* Appendix to Employment of Children, 28, 30–31, 32. No concerns were expressed about the workers' constant exposure to chlorine and other chemicals.

50. It would be unusual, however, for a bleacher to actually be in work for a full year, since the bleachers were subject to both very slow and very "throng" times. Nevertheless, migrants comparing the benefits would see the potential for a much higher wage in the bleachfields. Without a good estimate of Scottish servants' wages in the 1840s, this comparison is necessarily made to the servants' fees recorded in Paisley's newspapers in the 1860s.

51. On strategic payment of wages to prevent intemperance, *P.P.* Appendix to Employment of Children, 29; On overindulgence after payday, *P.P.* Appendix to Employment of Children, 32; On bleachfield company stores, *P.P.* Appendix to Employment of Children, 25–26, 29.

52. *P.P.* Bleach and Dye, 155, 169.

53. *P.P.* Employment of Children, 28.

54. Regarding living conditions in the womanhouses, see *P.P.* Appendix to Employment of Children, 25–26, 28, 29. Regarding the low rent, see *P.P.* Bleach & Dye, 169; *P.P.* Appendix to Employment of Children, 25.

55. The remainder lived with their parents or other family members (32 percent) or lodged with an unrelated family (13 percent). In each census year a few unmarried bleachers were recorded in a hospital or poorhouse.

56. Womanhouse statistics come from a person-by-person analysis, including those under fifteen years old, of the Lounsdale, Blackland Mill, Foxbar and Nethercraigs womanhouses in each of the four census years (Lounsdale was not present in 1881). The bleachworks were in the first ring of enumerators' districts outside Paisley Burgh boundaries, technically a part of the area known as Abbey Parish Landward, but practically more closely associated with Paisley than any other village or town. The place where they stood has since been swallowed up by the city. *Paisley Street Plan*, fourth ed. (Linlithgow: R.P.A. Smith, 1995).

57. *P.P.* Appendix to Employment of Children, 26. As the 1851 census statistics show, many more Irishwomen entered the bleachworks later in the 1840s, probably in response to the Famine.

58. In 1871, only 40 percent of the Highland-born womanhouse residents were under thirty, compared to 54 percent in 1861. Witnesses interviewed by Tancred maintained that 13 or 14 was the usual age for Highland women to come to the bleachfields. *P.P.* Appendix to Employment of Children, 24, 26. The 1851 census, however, reported only 7.2 percent of the bleachfield residents were younger than fifteen while 54.4 percent were between fifteen and thirty years old. Tancred's commission to examine children's employment may have led him to overemphasize the presence of a few very youthful bleachers.

59. See Appendix for definitions of these terms as they were used for the census sample.

60. In 1851, 1861, and 1871, more than 50 percent of the independent female Irish immigrants in Paisley lived as boarders or lodgers. In the 1881 census, however, there was a dramatic shift away from boarding. Just 17.4 percent of the Irish women were boarders that year, and significantly more lived either with employers or with relatives.

61. The "Renfrew-born" category does include some migrants to Paisley from elsewhere in Renfrewshire, many of whom worked as domestic servants. Most of the women in the group, however, were Paisley natives.

62. *P.P.* Employment of Children, 25, 30.

63. *P.P.* Appendix to Employment of Children, 24, 28.

64. *Saturday Post*, 17 September 1853.

65. *P.P.* Employment of Children, 25. Which is not to say domestic servants did not cause some anxiety in middle-class households. Their anxiety was not directed so much at migrants per se as at all young working-class women. Theresa McBride, *The Domestic Revolution: The Modernisation of Household Service in England and France 1820–1920* (New York: Holmes & Meier Publishers, 1976), 113–114.

66. Highland migrants in Glasgow in the 1830s reportedly sent "a great portion of their wages home to the Highlands to assist their aged parents." C. R. Baird in *P.P.* Island and Highlands.

67. Deborah Valenze, *The First Industrial Woman* (New York and Oxford: Oxford University Press, 1995), 178; Pamela Horn, *The Rise and Fall of the Victorian Servant* (New York: St. Martin's Press, 1975), 114; David M. Katzman, *Seven Days a Week: Women and Domestic Service in Industrializing America* (New York: Oxford University Press, 1978), 240.

68. *P.P.* Appendix to Employment of Children, 24.

69. *P.P.* Appendix to Employment of Children, 26.

70. *P.P.* Employment of Children, 28, Appendix to Employment of Children, 27, 25, 28. *P.P.* Bleach and Dye, 169.

71. Figure 4.13 is derived from *P.P.* Appendix to Employment of Children, passim; *P.P.* Bleach and Dye, 169.

72. *P.P.* Appendix to Employment of Children, 25, 29, 27; *P.P.* Employment of Children, 29. Tancred's survey was conducted well before there was any hint of potato blight in the British Isles. Migrants' spending habits probably changed drastically during the famine, but there is no reason to think they did not revert to buying items for themselves when the emergency was over.

73. Valenze, *Industrial Woman*, 163–165; McBride, *Domestic Revolution*, 95.

74. [Augusta Worthen], *The History of Sutton, New Hampshire* (Concord, N.H.: Republican Press Association, 1890), p. 192, quoted in Thomas Dublin, *Farm to Factory: Women's Letters, 1830–1860*, 2nd ed. (New York: Columbia University Press, 1993), 34.

75. Dunbar's story and several others in this chapter from the Paisley Sheriff's Court were reconstructed from the "Criminal Libels" published by the Procurator-Fiscal (public prosecutor) in Paisley in conjunction with a criminal trial. They include the charges against the accused, the evidence to be presented, and a list of the witnesses. The defense, however, had no voice in these records, nor were verdicts recorded, so they should not be considered indicative of guilt. Paisley Sheriff's Court, 9 February 1854, SC58/50/12, Scottish Record Office (hereafter SRO).

76. Paisley Sheriff's Court, Small Debt Court, 23 December 1852, 18 May 1854, SC58/32/16–18. Interestingly, Margot Finn found that in similar cases in English courts single women frequently played on their perceived weakness and naïveté, claiming they had been coerced into purchases by unscrupulous shopkeepers and winning the judge's sympathy. It is unclear from the Scottish cases if single women were able to argue down their debts in this way. Margot Finn, "Working-Class Women and the Contest for Consumer Control in Victorian County Courts," *Past and Present*, 161 (1998): 116–154.

77. *P.P.* Appendix to Employment of Children, 27 (emphasis added).

78. I have been unable to locate the Paisley Savings Bank records to determine if domestic servants in Paisley, like those in Preston, opened savings accounts.

79. John Cunningham, a bleacher in Barrhead, complained to Tancred about the rapidly multiplying pawnbrokers in the area, *P.P.* Appendix to Employment of Children, 29, and no fewer than five different pawnbrokers testified at Jane Lindsay's trial regarding Dunbar's stolen goods, Paisley Sheriff's Court, 9 February 1854, 5. On the pawnshop as part of the working-class economy, see Ellen Ross, "'Fierce Questions and Taunts': Married Life in Working-Class London, 1870–1914," *Feminist Studies* 8, no. 3 (1982): 575–602 and John Benson, "Working-Class Consumption, Saving, and Investment in England and Wales, 1851–1911" *Journal of Design History* 9, no. 2 (1996): 87–99.

80. Poor Law, 11–18, 25 July 1854, 7077.

81. Paisley Sheriff's Court, 23 June 1880, SC58/50/19, SRO.

82. *P.P.* Employment of Children, 29.

83. [Augusta Worthen], *The History of Sutton, New Hampshire* (Concord, N.H.: Republican Press Association, 1890), 192; quoted in Dublin, *Farm to Factory*, 34.

84. Devine, "Temporary Migration," 358; see also discussion of individual migration patterns below.

85. The question of Highland migrants' degree of assimilation into Lowland communities is an important question in Scottish migration

history. I have not addressed it directly in the body of this study for three reasons. First, because assimilation into an unfamiliar culture was not a problem for most of the migrants I have studied, assessing the independent Highland women's assimilation experience neither fit the structure nor facilitated the comparison I constructed. Second, all the evidence, statistical and qualitative, I have examined shows very little difference between the Highland migrants and their Lowland counterparts except in terms of the migration patterns themselves. The experiences of the two groups of women in terms of motivation and actions after migration were extremely similar, and I believe addressing the question of assimilation at any length would introduce an artificial element of difference. Finally, the evidence in Paisley is that there was little interest among all Highland migrants in creating an exclusive community similar to that maintained by Irish immigrants. Only about one-fifth of all the Highland women at Foxbar, for example, attended Gaelic church services (an indication of connections with the Highland community), services which were close to being discontinued in 1877 due to lack of interest. (*P.P.* Appendix to Employment of Children, 27; *Gazette*, 24 November 1877.) Since the Highland migrants were apparently willing to integrate themselves into the Lowland community, and were welcome to do so by the Lowlanders, there is little need to differentiate between the Highland and Lowland migrants in the issues of motivation and experience I am addressing here. See Gordon, "Highland Daughters, Lowland Wage," Chapter 5, for a more complete treatment of Highland women's assimilation in Paisley.

86. Devine, *Highland Famine*, 317.

87. Devine, *Highland Famine*, 158–159.

88. Census of the Island of Mull, Nov. 1847, SRO GD1/1003/158/5.

89. Poor Law 11-7, 2 August 1852, 6224. The Poor Law statement actually gives two spellings for Cameron's home: Kilmanivae in the testimony (probably a literal rendering of the pronunciation Agnes gave) and Kilmonivaig as the parish of settlement. Although the testimony claims Agnes was from Argyllshire, I could find no such parish in Argyll. Kilmonivaig is near the Lochaber district of Inverness, at the foot of the Great Glen. I was unable to trace Agnes in the 1851 census, but Cameron was a common family name in the district, which was mentioned to Tancred as one that sent many migrants to Paisley. *P.P.* Appendix to Employment of Children, 24.

90. Poor Law 11-16, 13 November 1868, 14926.

91. Joan Perkin, *Victorian Women* (New York: New York University Press, 1993), 178; George Alter, *Family and the Female Life Course: The Women of Verviers, Belgium, 1849–1880* (Madison: University of Wisconsin Press, 1988), 113–114, 139.

92. Poor Law 11-6, 4 February 1851, 4547. "Banns" were a public declaration of a couple's intent to marry, required by the Church of Scotland

to be announced and posted in church for three consecutive Sundays preceding the marriage ceremony.

93. See Rachel G. Fuchs and Leslie Page Moch, "Pregnant, Single, and Far from Home: Migrant Women in Nineteenth-Century Paris" *American Historical Review* 95:4 (1990), 1007–1031, for a detailed discussion of this phenomenon in nineteenth-century Paris.

94. T. C. Smout, "Scottish Marriage, Regular and Irregular: 1500–1940," in *Marriage and Society: Studies in the Social History of Marriage*, R. B. Outhwaite, ed. (New York: St. Martin's Press, 1982), 206.

95. *P.P.* Appendix to Employment of Children, 31; *P.P.* Employment of Children, 27. There are other explanations possible, such as that Murphy raped or otherwise took advantage of a naive new arrival from the Highlands, but there is no indication of violence or other foul play in the Poor Law report.

96. Poor Law, 11-11, 9 June 1858, 9738; 11-13, 23 November 1863, 12421; 11-17, 8 November 1871, 16113; In addition to those already cited, for just one calendar year see Poor Law 11-6, 14 January 1852, 5055; 19 January 1852, 5064; 11-7, 7 July 1852, 6202; 23 September 1852, 6292; 14 January, 1853, 6418.

97. *P.P.* Appendix to Employment of Children, 28, 34.

98. *P.P.* Appendix to Employment of Children, 35; *P.P.* Employment of Children, 30.

99. For a more detailed discussion of personal information field see: Leslie Page Moch, *Moving Europeans: Migration in Western Europe Since 1650* (Bloomington & Indianapolis: Indiana University Press, 1992), 15–16 and Thorsten Hägerstrand, "Migration and Area," *Lund Studies in Geography*, series b. 13 (1957): 27–158.

100. *P.P.* Appendix to Employment of Children, 26, 28.

101. Poor Law, 11-17, 4 September 1872, 16375.

102. The Church of Scotland encouraged teaching children to read, but few migrants had the luxury of remaining in school long enough to learn to write. *P.P.* Appendix to Employment of Children, 27, 29, 30; *P.P.* Bleach and Dye, 169. The Poor Law also irregularly recorded applicants' state of education (there was a space in the form for it, which was not always completed), and an unscientific perusal of the statements shows many more who were able to read than could write. Certainly no known letters have survived from migrants to Paisley.

103. Poor Law, 11-16, 23 February 1870, 15467.

104. Poor Law, 11-13, 23 February 1863, 12008.

105. On this statement dates were not provided for each move, but only the number of months or days spent in each location. Ruthven had been in Paisley for five days when she applied for relief, and it had been three months since she left Risk, putting her departure there on or near 18 November, within a few days of Martinmas.

106. On prior engagements, *Gazette*, 18 May, 1867. On the decline of feeing fairs, 19 May 1866, 14 November 1874.

107. *Paisley Herald and Renfrewshire Advertiser*, 20 May 1876.

108. Poor Law, 11-14, 27 April 1864, 12654.

109. *P.P.* Appendix to Employment of Children, 25, 30.

110. Poor Law, 11-14, 1 December 1865, 13452.

111. This is similar to the pattern George Alter described in Verviers, Belgium. *Female Life Course*, 83.

112. Poor Law, 11-17, 7 September 1874, 16973.

113. Poor Law, 11-11, 19 January 1860, 10382.

114. *P.P.* Appendix to Employment of Children, 26, 33, 35–36.

115. For example, Poor Law 11-7, 12 January 1854, 6855 (fever); 11-9, 26 May 1856, 8213 ("apparent consumption"); 11-9, 5 May 1857, 8573 (fever); 11-13, 23 December 1861, 11381 ("complains of pain in side"); 11-16, 29 October 1868, 14905 (consumption); 11-18, 31 August 1875, 17253 ("diseased foot").

116. For mill girls recovering their health, see Mattie Weymouth, Lowell, to Emma Page, No. Belgrade, Maine, 19 December 1869; Ella Sanders, Swanville, Maine, to Page and Weymouth, Lowell, 12 June 1867; Ella Y. Hunt, North Troy, Vermont, to Page, Lowell, 23 August 1874. "Grandmother's Friends: Letters of Maine Girls in the Lowell Mills 1864–1876," ed. Lawrence Sturtevant, unpublished typescript, Special Collections, Colby College Library, Waterville, Maine part I, 56, 74; part II, 23. For Preston's water, sanitation, and disease problems in the mid-nineteenth century, see David Hunt, *A History of Preston* (Preston: Carnegie Publishing, 1992), 166–168.

117. Bleachers' leisure hours, *P.P.* Appendix to Employment of Children, 24, 25, 28. Domestic servants' schedules, McBride, *Domestic Revolution*, 55–56; Horn, *Victorian Servant*, 50–53.

118. *P.P.* Appendix to Employment of Children, 25.

119. *Saturday Post*, 14 May 1864.

120. *Law of Master and Servant*, 55. See below for discussion of employers' responses to "immorality."

121. Poor Law, 11-9, 9 November 1857, 8817.

122. Poor Law, 11-9, 9 November 1857, 8817.

123. Poor Law, 11-14, 8 March 1865, 13093 and 13094.

124. Paisley Sheriff's Court, Small Debt Court, 15 June 1854, SRO SC 58/32/18.

125. It is possible that in some cases where the putative father denied paternity that the servant was trying to find an appropriate mate when marriage with the child's actual father was out of the question. Wealthier fathers, too, may have been more willing to pay off a pregnant servant, thus avoiding the embarrassment of being named to the Poor Law authorities.

126. Poor Law 11-9, 6 January 1857, 8429. On other servant-employer relations, see Jill Barber, "'Stolen Goods:' The Sexual Harassment of Female Servants in West Wales During the Nineteenth Century," *Rural History* 4, no. 2 (1993): 123–136.

127. *Master and Servant*, 35.

128. Poor Law, 11-13, 23 February 1863, 12008; see 11-9, 6 January 1857, 8429; 11-11, 18 November 1858, 9921 for other examples.

129. Barbara Littlewood and Linda Mahood, "Prostitutes, Magdalenes and Wayward Girls: Dangerous Sexualities of Working Class Women in Victorian Scotland," *Gender & History* 3, no. 2 (1991): 162; *Law of Master and Servant*, 35.

130. *P.P.* Appendix to Employment of Children, 28, 31.

131. Poor Law, 11-17, 7 September 1874, 16973.

132. Poor Law, 11-17, 4 August 1874, 16951.

133. *P.P.* Appendix to Employment of Children, 31.

134. Poor Law, 11-6, 28 November 1851, 4989. McPhee was apprehended in Greenock before she could return to her parents. There is no record of the case's outcome. For other migrants abandoning children, see 11-7, [March 1852], 6061; 11-7, 7 July 1852, 6202; 11-11, 28 March 1859, 10088.

135. Littlewood and Mahood, "Magdalenes, Prostitutes," 161, explored the fear of venereal disease in nineteenth-century Glasgow and its connection with the control of prostitution. There is a growing historiography of venereal disease in Europe and the United States, especially in connection with gender and the control of women. See Allan M. Brendt, *No Magic Bullet: A Social History of Venereal Disease in the United States Since 1880* (New York & Oxford: Oxford University Press, 1985); Gail Savage, "'The Wilful Communication of a Loathsome Disease:' Marital Conflict and Venereal

Disease in Victorian England," *Victorian Studies* 34, no. 1 (1990); Linda E. Merians, ed., *The Secret Malady: Venereal Disease in Eighteenth-century Britain and France* (Lexington: University Press of Kentucky, 1996); Mary Spongberg, *Feminizing Venereal Disease: The Body of the Prostitute in Nineteenth-century Medical Discourse* (New York: New York University Press, 1997).

136. Poor Law, 11-13, 7 December 1861, 11358.

137. Founded in the 1860s, the House of Refuge did not appear in earlier censuses.

138. Littlewood and Mahood, "Prostitutes, Magdalenes," 165–167.

139. Highland migrants, however, were not well represented among the inmates, corresponding to their low numbers in the population as a whole.

140. Poor Law, 11-17, 16 April 1872, 16250, emphasis in original. Linda Gordon found in late nineteenth-century (and later) Boston that victims of incest were more likely than other girls to become sexually delinquent, through promiscuity or outright prostitution. *Heroes of Their Own Lives: The Politics and History of Family Violence* (New York: Penguin Books, 1988), 240–244.

141. This estimate derived from the number of migrant women over 40 married to men born in different counties than themselves. Due to limitations of the statistics some family migrants were unavoidably included in this estimate.

142. *Gazette*, 2, 9, 23 December 1871.

143. Paisley Sheriff's Court, 14 November 1873, SC58/50/18, SRO.

Chapter Five. Comparisons

1. Only in Lowell in the 1880 census did the average age of recent migrants edge up to twenty-two years. The average for every other census in every city was between 20.7 and 21.8 years.

2. The agricultural depression was likely a greater influence on Preston than Paisley, as Scottish farmers were more likely to rely on mixed farming or pastoral husbandry, which cushioned the effect of the fall in the price of grain. Nevertheless, there was a substantial drop in the number of Lowland Scots employed in agriculture in the latter part of the century. J. D. Mackie, *A History of Scotland*, reprint of 2nd ed. (London: Penguin Books, 1991), 344–345.

3. Deborah Valenze, *The First Industrial Woman* (New York and Oxford: Oxford University Press, 1995), 98–100.

4. *Ninth Census of the United States*, Enumerator's Book (microfilm), Troy, Orleans County, Vermont, National Archives.

5. Poor Law, 11-17, 4 September 1872, 16375.

6. Hattie, Lowell, to Emma Page, No. Belgrade, Maine, 19 November 1871, Lawrence Sturtevant, ed., "Grandmother's Friends: Letters of Maine Girls in the Lowell Mills," part II, Special Collections, Miller Library, Colby College, Waterville, Maine, 68.

7. Because of Lowell's very large migrant community, this figure was arrived at by determining the number of married migrant women of the appropriate age who were married to men born in different states than themselves, rather than only men born in Massachusetts.

8. Emma Page and her older sister (also a mill girl) both married in Maine, as did several other of the correspondents. "Grandmother's Friends," part I, front matter.

9. In the 1880 census parents' place of birth was recorded, and migrants whose parents were immigrants were excluded from the "married migrant" sample for that year.

10. In Preston and Paisley the ratio averaged 1.4 single women per unmarried man, and from 85 to 90 per cent of the single men were native born.

11. Alun Howkins, *Reshaping Rural England: A Social History* (London: HarperCollins Academic, 1991), 96–97; Malcolm Gray, "Scottish Emigration: The Social Impact of Agrarian Change in the Rural Lowlands, 1775–1875," *Perspectives in American History* VII (1973): 132–133.

12. Good health was usually equated with weight gain: Mattie Weymouth wrote to Emma Page after Mattie's return to Lowell, "all I heard that evening was ['']how fat you are[!']" Other correspondents related to Emma that they were "getting along nicely. Have gained five pounds since I came to Maine," or "O! you would hardly know me I am so *fat* I don't do anything but *eat* so you may know I am *fat*." Weymouth, Lowell, to Page, No. Belgrade, 19 December 1869; Ella Sanders, Swanville, Maine, to Page and Weymouth, Lowell, 12 June 1867; Ella Y. Hunt, North Troy, to Page, Lowell, 23 August 1874. "Grandmother's Friends," part I, 56, 74; part II, 23. The countryside was also believed to be healthier for women than the city: Linda J. Borish, "Farm Females, Fitness, and the Ideology of Physical Health in Antebellum New England," *Agricultural History* 64, no. 3 (1990): 17–30.

13. Hulda Farnsworth, Lowell, to Abagail Farnsworth, Danville, Vermont, 6 August [1848], Letters Collection, CLH.

14. Aside from the complaints voiced Parliamentary inquiries in response to direct questions (one of the subheadings of Tancred's report to Parliament was "Moral Condition" [*Parliamentary Papers*, Second Report of the Commissioners for Enquiring into the Employment of Children (Trades and Manufactures), 1843 [430.] XIII.307, 30]), I found no public comments from the citizens of Paisley complaining about moral danger from the womanhouses.

15. Thomas Bender, *Toward an Urban Vision: Ideas and Institutions in Nineteenth-Century America* (Lexington: University Press of Kentucky, 1975), 35.

Appendix

1. Michael Anderson, *Family Structure in Nineteenth Century Lancashire* (Cambridge: Cambridge University Press, 1971).

2. Thomas Dublin, *Women at Work: The Transformation of Work and Community in Lowell, Massachusetts, 1826–1860* (New York: Columbia University Press, 1979), 233–234; Alan Armstrong, *Stability and Change in an English County Town: A Social Study of York 1801–51* (Cambridge: Cambridge University Press, 1974), 246, n.7.

3. Armstrong considered three or more lodgers to be a "larger group of lodgers" (*Stability and Change*, 181). Most English families that took in boarders or lodgers kept three or fewer (Lenore Davidoff, "The Separation of Home and Work? Landladies and Lodgers in Nineteenth- and Twentieth-century England," in *Fit Work for Women*, ed. Sandra Burman [New York: St. Martin's Press, 1979], 86), and houses with more were more likely to be recorded as lodging houses. Mark Peel ("On the Margins: Lodgers and Boarders in Boston, 1860–1900," *Journal of American History* 74, no. 4 [1986]) defined five or more tenants as a "larger boardinghouse." John Modell and Tamara K. Hareven, "Urbanization and the Malleable Household: An Examination of Boarding and Lodging in American Families" in *Family and Kin in Urban Communities, 1700–1930*, ed. Tamara K. Hareven (New York: New Viewpoints, 1977), distinguished between boarders in families and in boardinghouses, but did not define the two groups. I divided the boardinghouses into small and large based on an estimate of how many lodgers could be accommodated in a house or apartment built to hold a single family ("small") and how many would require a building constructed as a large house or boardinghouse ("large"). The divisions are necessarily arbitrary. See the works cited for some of the difficulties involved in analyzing boarders and lodgers, one of which is distinguishing between the two. For this project they were considered (somewhat inaccurately) as a single group (see Modell and Hareven, 183, n.1).

Bibliography

Primary Sources

Archival

PRESTON

Harris Library, Preston Preston
    Penny Bank Minute Book

Lancashire Record Office, Preston
    Preston Savings Bank Records, DDP 144.

LOWELL

Baker Library, Harvard Graduate School of Business, Boston, Mass.
    Hamilton Manufacturing Company Records, 1860–1887.
    Payrolls, correspondence.
    Lawrence Manufacturing Company Records, 1860–1900.
    Payrolls, correspondence.
    "The Merrimack River Group and the Lawrence Manufacturing
    Company (1811–1865)."

Center for Lowell History, University of Massachusetts, Lowell
    Statistics on the Nativity of Mill Workers

Lowell National Historic Park
    Eliza Smith Collection
    Letters Collection.

Miller Library Special Collections, Colby College, Waterville, Maine.
    "Grandmother's Friends: Letters of Maine Girls in the Lowell Mills
    1864–1876," parts I and II. Lawrence Sturtevant, ed.

PAISLEY

General Register Office, Edinburgh
    Paisley Sheriff's Court Records SC58/50
    Small Debt Court.
    Criminal Cases.

Paisley Public Library
    Paisley Parish Poor Law, Statements of Cases. Vols. 11-6–11-18

Published

CENSUS ENUMERATORS' BOOKS (MICROFILM)

Census of Great Britain, 1851. Preston, Lancashire and Paisley, Renfrewshire Genealogical Society of the Church of Jesus Christ of Latter Day Saints, Salt Lake City, Utah. Originals held by Public Record Office, London.

Census of England and Wales, 1861, 1871, and 1881. Preston, Lancashire. Genealogical Society of the Church of Jesus Christ of Latter Day Saints, Salt Lake City, Utah. Originals held by Public Record Office, London.

Census of Scotland, 1861, 1871, and 1881. Paisley, Renfrewshire. Genealogical Society of the Church of Jesus Christ of Latter Day Saints, Salt Lake City, Utah. Originals held by Scottish Record Office, Edinburgh.

Seventh, Eighth, Ninth, and *Tenth Census of the United States,* Lowell, Mass. National Archives.

Ninth Census of the United States, Troy, Vermont. National Archives.

Massachusetts State Census, 1865, Lowell, Mass. Massachusetts State Archives.

CITY DIRECTORIES

Oakey's Commercial Directory of Preston. Preston: Henry Oakey, 1851.

Mannex, P. *Preston and District: Being the First Volume of the Directory and Topography of North Lancashire.* Preston: J. Harkness, 1865.

Geo. A. Gillett. *Commercial and General Directory of Preston.* Preston: Chas. Greenall, 1869.

Mannex & Co. *Directory of Preston and District.* Preston: T. Snape & Co., 1877.

Mannex & Co. *Directory of Preston and Fylde District*. Preston: P. Mannex & Co., 1880.

NEWSPAPERS

Glasgow Saturday Post and Paisley and Renfrewshire Reformer. September 1853–June 1864.

Paisley and Renfrewshire Gazette. May 1867–December 1881.

Paisley Herald and Renfrewshire Advertiser. July 1853–June 1855; and September 1865–October 1878.

Plattsburgh Republican. 31 July 1847.

Preston Guardian. July 1855–July 1880.

PARLIAMENTARY PAPERS

Report from the Select Committee Appointed to Inquire into the Condition of the Population of the Islands and Highlands of Scotland, and into the Practice of Affording the Proper Relief by Means of Emigration. 1841(182.)VI.1.

Second Report from the Select Committee Appointed to Inquire into the Condition of the Population of the Islands and Highlands of Scotland. 1841(333.)VI.229.

Second Report of the Commissioners for Enquiring into the Employment of Children [Trades and Manufactures]. 1843[430.]XIII.307.

Appendix to the Second Report of the Commissioners for Enquiring into the Employment of Children, West of Scotland, Part II. 1843[432.]XV.1.

Census of Great Britain, 1851. Population Tables II. LXXXVIII.[c.1691.II]. 1852–53.

First Report from the Select Committee on Bleaching and Dyeing Works; Together with the Minutes of Evidence. 1857(151 Sess. II) XI.

Census of Scotland, 1871. Tables of the Number of the Population. LXVIII.[c.592].1872.

Census of England and Wales, 1871. Population Tables III. LXXI.[c.872.I].1873.

Census of England and Wales 1891. Preliminary Report. XCIV.[c.6422]. 1890–91.

MAPS

Boynton, G. W. *Plan of the City of Lowell, from a Survey Ordered by the City, 1845.* Lowell: Lowell Historical Society, n.d.

Lowell, Massachusetts in 1876. Reproduced by Historic Urban Plans, Ithaca, New York, from a lithograph in the Merrimack Valley Textile Museum, North Andover, Massachusetts.

Map of Preston Published for Barrett's Directory. Preston: W. Brown, 1895.

New Survey of the Town of Preston. Preston: Henry Oakey, 1851.

Paisley Street Plan. Fourth edition. Linlithgow: R. P. A. Smith, 1995.

Renfrewshire 12: Abbey Parish. Ordnance Survey [Great Britain], 1858.

BOOKS AND PAMPHLETS

Aiken, John. *Labor and Wages, At Home and Abroad: In a series of Newspaper Articles.* Lowell: D. Bixby & Co, 1849.

Aspden, Thomas and Joseph Dearden. *The Preston Guide.* Preston: M. Mather, 1868.

Colston, James. *The Domestic Servant of the Present Day.* Edinburgh: National Association for the Promotion of Social Sciences, 1864.

The Law of Master and Servant Familiarly Explained: So Far as Applicable to Domestic and Farm Servants, etc. Glasgow: n.p. 1841.

Lowe, J. "An Account of the Strike in the Cotton Trade at Preston, in 1853," in *Trade Societies and Strikes*, presented at the fourth annual meeting of the National Association for the Promotion of Social Science. 1860. Reprint New York: Augustus M. Kelly, 1968.

Miles, Henry A. *Lowell, As It Was and As It Is.* 1845. Reprint New York: Arno Press, 1972.

The Seventh Census of the United States: 1850. 1853. Reprint, New York: Norman Ross Publishing, 1990.

Souvenir: Preston Savings Bank, 1816–1907. Preston: C. W. Whitehead, 1907.

The Tenth Census of the United States: 1880. 1883. Reprint, New York: Norman Ross Publishing, 1990.

Wood, Horatio. *Reports of the Minister at Large in Lowell to the Missionary Society Connected with the South Parish.* Bound pamphlets, two volumes. Lowell: Various Publishers, 1845–54; 1857–68.

Secondary Sources

Unpublished Theses and Dissertations

Collins, B. E. A. "Aspects of Irish Immigration into Two Scottish Towns (Dundee and Paisley) During the Mid-Nineteenth Century." M.Phil., University of Edinburgh. 1978.

Docherty, Denis. "The Migration of Highlanders into Lowland Scotland 1780/1850 with Particular Reference to Paisley." B.A. (Honors), University of Strathclyde, Glasgow. 1977.

Gaudie, Enid. "Scottish Bleachworks 1718–1862," Bachelor of Philosophy, Queen's College, University of St. Andrews. 1966.

Gordon, Wendy. "Highland Daughters, Lowland Wage: The Migration of Single Highland Women to Abbey Parish, Paisley, c. 1851." Postgraduate Diploma, University of Strathclyde and Central Michigan University. 1995.

Lawson, Elizabeth Zoë. "Working-Class Shopkeeping in Preston, 1860–1890." Dissertation for Diploma in Local History [Preston Polytechnic]. 1989.

Lobban, R. D. "The Migration of Highlanders into Lowland Scotland (c. 1750–1890) with Particular Reference to Greenock." Ph.D., University of Edinburgh. 1969.

MacKenzie, Joan. "The Highland Community in Glasgow in the Nineteenth Century: A Study of Non-Assimilation." Ph.D., University of Stirling. 1987.

Sloan, William. "Aspects of the Assimilation of Highland and Irish Migrants in Glasgow, 1830–1870. M. Phil., University of Strathclyde, Glasgow. 1987.

Spencer, Kenneth M. "A Social and Economic Geography of Preston, 1800–1865." M.A., University of Liverpool. 1968.

Articles and Chapters

Abell, Peter. "Foundations for a Qualitative Comparative Method." *International Review of Social History* 34, no. 1 (1989): 103–109.

Anderson, Margo. "The History of Women and the History of Statistics." *Journal of Women's History* 4, no. 1 (Spring 1992): 14–36.

Anderson, Michael. "Household Structure and the Industrial Revolution: Mid-nineteenth-century Preston in Comparative Perspective." In

Household and Family in Past Time, ed. Peter Laslett and Richard Wall, 215–235. Cambridge: Cambridge University Press, 1972.

Archer, John. "Country and City in the American Romantic Suburb." *Journal of the Society of Architectural Historians* 42, no. 2 (1983): 139–156.

Aya, Rod. "The Anatomy of 'Social' Revolution: Or the Comparative Method as a Confidence Game." *International Review of Social History* 37, no. 1 (1992): 91–98.

Barber, Jill. "'Stolen Goods:' The Sexual Harassment of Female Servants in West Wales During the Nineteenth Century." *Rural History* 4, no. 2 (1993): 123–136.

Bauman, Paula M. "Single Women Homesteaders in Wyoming, 1880–1930." *Annals of Wyoming* 58, no. 1 (1986): 39–53.

Beattie, Betsy. "'Going up to Lynn:' Single, Maritime-Born Women in Lynn, Massachusetts, 1879–1930." *Acadiensis* 22, no. 1: 65–86.

Beaudry, Mary C. "Public Aesthetics versus Personal Experience: Worker Health and Well-Being in 19th-Century Lowell, Massachusetts." *Historical Archaeology* 27, no. 2 (1993): 90–105.

Benson, John. "Working-Class Consumption, Saving, and Investment in England and Wales, 1851–1911." *Journal of Design History* 9, no. 2 (1996): 87–99.

Bloch, Marc. "A Contribution Toward a Comparative History of European Societies." In *Land and Work in Medieval Europe: Selected Papers by Marc Bloch*, trans. J. E. Anderson, 44–81. New York: Harper and Row, 1967.

Borish, Linda J. "Farm Females, Fitness, and the Ideology of Physical Health in Antebellum New England." *Agricultural History* 64, no. 3 (1990): 17–30.

Brettell, Caroline B. and Rita James Simon. "Immigrant Women: An Introduction." In *International Migration: The Female Experience*, ed. Caroline B. Brettell and Rita James Simon, 3–20. Totawa, N.J.: Rowman and Allanheld, 1986.

Ceaser, James W. "The City and Country in the American Tradition." *Journal of Political Science* 15, nos. 1–2 (1987): 21–35.

Chirot, Daniel. "The Social and Historical Landscape of Marc Bloch." In *Vision and Method in Historical Sociology*, ed. Theda Skocpol, 22–46. Cambridge: Cambridge University Press, 1984.

Cooper, Di and Moira Donald. "Households and 'Hidden' Kin in Early Nineteenth-century England: Four Case Studies in Suburban

Exeter, 1821–1861." *Continuity and Change* 10, no. 2 (1995): 257–278.

Cronin, James E. "Neither Exceptional nor Peculiar: Towards the Comparative Study of Labor in Advanced Society." *International Review of Social History* 38, no. 1 (1993): 59–75.

Crunden, Robert M. "Theory and Practice in Intellectual and Comparative History." *Canadian Review of American Studies* 18, no. 4 (1987): 507–510.

Conk, Margo. "Labor Statistics in the American and English Census: Making some Invidious Comparisons." *Journal of Social History* 16, no. 4 (1983): 83–102.

Daniels, Bruce C. "Opportunity and Urbanism: Population Growth in New England's Secondary Cities." *Canadian Review of American Studies* 22, no. 2 (1991): 173–193.

Devine, T. M. "Temporary Migration and the Scottish Highlands in the Nineteenth Century." *Economic Historical Review* 39, no. 3 (1979): 344–359.

Dublin, Thomas. "The Lowell Mills and the Countryside: The Social Origins of Women Factory Workers, 1830–1850." In *Essays from the Lowell Conference on Industrial History, 1980 and 1981*, ed. Robert Weible, Oliver Ford and Paul Marion, 46–76. Lowell, Mass: Lowell Conference on Industrial History, 1981.

———. "Rural-Urban Migrants in Industrial New England: The Case of Lynn, Massachusetts, in the Mid-Nineteenth Century." *Journal of American History* 73, no. 3 (1986): 623–644.

Dubnoff, Steven. "Gender, the Family, and the Problem of Work Motivation in a Transition to Industrial Capitalism." *Journal of Family History* 4, no. 2 (1979): 121–136.

Early, Frances H. "The French-Canadian Family Economy and Standard-of-Living in Lowell, Massachusetts, 1870." *Journal of Family History* 7, no. 2 (1982): 180–199.

Elliott, Vivien Brodsky. "Single Women in the London Marriage Market: Age, Status and Mobility, 1598–1619" in *Marriage and Society: Studies in the Social History of Marriage*, ed. R. B. Outhwaite. New York: St. Martin's Press, 1982: 81–100.

Finn, Margot. "Working-Class Women and the Contest for Consumer Control in Victorian County Courts." *Past and Present* 161 (1998): 116–154.

Fisher, Trevor. "Respectability" *Modern History Review* 5, no. 2 (1993): 17–19.

Fredrickson, George M. "From Exceptionalism to Variability: Recent Developments in Cross-National Comparative History." *Journal of American History* 82, no. 2 (1995): 587–604.

Fuchs, Rachel G. and Leslie Page Moch. "Pregnant, Single, and Far from Home: Migrant Women in Nineteenth-Century Paris." *American Historical Review* 95, no. 4 (1990): 1007–1031.

Gordon, Wendy. "Highland Daughters, Lowland Wage: The Migration of Single Women from the Scottish Highlands to Abbey Parish, Paisley, c. 1851," *Scottish Labour History Society Journal* 32 (1997): 23–39.

Gray, Malcolm. "Scottish Emigration: the Social Impact of Agrarian Change in the Rural Lowlands, 1775–1875." In *Perspectives in American History VII, Dislocation and Emigration: The Social Background of American Immigration*, 95–174. Cambridge: Charles Warren Center for Studies in American History, 1973.

———. "Migration in the Rural Lowlands of Scotland, 1750–1850." In *Ireland and Scotland 1600–1850: Parallels and Contrasts in Economic and Social Development*, ed. T. M. Devine and David Dickson, 104–117. Edinburgh: John Donald Publishers, 1983.

Gamber, Wendy. "A Precarious Independence: Milliners and Dressmakers in Boston, 1860–1890." *Journal of Women's History* 4, no. 1 (1992): 60–88.

Gillespie, Joanna. "Mary Briscoe Baldwin, 1811–1877, Single Woman Missionary and 'Very Much My Own Mistress.'" *Anglican and Episcopal History* 57, no. 1 (1988): 63–92.

Green, Nancy L. "The Comparative Method and Poststructural Structuralism—New Perspectives for Migration Studies." *Journal of American Ethnic History* 13, no. 4 (1994): 3–22.

Grew, Raymond. "The Case for Comparing Histories." *American Historical Review* 85, no. 4 (1980): 763–778.

Grimshaw, Patricia. "Writing About White Women in New Societies: Americans in Hawaii, Anglo-Australians in Colonial Victoria." *Australasian Journal of American Studies* 9, no. 2 (1990): 20–32.

Hägerstrand, Thorsten. "Migration and Area" *Lund Studies in Geography*, series b. 13 (1957): 27–158.

Hakim, Catherine. "Census Reports as Documentary Evidence: The Census Commentaries, 1801–1951." *Sociological Review* 28, no. 3 (1980): 551–580.

Hallgarth, Susan A. "Women Settlers on the Frontier: Unwed, Unreluctant, Unrepentant." *Women's Studies Quarterly* 17, nos. 3–4 (1989): 23–34.

Herson, John. "Irish Migration and Settlement in Victorian England: A Small-town Perspective." In *The Irish in Britain*, ed. Sheridan Gilley and Roger Swift, 84–103. Savage, Maryland: Barnes and Noble Books, 1989.

Hill, Alette Olin and Boyd H. Hill, Jr.; William H. Sewell, Jr.; and Sylvia L. Thrupp. "*AHR* Forum: Marc Bloch and Comparative History." *American Historical Review* 85, no. 4 (1980): 828–857.

Hill, Bridget. "Rural-Urban Migration of Women and Their Employment in Towns." *Rural History* 5, no. 2 (1994): 185–194.

————. "Women, Work, and the Census: A Problem for Historians of Women." *History Workshop Journal* 35 (1993): 78–94.

Horowitz, Richard P. "Architecture and Culture: The Meaning of the Lowell Boarding House." *American Quarterly* 25, no. 1 (1973): 64–82.

Johnston, Alexander. "South Africa in Comparative Context: The Awkward Squad on Parade." *South African Historical Journal* 25 (1991): 218–226.

Junke, William. "Anabaptism and Mormonism: A Study in Comparative History." *Mennonite Life* 40, no. 4 (1985): 22–25.

Kennedy, Martha H. "Nebraska's Women Photographers." *Nebraska History* 72, no. 2 (1991): 62–77.

Kocolowski, Gary P. "Alternatives to Record Linkage." *Historical Methods* 14, no. 3 (1981): 139–142.

Lamar, Howard R. "Coming into the Mainstream at Last: Comparative Approaches to the History of the American West." *Journal of the West* 35, no. 4 (1996): 3–5.

Lee, Everett S. "A Theory of Migration." *Demography* 3, no. 1 (1966): 47–57.

Leeds, Anthony. "'Women in the Migratory Process:' a Reductionist Outlook." *Anthropological Quarterly* 49, no. 1 (1976): 69–76.

Lintelman, Joy K. "'America Is the Woman's Promised Land:' Swedish Immigrant Women and American Domestic Service." *Journal of American Ethnic History* 8, no. 2: 9–23.

Littlewood, Barbara and Linda Mahood. "Prostitutes, Magdalenes and Wayward Girls: Dangerous Sexualities of Working Class Women in Victorian Scotland." *Gender & History* 3, no. 2 (1991): 160–175.

McQuillan, Kevin. "Economic Factors and Internal Migration: The Case of Nineteenth-Century England." *Social Science History* 4, no. 4 (1980): 479–499.

Meyerowitz, Joanne, "Women and Migration: Autonomous Female Migrants to Chicago, 1880–1930." *Journal of Urban History* 13, no. 2 (1987): 147–168.

MacKenzie, John M. "European Imperialism: Comparative Approaches." *European Historical Quarterly* 22, no. 3 (1992): 415–429.

McQuilton, John. "Comparative Frontiers: Australia and the United States." *Australasian Journal of American Studies* 12, no. 1 (1993): 27–46.

Modell, John. "Mobility and Industrialization: Countryside and City in Nineteenth-century Rhode Island." In *Essays from the Lowell Conference on Industrial History, 1980 and 1981*, ed. Robert Wieble, Oliver Ford, and Paul Marion, 86–109. Lowell, Mass: Lowell Conference on Industrial History, 1981.

———and Tamara K. Hareven. "Urbanization and the Malleable Household: An Examination of Boarding and Lodging in American Families." In *Family and Kin in Urban Communities, 1700–1930*, ed. Tamara K. Hareven, 164–186. New York: New Viewpoints, 1977.

Morokvasic, Mirjana. "Birds of Passage are also Women . . ." *International Migration Review* 28, no. 4 (1984): 886–907.

Peel, Mark. "On the Margins: Lodgers and Boarders in Boston, 1860–1900." *Journal of American History* 74, no. 4 (1986): 813–834.

Rankin, Charles E. "Teaching: Opportunity and Limitation for Wyoming Women." *Western Historical Quarterly* 21, no. 2 (1990): 147–170.

Ross, Ellen. " 'Fierce Questions and Taunts': Married Life in Working-Class London, 1870–1914." *Feminist Studies* 8, no. 3 (1982): 575–602.

Savage, Gail. " 'The Wilful Communication of a Loathsome Disease': Marital Conflict and Venereal Disease in Victorian England." *Victorian Studies* 34, no. 1 (1990): 35–54.

Sewell, William H. "Marc Bloch and the Logic of Comparative History" *History and Theory* 6, no. 2 (1967): 208–218.

Skocpol, Theda. "Emerging Agendas and Recurrent Strategies in Historical Sociology." In *Vision and Method in Historical Sociology*, ed. Theda Skocpol, 356–391. Cambridge: Cambridge University Press, 1984.

Sloan, William. "Religious Affiliation and the Immigrant Experience: Catholic Irish and Protestant Highlanders in Glasgow, 1830–1850." In *Irish Immigrants and Scottish Society in the Nineteenth and Twentieth Centuries: Proceedings of the Scottish Historical Studies Seminar, University of Strathclyde 1989–90*, ed. T. M. Devine. Edinburgh: John Donald Publishers, Ltd., 1991.

Smout, T. C. "Scottish Marriage, Regular and Irregular: 1500–1940." In *Marriage and Society: Studies in the Social History of Marriage*, R. B. Outhwaite, ed. New York: St. Martin's Press, 1982: 204–236.

Thernstrom, Stephan and Peter R. Knights. "Men in Motion: Some Data and Speculations about Urban Population Mobility in Nineteenth-Century America." *Journal of Interdisciplinary History* 1, no. 1 (1970): 17–47.

Tilly, Louise, Joan Scott, and Miriam Cohen. "Women's Work and European Fertility Patterns. *Journal of Interdisciplinary History* 6, no. 3 (1976): 447–476.

VandenBraembussche, A. A. "Historical Explanation and Comparative Method: Towards a Theory of the History of Society." *History and Theory* 28, no. 1 (1989): 1–24.

Walker, Robert, Mark Ellis, and Richard Barff. "Linked Migration Systems: Immigration and Internal Labor Flows in the United States." *Economic Geography* 68, no. 3 (Jul. 1992): 234–248.

Whatley, Christopher A. "Women and the Economic Transformation of Scotland c. 1740–1830." *Scottish Economic and Social History* 14 (1994): 19–40.

Wilson, Franklin D. "Aspects of Migration in an Advanced Industrial Society." *American Sociological Review* 53, no. 1 (1988): 113–126.

Withers, Charles W. J. "Kirk, Club and Culture Change: Gaelic Chapels, Highland Societies and the Urban Gaelic Subculture in Eighteenth-Century Scotland." *Social History* 10, no. 2 (1985): 171–192.

———. "Highland Migration to Dundee, Perth, and Stirling, 1753–1891." *Journal of Historical Geography* 11, no. 4 (1985): 395–418.

———. "Destitution and Migration: Labour Mobility and Relief from Famine in Highland Scotland, 1836–1850." *Journal of Historical Geography*, 14, no. 2 (1988): 128–150.

——— and Alexandra J. Watson. "Stepwise Migration and Highland Migration to Glasgow, 1852–1989." *Journal of Historical Geography* 17, no. 1 (1991): 35–55.

Books

Alter, George. *Family and the Female Life Course: The Women of Verviers, Belgium, 1849–1880*. Madison: University of Wisconsin Press, 1988.

Anderson, Michael. *Family Structure in Nineteenth-Century Lancashire*. Cambridge: Cambridge University Press, 1971.

Armstrong, Alan. *Stability and Change in an English County Town: A Social Study of York, 1801–1851*. Cambridge: Cambridge University Press, 1974.

Baines, Dudley. *Migration in a Mature Economy: Emigration and Internal Migration in England and Wales, 1861–1900*. Cambridge: Cambridge University Press, 1985.

Barron, Hal S. *Those Who Stayed Behind: Rural Society in Nineteenth-Century New England*. New York and Cambridge: Cambridge University Press, 1984.

Baron, Ava, ed. *Work Engendered: Toward a New History of American Labor*. Ithaca and London: Cornell University Press, 1991.

Bender, Thomas. *Toward an Urban Vision: Ideas and Institutions in Nineteenth-Century America*. Lexington: University Press of Kentucky, 1975.

Benmayor, Rina and Andor Skotnes. *Migration and Identity*, International Yearbook of Oral History and Life Stories, vol. 3. Oxford: Oxford University Press, 1994.

Bingham, Caroline. *Beyond the Highland Line: Highland History and Culture*. London: Constable, 1991.

Black, G. Stewart. *The Story of Paisley*. Paisley: J & J Cook, Ltd, 1948.

Blewett, Mary H., ed. *The Last Generation: Work and Life in the Textile Mills of Lowell, Massachusetts, 1910–1960*. Amherst: University of Massachusetts Press, 1990.

———, ed. *Surviving Hard Times: The Working People of Lowell*. Lowell: Lowell Museum, 1982.

Boserup, Ester. *Woman's Role in Economic Development*. New York: St. Martin's Press, 1970.

Brown, Alan A. and Egon Neuberger, eds. *Internal Migration: A Comparative Perspective*. New York: Academic Press, 1977.

Burman, Sandra, ed. *Fit Work for Women*. New York: St. Martin's Press, 1979.

Bythell, Duncan. *The Handloom Weavers: A Study in the English Cotton Industry During the Industrial Revolution*. Cambridge: Cambridge University Press, 1969.

Cadwallader, Martin. *Migration and Residential Mobility: Macro and Micro Approaches*. Madison: University of Wisconsin Press, 1992.

Clark, Sylvia. *Paisley: A History*. Edinburgh: Mainstream Publishing Company, 1988.

Coolidge, John. *Mill and Mansion: Architecture and Society in Lowell, Massachusetts, 1820–1865.* 2nd ed. Amherst: University of Massachusetts Press, 1993.

Devine, T. M. *Clanship to Crofters' War: The Social Transformation of the Scottish Highlands.* Manchester and New York: Manchester University Press, 1994.

———, ed. *Farm Servants and Labour in Lowland Scotland, 1770–1914.* Edinburgh: John Donald Publishers, Ltd., 1984.

———. *The Great Highland Famine: Hunger, Emigration and the Scottish Highlands in the Nineteenth Century,* Edinburgh: John Donald Publishers, Ltd., 1988.

Dobson, William. *The Story of Proud Preston; Being a Descriptive and Historical Sketch of the Borough of Preston, In Lancashire.* Preston: J. E. Dobson, 1882.

Dublin, Thomas, ed. *Farm to Factory: Women's Letters, 1830–1860. 2nd ed.* New York: Columbia University Press, 1993.

———. *Transforming Women's Work: New England Lives in the Industrial Revolution.* Ithaca and London: Cornell University Press, 1994.

———. *Women at Work: The Transformation of Work and Community in Lowell, Massachusetts, 1826–1860.* New York: Columbia University Press, 1979.

Dudden, Faye E. *Serving Women: Household Service in Nineteenth-Century America.* Middletown, Conn.: Wesleyan University Press, 1983.

Eisler, Benita, ed. *The Lowell Offering: Writings by New England Mill Women.* New York: Harper Torchbooks, Harper & Row, Publishers, 1977.

Eno, Arthur L, Jr., ed. *Cotton Was King: A History of Lowell, Massachusetts* Somersworth: New Hampshire Publishing, 1976.

Foner, Phillip S., ed. *The Factory Girls.* Urbana, Chicago and London: University of Illinois Press, 1977.

Friedman-Kasaba, Kathie. *Memories of Migration: Gender, Ethnicity, and Work in the Lives of Jewish and Italian Women in New York, 1870–1924.* Albany: State University of New York, 1996.

Gabaccia, Donna. *From the Other Side: Women, Gender, and Immigrant Life in the U.S., 1820–1990.* Bloomington and Indianapolis: Indiana University Press, 1994.

Gamber, Wendy. *The Female Economy: The Millinery and Dressmaking Trades, 1860–1930.* Urbana: University of Illinois Press, 1997.

Ginswick, J., ed. *Labour and the Poor in England and Wales, 1849–1851*, vol. 1, London: Frank Cass, 1983.

Gordon, Eleanor and Esther Breitenbach, eds. *Out of Bounds: Women in Scottish Society, 1800–1945*. Edinburgh: Edinburgh University Press, 1992.

———, eds. *The World is Ill Divided: Women's Work in Scotland in the Nineteenth and Early Twentieth Centuries*. Edinburgh: Edinburgh University Press, 1990.

Gordon, Linda. *Heroes of Their Own Lives: The Politics and History of Family Violence, Boston 1880–1960*. New York: Penguin Books, 1988.

Gray, Malcolm. *Scots on the Move: Scots Migrants 1750–1914*. Edinburgh: The Economic and Social History Society of Scotland, 1990.

Green, Nancy. *Ready-to-Wear and Ready-to-Work: A Century of Industry and Immigrants in Paris and New York*. Durham: Duke University Press, 1997.

Gump, James O. *The Dust Rose Like Smoke: The Subjugation of the Zulu and the Sioux*. Lincoln: University of Nebraska Press, 1994.

Handlin, Oscar. *Boston's Immigrants: A Study in Acculturation*. Revised and enlarged ed. New York: Atheneum, 1972.

———. *The Uprooted*. 2nd ed. Boston: Little, Brown, 1973.

Hareven, Tamara K. *Family Time and Industrial Time: The Relationship Between the Family and Work in a New England Industrial Community*. Cambridge and New York: Cambridge University Press, 1982.

Harzig, Christiane, ed. *Peasant Maids—City Women: From the European Countryside to Urban America*. Ithaca and London: Cornell University Press, 1997.

Henderson, W. O. *The Lancashire Cotton Famine, 1861–1865*. 2nd ed. New York: Augustus M. Kelley, 1969.

Higgins, S. H. *A History of Bleaching*. London: Longmans, Green and Co., 1924.

Hoerder, Dirk and Leslie Page Moch, eds. *European Migrants: Global and Local Perspectives*. Boston: Northeastern University Press, 1996.

Horn, Pamela. *The Rise and Fall of the Victorian Servant*. New York: St. Martin's Press, 1975.

Howkins, Alun. *Reshaping Rural England: A Social History, 1850–1925*. London: HarperCollins Academic, 1991.

Hunt, David. *A History of Preston*. Preston: Carnegie Publishing in conjunction with Preston Borough Council, 1992.

Hunter, James. *The Making of the Crofting Community*. Edinburgh: John Donald, 1976.

Jackson, John Archer. *The Irish in Britain*. Cleveland: Press of Western Reserve University, 1963.

Jones, Donald W. *Migration and Urban Unemployment in Dualistic Economic Development*. Chicago: University of Chicago, 1975.

Kasson, John F. *Civilizing the Machine: Technology and Republican Values in America 1776–1900*. New York: Grossman Publishers, 1976.

Katzman, David M. *Seven Days a Week: Women and Domestic Service in Industrializing America*. New York: Oxford University Press, 1978.

Knox, W. W. *Hanging by a Thread: The Scottish Cotton Industry, c. 1850–1914*. Lancashire: Carnegie Publishing, 1995.

Laslett, Peter and Richard Wall, eds. *Household and Family in Past Time*. Cambridge: Cambridge University Press, 1972.

Layer, Robert G. *Earnings of Cotton Mill Operatives, 1825–1914*. Cambridge: Harvard University Press, 1955.

Lowe, W. J. *The Irish in Mid-Victorian Lancashire: The Shaping of a Working Class Community*. New York: Peter Lang, 1989.

Lown, Judy. *Women and Industrialization: Gender at Work in Nineteenth-Century England*. Minneapolis: University of Minnesota Press, 1990.

Lumb, Rosemary. *Migration in the Highlands and Islands of Scotland*. Aberdeen: Institute for the Study of Sparsely Populated Areas, University of Aberdeen, 1980.

MacDonald, D. F. *Scotland's Shifting Population, 1770–1850*. Glasgow: n.p., 1937.

Mahood, Linda. *The Magdalenes: Prostitution in the Nineteenth Century*. London and New York: Routledge, 1990.

McBride, Theresa M. *The Domestic Revolution: The Modernisation of Household Service in England and France 1820–1920*. New York: Holmes & Meier Publishers, Inc., 1976.

McCarthy, Mary. *A Social Geography of Paisley*. Paisley: Committee of Management, Paisley Public Library, 1969.

McGouldrick, Paul F. *New England Textiles in the Nineteenth Century: Profits and Investment*. Cambridge, Mass.: Harvard University Press, 1968.

Meyerowitz, Joanne J. *Women Adrift: Independent Wage Earners in Chicago, 1880–1930*. Chicago and London: University of Chicago Press, 1988.

Mitchell, Brian C. *The Paddy Camps: The Irish of Lowell, 1821–61*. Urbana and Chicago: University of Illinois Press, 1988.

Moch, Leslie Page. *Moving Europeans: Migration in Western Europe Since 1650*. Bloomington and Indianapolis: Indiana University Press, 1992.

——— *Paths to the City: Regional Migration in Nineteenth-Century France*. Beverly Hills, London, and New Delhi: Sage Publications Ltd., 1983.

Montgomery, J. *The Cotton Manufacturing of the USA Compared with that of Great Britain*. Glasgow: n.p., 1840.

Parkhill, John. *The History of Paisley*. Paisley: n.p., 1857.

Perkin, Joan. *Victorian Women*. New York: New York University Press, 1993.

Pinchbeck, Ivy. *Women Workers and the Industrial Revolution: 1750–1850*. Reprint ed. London: Frank Cass, 1977.

Prude, Jonathan. *The Coming of Industrial Order: Town and Factory Life in Rural Massachusetts 1810–1860*. Cambridge and New York: Cambridge University Press, 1983.

Ragin, Charles C. *The Comparative Method: Moving Beyond Qualitative and Quantitative Strategies*. Berkeley: University of California Press, 1987.

Ravenstein, E. G. *The Laws of Migration*. 1885. Reprint New York: Arno Press, 1976.

Redford, Arthur. *Labor Migration in England*. Manchester: Manchester University Press, 1964.

Reilly, Valerie. *The Paisley Pattern: The Official Illustrated History*. Salt Lake City: Peregrine Smith Books, 1989.

Rendall, Jane. *Women in an Industrializing Society: England 1750–1880*. London: Basil Blackwell, 1990.

Richards, Eric. *A History of the Highland Clearances: Agrarian Transformation and the Evictions 1746–1886*. London: Croom Helm, Ltd., 1982.

Robinson, Harriet H. *Loom and Spindle or Life Among the Early Mill Girls, with a Sketch of "The Lowell Offering" and Some of Its Contributors*. Revised ed. with introduction by Jane Wilkins Pultz. Kailua, Hawaii: Press Pacifica, 1976.

Rock, C. H. *Paisley Shawls: A Chapter of the Industrial Revolution*. Paisley: Maisley Museum & Art Galleries, 1966.

Rose, Mary B., ed. *The Lancashire Cotton Industry: A History Since 1700*. Preston: Lancashire County Books, 1996.

Schapiro, Morton Owen. *Filling Up America: An Economic-Demographic Model of Population Growth and Distribution in the Nineteenth-Century United States*. Greenwich, Conn. and London: JAI Press, Inc., 1986.

Scott, Joan. *Gender and the Politics of History*. New York: Columbia University Press, 1988.

Sewell, William Jr. *Structure and Mobility: The Men and Women of Marseille, 1820–1870*. Cambridge: Cambridge University Press, 1985.

Skocpol, Theda. *States and Social Revolutions: A Comparative Analysis of France, Russia and China*. Cambridge: Cambridge University Press, 1979.

Spongberg, Mary. *Feminizing Venereal Disease: The Body of the Prostitute in Nineteenth-Century Medical Discourse*. New York: New York University Press, 1997.

Taylor, James. *Poverty, Migration and Settlement in the Industrial Revolution: Sojourners' Narratives*. Palo Alto, Calif.: SPSS, 1989.

Thomas, Brinley. *Migration and Economic Growth: A Study of Great Britain and the Atlantic Economy*. 2nd ed. Cambridge: Cambridge University Press, 1973.

———. *Migration and Urban Development: A Reappraisal of British and American Long Cycles*. London: Methuen & Co., Ltd., 1972.

Tilly, Louise and Joan W. Scott. *Women, Work, and Family*. New York: Holt, Rinehart and Winston, 1978.

Timmins, Geoffrey. *The Last Shift: The Decline of Handloom Weaving in Nineteenth-Century Lancashire*. Manchester and New York: Manchester University Press, 1993.

Treble, James H. *Urban Poverty in Britain 1830–1914*. New York: St. Martin's Press, 1979.

Tucker, Cynthia Grant. *Prophetic Sisterhood: Liberal Women Ministers of the Frontier, 1880–1930*. Boston: Beacon Press, 1990.

Valenze, Deborah. *The First Industrial Woman*. New York and Oxford: Oxford University Press, 1995.

Vicinus, Martha. *Independent Women: Work and Community for Single Women, 1850–1920*. Chicago: University of Chicago Press, 1985.

Ward, David. *Cities and Immigrants: A Geography of Change in Nineteenth-Century America*. New York & London: Oxford University Press, 1971.

Weible, Robert, ed. *The Continuing Revolution: A History of Lowell, Massachusetts*. Lowell: Lowell Historical Society, 1991.

Williams, Glyn and John Ramsden. *Ruling Britannia: A Political History of Britain 1688–1988*. London and New York: Longman, 1990.

Withers, C. W. J. *Highland Communities in Dundee and Perth, 1787–1891: A Study in the Social History of Migrant Highlanders*. Dundee: Abertay Historical Society, 1986.

Wrigley, E. A., ed. *Nineteenth-Century Society: Essays in the Use of Quantitative Methods for the Study of Social Data*. Cambridge: Cambridge University Press, 1972.

Index